AF478857

NEW MOONS

ERIKA VERZUTTI

NEW
MOONS

ERIKA
VERZUTTI

Center for Curatorial Studies,
Bard College, Annandale-on-Hudson, New York

Institute for Studies on Latin American Art
(ISLAA), New York

Dancing Foxes Press,
Brooklyn, New York

TABLE OF CONTENTS

FOREWORD

New Moons is the largest and most comprehensive US survey to date of Brazilian artist Erika Verzutti, who makes original, intelligent "sculptures out of sculptures," as she describes them—material pleasures in bronze, plaster, papier-mâché, aluminum, clay, stone, and polystyrene, for example. Surveying the past fifteen years of Verzutti's diverse practice, this publication investigates her many lines of inquiry— art history, existence, the natural world, and the cosmos. Evocatively suspended between figuration and abstraction, her works combine surprisingly heterogenous elements. Allusions to human, animal, and plant life merge with references to the work of architects and other artists, such as painter Tarsila do Amaral, sculptor Constantin Brancusi, and landscape architect Roberto Burle Marx. Unlike many of her citations, Verzutti's distinctive forms often point to the process of their own making, revealing the trace of her hand—sometimes even her fingerprints. Her works open pathways to consider the possibilities of form and medium, broaching questions related to what curator and writer André Mesquita has called the "indiscipline of sculpture."

Erika Verzutti: New Moons continues a series of monographic exhibitions of midcareer and underrepresented artists initiated by Lauren Cornell, director of the graduate program and chief curator at the Center for Curatorial Studies, Bard College. These include Dara Birnbaum, Leidy Churchman, Sky Hopinka, Daniel Steegmann Mangrané, Martine Syms, and Nil Yalter. With fresh insight and deft curatorial strategies, Cornell has created a vital platform for artists breaking new aesthetic ground. The school she leads is an incubator for exhibition research and critical thinking, and we are grateful for the contributions to this book from graduates Ruba Katrib (CCS Bard '07) and Bernardo Mosqueira (CCS Bard '21).

The exhibition was produced with great commitment, care, and excellence by our exhibitions team, led by Ian Sullivan, director of exhibitions and operations; Andy Gabrysiak, head preparator; Martha Hart, museum registrar; and Amy Linker, head of collections and registration, all of whom extensively contributed to making this exhibition a reality, along with registration assistants Ray Camp and Kyle Herrington (CCS Bard '23). Our colleagues in administration have energetically and resourcefully supported many foundational aspects of the entire project, and I would like to thank Shane Brennan, director of administration; Victoria Chou, administrative coordinator and development assistant; Andrés Laracuente, graduate program and exhibitions assistant; Casey Robertson, public engagement manager; and Ramona Rosenberg, director of external affairs.

This exhibition would not have been possible without the enthusiastic support of the artist's galleries and their staffs: Danielle Bruce, Alice Conconi, Connor Creagan, Andrew Kreps, and Rob Smith from Andrew Kreps Gallery, New York; and Luiza Calmon, Ligia Carvalhosa, Gabriela Carvalho, and Márcia Fortes from Fortes D'Aloia & Gabriel. We would also like to acknowledge the generous lenders who contributed to this expansive presentation of Verzutti's art: Ricard Akagawa, Maria Rita and Rodolfo Barreto, Luiz Antonio Campos, Compound LB, Beth Rudin DeWoody, Martin and Rebecca Eisenberg, Camille Henrot, the Hollander-Yehudi Collection, the Inhotim Institute, Jay and Claudia Khalifeh, Kaitlyn and Mike Krieger, Paulus Magnus, Patrícia and Ricardo Lacaz Martins, Luís Paulo Montenegro, Tracy O'Brien and Thaddeus Staber, Andrea and José Olympio Pereira, the Ernesto Poma Family Collection, Rodman Primack and Rudy Weissenberg, Marcelino Rafart de Seras, Ana Luiza and Gregory Reider, Sergio Renault and Junio Oliveira, Paola Ricci and Henrique Miziara, Laura Skoler, Cecilia Tanure, and Adriana Varejão.

CCS Bard is committed to experimentation and innovation in exhibition making, and we are fortunate to have visionary funders to bolster our initiatives. Exhibitions at CCS Bard and the Hessel Museum of Art are made possible with generous support from Lonti Ebers, the Marieluise Hessel Foundation, the Robert Mapplethorpe Foundation, the Board of Governors of the Center for Curatorial Studies, and the Center's Patrons, Supporters, and Friends.

Additional support for *Erika Verzutti: New Moons* and the accompanying catalogue was generously provided by the Institute for Studies on Latin American Art (ISLAA). We would particularly like to thank Ariel Aisiks, founder; Lucy Hunter, executive director; and Nicole Kaack, editorial program manager, with whom we are proud to partner on this project and other educational initiatives that support new and timely narratives around Latin American artists.

Tom Eccles
Executive Director, Center for Curatorial Studies, Bard College, and Founding Director, Hessel Museum of Art

NEW MOONS

Lauren Cornell

Moon watching, communing with our closest celestial body, humbles and awakens perception. "How intimate the Moon is, she being / Far from the glory-jealous Sun!"[1] This line, from "Moonrise after Midnight" (1935) by poet Welborn Hope, conscripts the moon into tropes of femininity: the shining orb is guileless and hushed, as opposed to the brash and ascendant male sun. As a reliable muse, the moon has often been projected upon and personified. Night light braids into religion and myth and also fuels fantasies of space conquest. Georges Méliès's film *Le Voyage dans la Lune* (*A Trip to the Moon*, 1902), in which a hapless group of astronomers raids the moon and takes an alien hostage, satirizes imperial takeover and space showmanship. Roughly a half century later, Cold War superpowers positioned space as the next frontier, with expeditions to the lunar surface broadcast for home-viewing audiences. Skip ahead to 2023 and billionaire rocket men Jeff Bezos and Elon Musk are in another headline-grabbing race to space, this time with the intention of closing the distance for all by commercializing the path between our planet and its storied, elusive lunar counterpart.

Representing an inverse strand of thinking, novelist Clarice Lispector perceives the moon as an impervious witness to the agonizing churn of life on Earth. In 1965, she wrote:

> That moonlight, think about it, that moonlight, paler than a corpse's face, so silent and far away, that moonlight witnessed the cries of the first monsters to walk the earth, surveyed the peaceful waters after the deluges and the floods, illuminated centuries of nights and went out at dawns throughout centuries . . . Think about it, my friend, that moonlight will be the same tranquil ghost when the last traces of your great-grandsons' grandsons no longer exist.[2]

If we follow Lispector and think about *that moonlight*, in its constancy and capacity to outlast us, might it alter the way we understand ourselves in relation to others?

Twenty years ago, the scholar Gayatri Spivak elaborated such a perspective, offering the concept of "planetarity" in her book *Death of a Discipline* (2003) as a means of thinking differently about connections between people and worldly species across time and during an unfolding ecological crisis. Planetarity is a means to map collectivity and subjectivity through categories of belonging outside those inscribed by colonialism, such as nationalism and race, which were developed on the premise of exclusion: to divide and to segregate. Spivak's argument is firstly an academic one, aimed at the demarcations of "area studies" (for example, Asian, Latin American, Middle Eastern, and Women's Studies) that have shaped the production of knowledge within higher education. But it also offers routes through which to see oneself in a new state of collective being. Setting off a debate that has reverberated since, Spivak wrote,

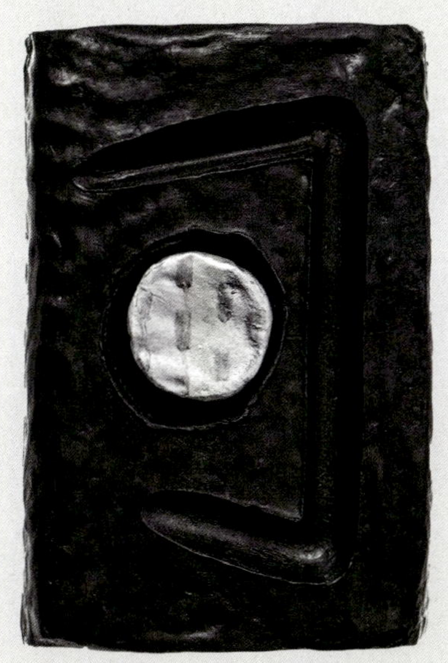

Erika Verzutti, *Water*, 2015. Bronze, aluminum, and oil, 12 ¼ × 8 ¼ × 2 ¾ inches (31.1 × 21 × 7 cm)

<hr>

1   Welborn Hope, "Moonrise after Midnight," *Poetry* 46, no. 6 (September 1935): 316.
2   Clarice Lispector, "Another Couple of Drunks," in *Complete Stories*, ed. Benjamin Moser, trans. Katrina Dodson (New York: New Directions, 2018), 101.

In this era of global capital triumphant, to keep responsibility alive in the reading and teaching of the textual is at first sight impractical. It is, however, the right of the textual to be so responsible, responsive, answerable. The "planet" is, here, as perhaps always, a catachresis for inscribing collective responsibility as right. Its alterity, determining experience, is mysterious and discontinuous—an experience of the impossible. It is such collectivities that must be opened up with the question "How many are we?" when cultural origin is detranscendentalized into fiction.[3]

Since the publication of *Death of a Discipline*, and amid an escalation of environmental precarity and concern, numerous writers and thinkers have called for a reconsideration of humanity in greater relation to the organisms and species that populate the planet. Contemporary discourse on planetarity and on what we might learn from multispecies coevolution and nonhuman perspectives has a corollary in art that scrambles language, ontology, order, and medium, such as the work of Erika Verzutti. Through her practice, Verzutti builds new collectivities, offering an antitaxonomy for being that eschews species autonomy and established hierarches in favor of reinvention and ongoing recombination. The exhibition *New Moons* at the Center for Curatorial Studies, Bard College—the first major US survey of the artist's work—considers how the "mystery and discontinuity" of Verzutti's art provides a bold new vision on sculpture, as well as a planetary-inspired perspective on earthly life and the prevailing systems and divisions of knowledge classification.

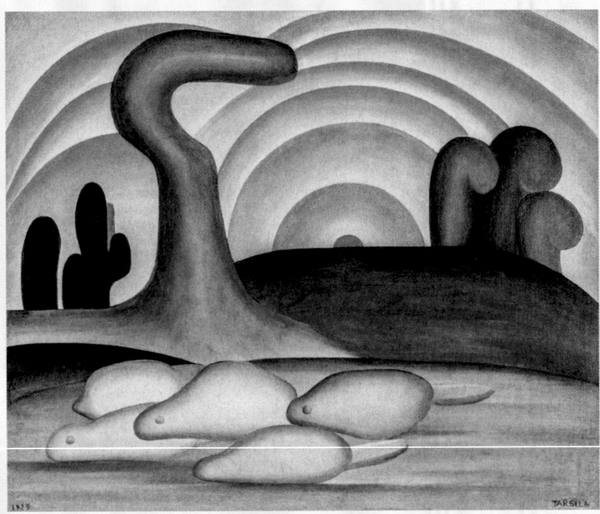

Tarsila do Amaral, *Sol Poente* (*Setting Sun*), 1929. Oil on canvas, 21 ¼ × 25 ⅝ inches (54 × 65 cm)

Asked to reflect on the persistent theme of the planetary in her work, Verzutti describes an affinity for a "loss of control" or a "loss of gravity." Pressed to explain further, she replies, "I don't feel the opposition between things so much."[4] Indeed, the lack of oppositional tension is key to her work. Take, for instance, *Water* (2015; page 9), a wall relief made of bronze and painted deep black except for a sunken white orb striped with pale blue lines. If it looks like a view of Earth from above, its rough-hewn shapes and small scale still make it hard to fully discern as an image. Where is the titular water? Is it to be found in the expanse of black or in the pale blue stripes? Or is it all-encompassing? *Water* hovers between the familiar and the enigmatic, fading in and out of legibility.

3   Gayatri Chakravorty Spivak, *Death of a Discipline* (New York: Columbia University Press, 2003), 101–2.

4   Erika Verzutti, phone conversation with the author, March 2, 2023.

This physical and conceptual weightlessness is tangible in the experience of Verzutti's work because it is rooted in her approach. Her use of materials levels what is considered high or low, permanent or expendable in form and she lifts and recasts references freely. Diverse materials intermingle, for instance, in *Rabisco* (2007; page 21), which shows a heavy bronze rabbit's head sitting atop a colorful body of clay. In *Boyfriend* (2014; page 56), a thick bronze layer holds two delicate ostrich eggshells that threaten to drop from its grip. In *Torre de Cacau* (2021; page 119), a tall column of oversize bronze cacao fruits rises from the ground in an exquisite balancing act. The play with mass, load, and suspension is disorienting, while the lack of categorical difference makes for works that are daring and stark in their collisions. Verzutti's titles, meanwhile, suture terms that have no clear association aside from what is manifest in the work—consider *Fauve Zombie* (2018), *Starfruit Lamp* (2009–17), and *Tapioca Magritte* (2022). Distinctions that would otherwise be sensitive between artists, life forms, and period are discarded, as if the object were untethered to origin or provenance. On the dynamism in her practice, curator André Mesquita has said, "The narratives in her works are not reductionist, nor are they closed in [on] themselves as unshakeable truths."[5] Her objects are animated and unstable: they multiply and reproduce.

Notable in Verzutti's art is the fact that all her pieces—which encompass earthly subjects such as animals and fruit, legs swirling in colorful compositions, and bulbous, plant-like objects—are endowed with their own sense of integrity or sentience. Relatedly, there is the concept of "families" in her work, or works that share affinities and kinships, as a number of scholars have noted.[6] In *New Moons*, pieces from prominent families demonstrate the range of the artist's preoccupations and the significance of multiplication and versioning across her practice. Her jackfruit series, for instance, includes *Brasília TV* (2011; page 40), a jackfruit with a square space cut into it, as if to fit a monitor; *Brasília Teatro* (*Brasília Theater*, 2014), two worn jackfruits evoking a pair of old shoes; *Brasília Cadeira* (*Brasília Chair*, 2012), a jackfruit sliced to suggest the seat of a chair; and the list goes on (*Brasília Colher* [*Brasília Spoon*, 2012], *Brasília Rosto* [*Brasília Face*, 2012], *Brasília Azulejo* [*Brasília Tile*, 2012], *Brasília Pintura* [*Brasília Painting*, 2019] . . .). The *Brasília* family reproduces endlessly and horizontally, crossbreeding with nonorganic matter, from commercial products to gemstones, and troubling the singularity of the art object to instead fashion sculpture as an open-ended chain of associations. Her *Tarsilas* family adapts a vegetal form from Tarsila do Amaral's painting *Sol Poente* (*Setting Sun*, 1929; page 10) across an extensive number of sculptures of varying scales and assorted materials. Sometimes she deploys Tarsila's form as a cradle for other elements, as in *Tarsila com Koons* (2015; page 67), where it holds a shiny, iridescent ball and brings two seemingly dissimilar artists together in an intimate embrace. In *Cisne com Palco* (*Swan with Stage*, 2015; page 72), it becomes a twelve-by-eleven-and-a-half-foot-wide sculpture with a platform for live performance, emphasizing the very performativity of the influences, characters, personae, and sentient bodies that span her work.

5   André Mesquita, "The Indiscipline of Sculpture," in *Erika Verzutti: The Indiscipline of Sculpture* (São Paulo: Museu de arte de São Paulo Assis Chateaubriand, 2021), 21.
6   See, for instance, Mesquita, "The Indiscipline of Sculpture," and Christine Macel, "Sculpture as a Vital Process," in *Erika Verzutti*, ed. Christine Macel (Paris: Editions Centre Pompidou, 2019), 33.

Verzutti's genealogies intersect with motifs including eggs and orbs, the outlines of body parts (breasts, hips, legs, genitalia), and traces of the work's making, evidenced in the markings of tools and swarms of the artist's fingerprints. Strikingly, relations break down around art histories as she picks up and plays out myriad historical styles. Strongest and most pervasive in her practice are references to Brazilian art and architecture across multiple trajectories. *Gato* (2008; page 32), for instance, a cross topped with a feline head, nods to the sacred sculptures of artist and priest Mestre Didi, while her many egg allusions align her with the teacher and feminist Celeida Tostes, who made works with small clay eggs, her preoccupation with these culminating in a performance, documented in a series of twenty-one photographs, in which she covered her nude body in liquid clay and crawled inside a womb-like vat of unbaked clay (*Passagem* [*Passage*], 1979). Squinting, one can see glints of the bodies and orbs of Cristina Salgado, the bright, graphic language of Rubem Valentim, and

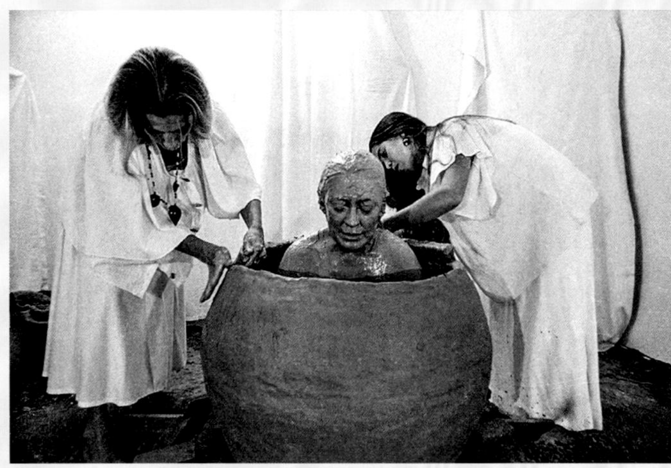

Celeida Tostes, *Passagem* (*Passage*), 1979. Photographs, 21 parts: dimensions variable

the totems of Sergio Castillo, among other notable artists, in a free-flowing, sometimes absurd, relation to key figures from the Global North. In *Turtle Modern* (2007; page 27), a humble reptile seems to have been grabbed and shoved into a more northerly modernist canon, its shell replaced with the bronze cast of a pineapple and its legs swapped out for chunks of clay; unnaturally shining and minimal, like an ovoid sculpture by Brancusi, it retains the self-contained air of a creature that can outlive its present indignities. In *Homeopatia Mondrian* (2020; page 105), a slab of concrete resembles a painter's palette with a more expansive and vibrant color scheme than the one used by the de Stijl artist. This swirl of references hews close to the notion of artistic process expressed in Oswald de Andrade's "Manifesto Antropófago" (Cannibalist Manifesto, 1928), about metabolizing and resynthesizing disparate cultural influences: "Cannibalism alone unites us. Socially. Economically. Philosophically."[7] This process, in de Andrade's estimation, is distinctly Brazilian owing to the country's hybridity. For Verzutti, these art historical references become material, combined fiercely with other disciplines and life forms, to transcend beyond quotation into a unique hybrid vocabulary.

7   Oswald de Andrade, "Cannibalist Manifesto," trans. Leslie Bary, *Latin American Literary Review* 19, no. 38 (July–December 1991), 38. First published as "Manifesto Antropófago," in *Revista de Antropofagia*, May 1928, São Paulo.

In *Imaginary Ethnographies*, theorist Gabriele Schwab writes, "What we can know about [others] always bears the traces of our own transference. To realize this may be at least a first step toward a less cannibalistic ethics of otherness."[8] The pervasive evidence of Verzutti's tools and hands repeatedly pressing into firm, wet clay reminds us that the artist is not just taking—not just absorbing her references into her creations—but rather that she is emphasizing a relation of transference, projection, and personification. We see her retooling different objects, forms, and styles, as the traces of her hands impart her own imagination while emphasizing the sensuality that undergirds all the genealogies and interwoven parts that make up her objects. Verzutti will tease out latent sexual innuendo, or add it, as in *Pavão* (*Peacock,* 2008; pages 26–27), where an array of paintbrushes becomes a resplendent train; *Missionary* (2011; pages 48 and 49), a sliced papaya affixed to a cast of a zucchini reminiscent of Brancusi's phallic *Princess X* (1915–16); or *Henry Branco* (2010; page 37), where a miniature bronze figure twists to examine a protuberance on its backside. These are heavily handled, desiring objects, unbound and ripe with traces of interconnection, feeling, and sensation.

The soft marks of the artist's hand are evident in *Lua Oleo* (*Oil Moon*, 2020; page 14), a wall work rife with double meanings and material play. Made of concrete, it is rough and uneven and suggests a planet formed by cosmic blast. The "oil" in the title references both paint and fuel, conjuring an image of an oil-slicked planet and casting the moon as a resource in danger of extraction. As a lunar landscape, it appears equal parts faithful and imagined, evoking the moon's surface as seen through a telescope, except in warmer hues and with cratered impressions arranged in neat lines like those of an egg carton. Beholding *Oil Moon* feels something like watching oneself watch the moon—a communion with Lispector's sense of the moon as a witness that will outlast us all.

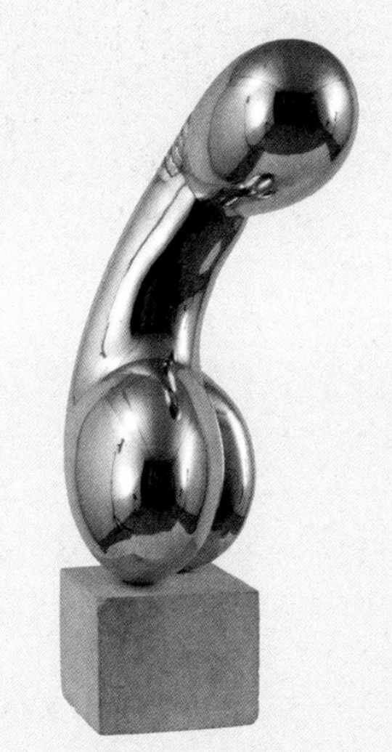

Constantin Brancusi, *Princess X*, 1915–16. Polished bronze and limestone block: 24 5/16 × 15 15/16 × 8 3/4 inches (61.7 × 40.5 × 22.2 cm), base (block): 7 1/4 × 7 1/4 inches (18.4 × 18.4 cm), base (pedestal): 39 3/8 inches (100 cm)

8   Gabriele Schwab, *Imaginary Ethnographies: Literature, Culture, and Subjectivity* (New York: Columbia University Press, 2012), 94.

Moons recur throughout Verzutti's work as symbols of rebirth and the multiple phases and cycles one entity can take. On *Skin Moon* (2019; page 97), a dark black moon waxes and wanes on a fleshy, pink surface, as if cosmic time were imprinted on us. But the artist also reflects on her own material processes by producing works from her own studio refuse, elevating ideas that have "died" into permanence through her series of "cemeteries," which she also calls "flat topography." In 2008, in conjunction with the exhibition *Pet Cemetery* at Galeria Fortes Vilaça in São Paulo, she assembled her first such collection of objects, *Indigentes*, from the discarded remains of works made for the exhibition. *Indigentes* is composed primarily of brick rows interspersed with random play skeletons, an ostrich eggshell, a miniature drawer, and a soapbox, among other things—an altogether solemn and mysterious gathering. Featured in the CCS Bard exhibition, *Cemitério com Franja* (*Cemetery with Fringe*, 2014; pages 60–61) is a vast grid of 632 pieces, mostly smooth, round stones of assorted sizes, which are mounted on bricks like small towers or placed between the individual paintbrushes that line one edge to make a fringe. If arranging these pieces is a funereal process ("ideas die in that corner," she has said of the studio area designated for this work[9]), it is one that elevates detritus into radiant new configurations.

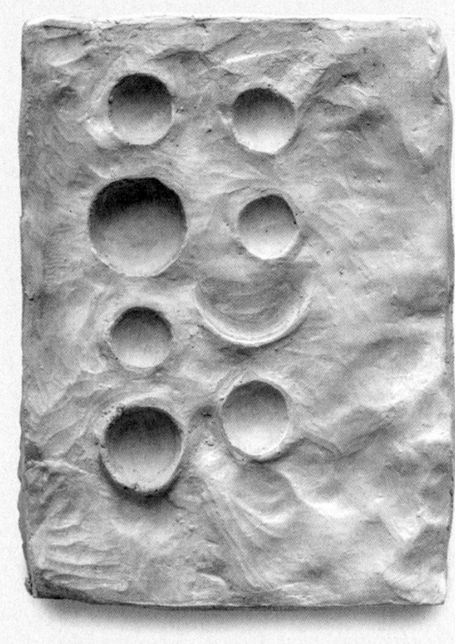

Erika Verzutti, *Lua Oleo* (*Oil Moon*), 2020. Oil on concrete, 10 × 7 × 1 inches (26 × 19 × 4 cm)

"Assemblages are open-ended gatherings. They allow us to ask about communal effects without assuming them. They show us potential histories in the making. . . . Assemblages don't just gather lifeways; they make them," writes anthropologist Anna Lowenhaupt Tsing in her widely cited book *The Mushroom at the End of the World* (2015), which considers the precarity and indeterminacy of life on Earth and what we might learn from the life of the matsutake mushroom—a fungus born of an inorganic cross-fertilization with pine trees enabled by climate change.[10] Verzutti has said she appreciates the effort to zoom out, in a telescopic sense, to the point where relations that we take so seriously can be rethought; this sentiment dovetails with Lispector's passage on the triviality of human dramas in the light of cosmic time.[11] While Verzutti's work appears playful, even humorous, its assertions around the porousness of life are pointed. Her sculpture and wall works deprivilege the cohesion and centrality of human beings and remove logics from existing orders, be they related to animal or plant life, history or culture. Within Verzutti's work exists a novel way of perceiving interrelations—through a planetarity that orbits outside set systems of being.

9   Verzutti, phone conversation with the author.

10   Anna Lowenhaupt Tsing, *The Mushroom at the End of the World: On the Possibility of Life in Capitalist Ruins* (Princeton, NJ: Princeton University Press, 2015), 22–23.

11   Erika Verzutti, phone conversation with the author, February 10, 2023.

Jaspera na Escola (Jaspera at School), 2006–8
Bronze, acrylic, and paper
21 5/8 × 9 13/16 × 9 13/16 inches (55 × 25 × 25 cm)

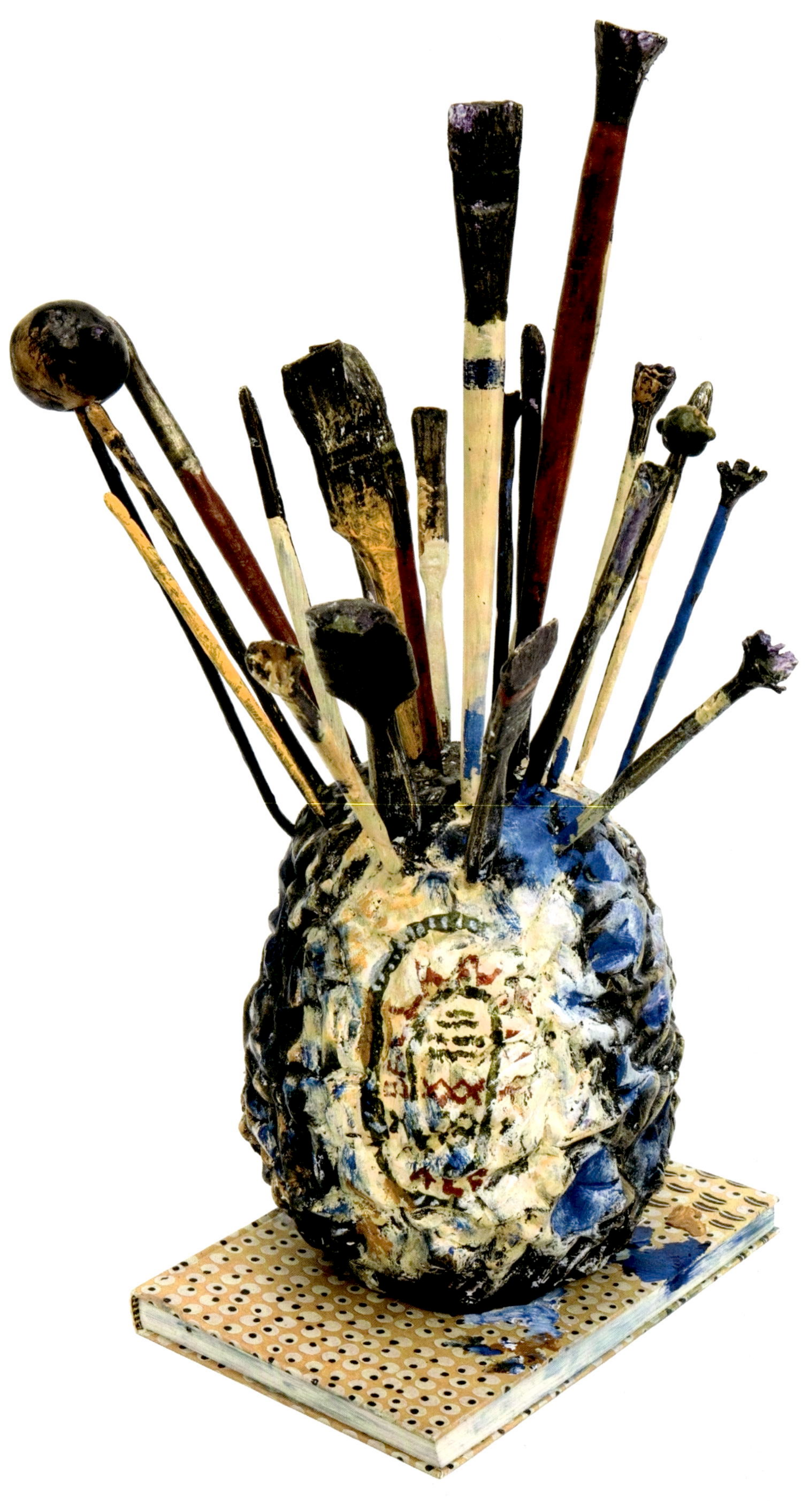

Saramandaia, 2006
Polychromatic bronze
18 ⅞ × 14 ³⁄₁₆ × 17 ¹¹⁄₁₆ inches (48 × 36 × 45 cm)

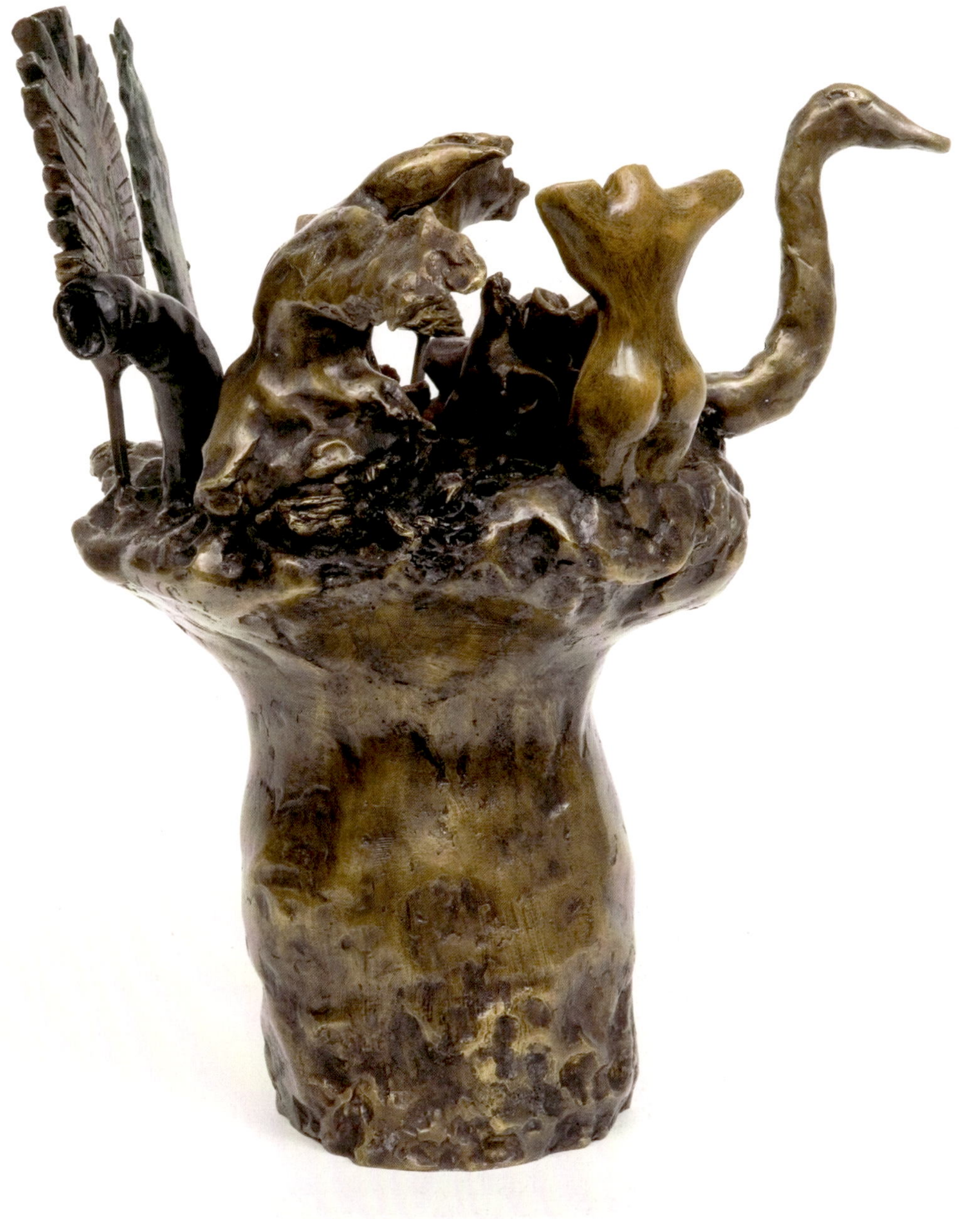

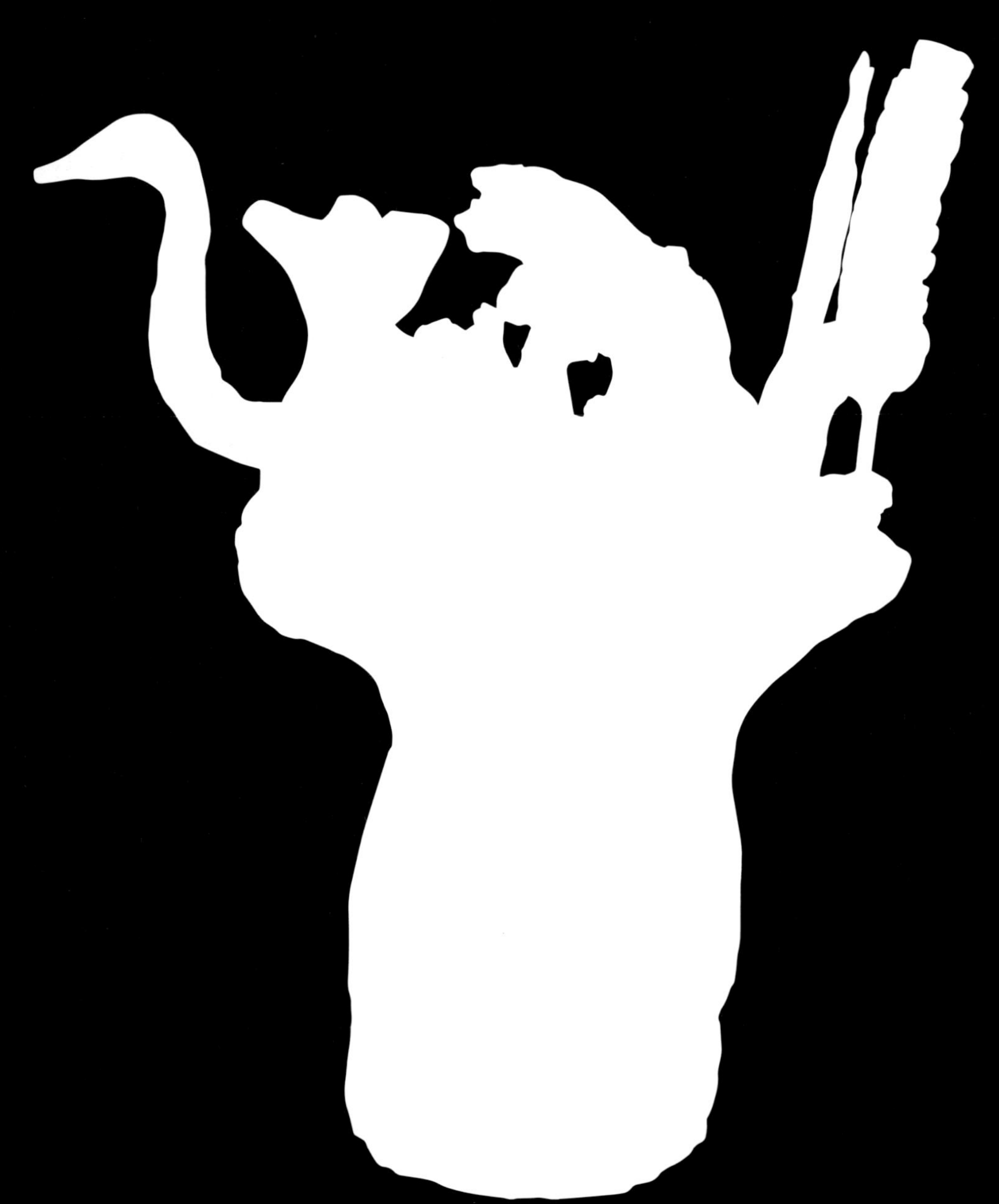

SARAMANDAIA

Saramandaia (2006) is my first bronze sculpture, named after a soap opera that aired in Brazil in 1976. I wasn't allowed to watch it, as it was "prohibited to minors." At the time, all TV programs started with a screen that showed a hand-signed document titled "Censura Federal" (Federal Censorship), which stated the program's age allowance. I grew up seeing that screen, not realizing

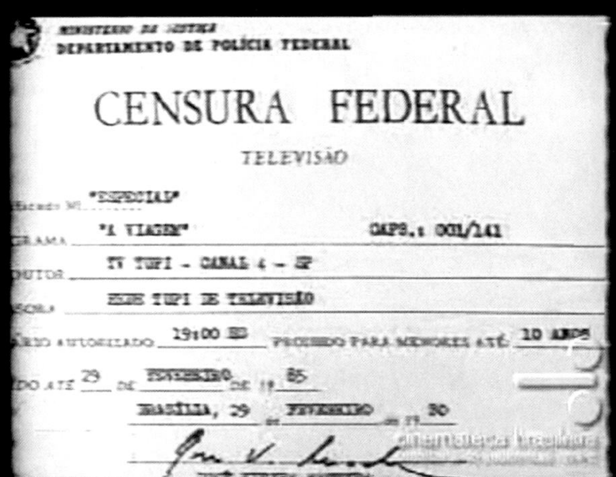

Mandatory certificate of approval issued by Brazil's Ministry of Justice, shown before any broadcast on Brazilian television during the military dictatorship, 1964–85

Brazil lived under a military dictatorship with strict control over all media. Many television shows were censored or banned, and artists and writers were imprisoned and tortured, or exiled.

The soap opera *Saramandaia* used satire and surrealism to criticize society without risking censorship. A corrupt farmer was ridiculed in a famous scene where an army of ants started coming out of his nose. There was also Dona Redonda (roughly, "Ms. Round"), a beloved character who loved food so much she exploded in the last episode. This grotesque scene, one of the most iconic moments in Brazilian television history, seems to me now a good theatrical critique of consumerism.

Such vivid scenes taught me that absurdities are possible. That was my mood when I created my first bronze sculpture: I felt urged to make all sculptures, all formats and genres, as ravenous as Dona Redonda. As a shape, my *Saramandaia* started as a bulky silhouette intended to contain all my ideas. In fact, *Saramandaia* was conceived as the vase from which all the world's sculptures would blossom.

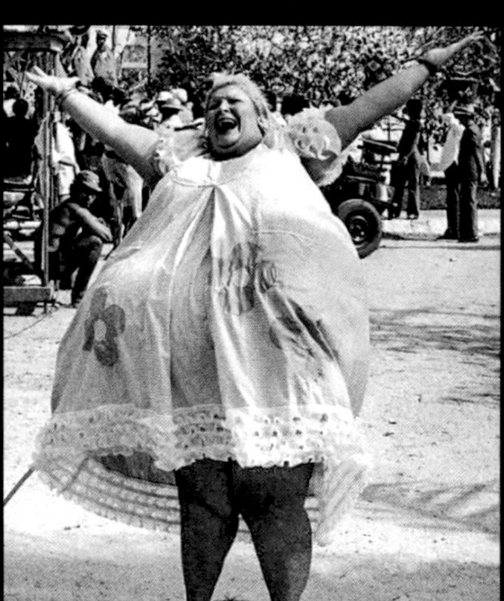

Sônia Braga as Dona Redonda in the TV series *Saramandaia*, 1976

I see that work now as if it were something I made as a child—clumsy shapes with so much belief in them. I just kept modeling, incorporating elements like angel wings, a female torso, tropical vegetation, something that resembles a periscope, flowers, a pine tree/Popsicle, two geometric braces mimicking a Henry Moore sculpture, an ostrich. It was all confident and arbitrary. I also like the fact that the figures don't respect scale—the bird is a giant monster in relation to the human figure. I'm happy to have started from absurdity.

—E.V.

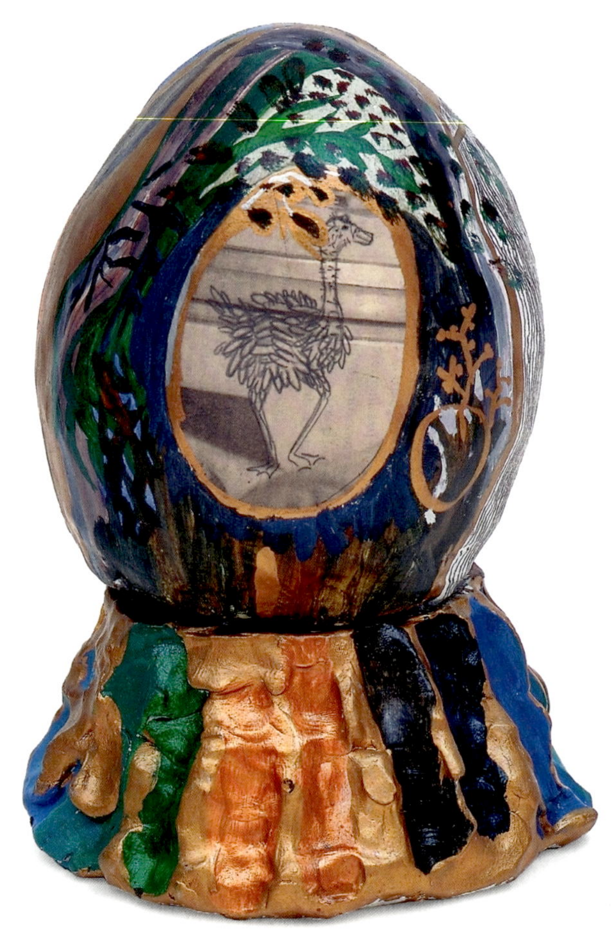

Rabisco, 2007
Bronze and cold porcelain clay
18 ⅛ × 14 ³⁄₁₆ × 10 ¼ inches (46 × 36 × 26 cm)

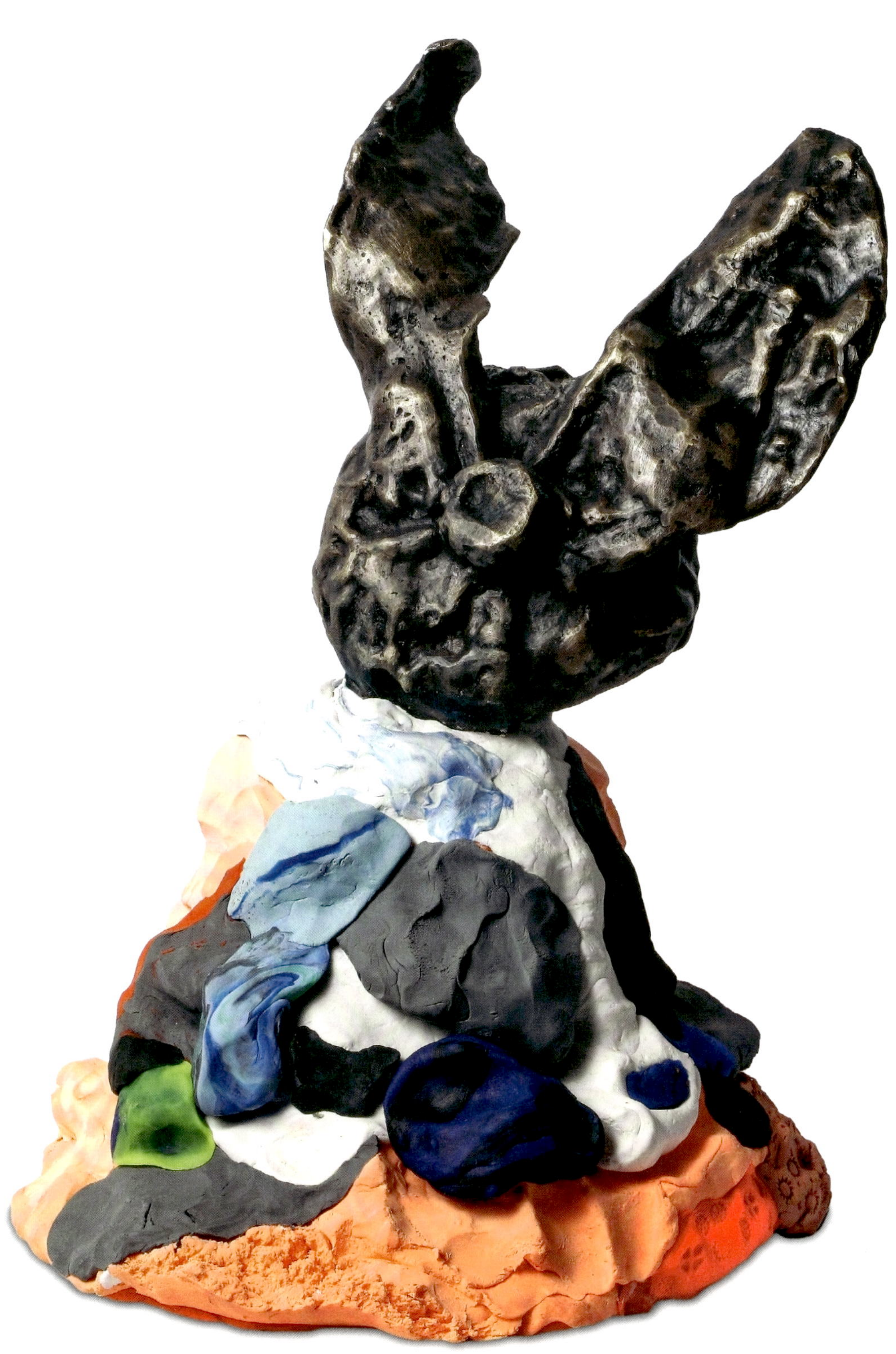

Nessie, 2008
Cold porcelain clay, wood, and acrylic
101 ³⁄₁₆ × 15 ¾ × 19 ¹¹⁄₁₆ inches (257 × 40 × 50 cm)

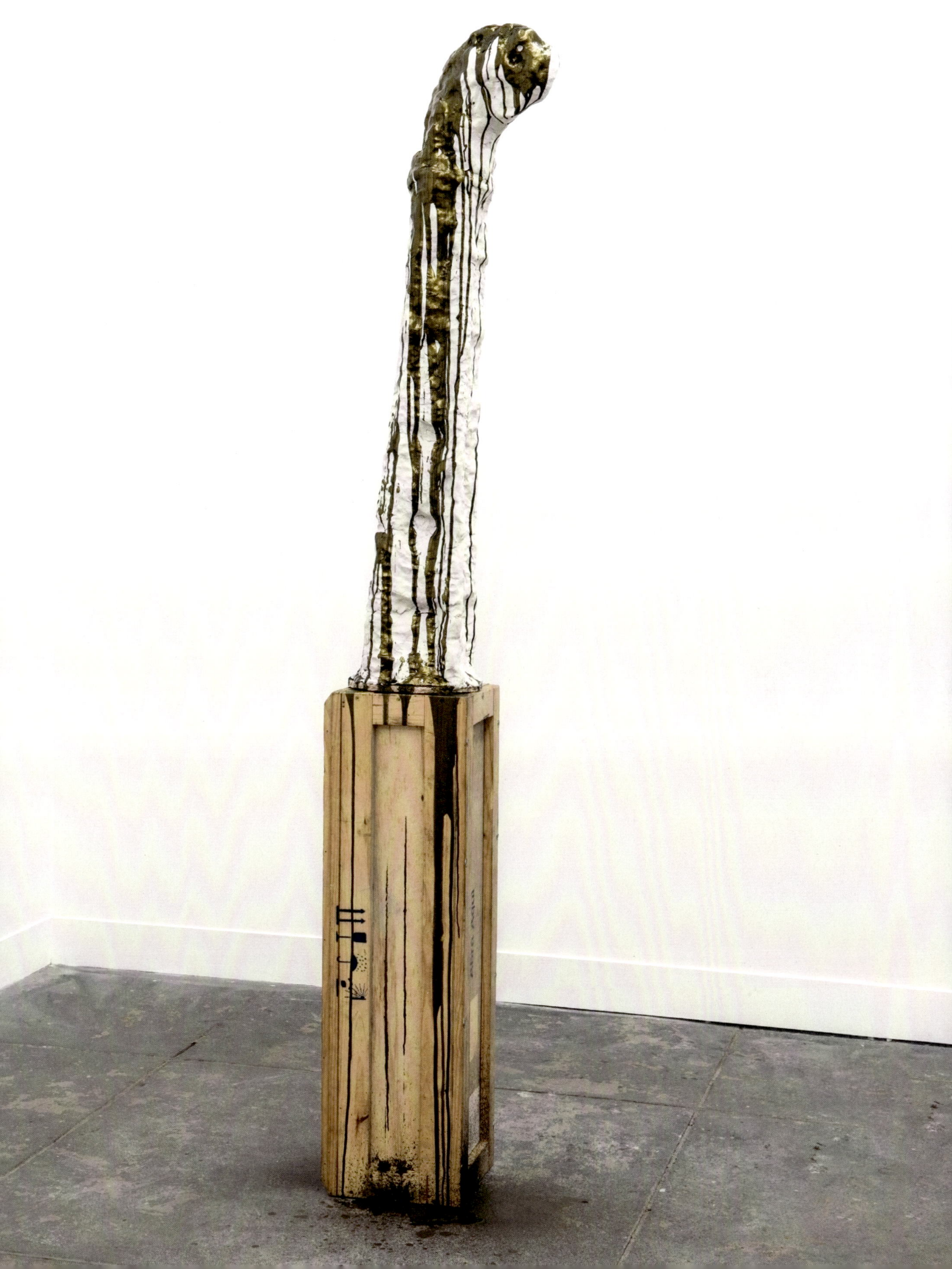

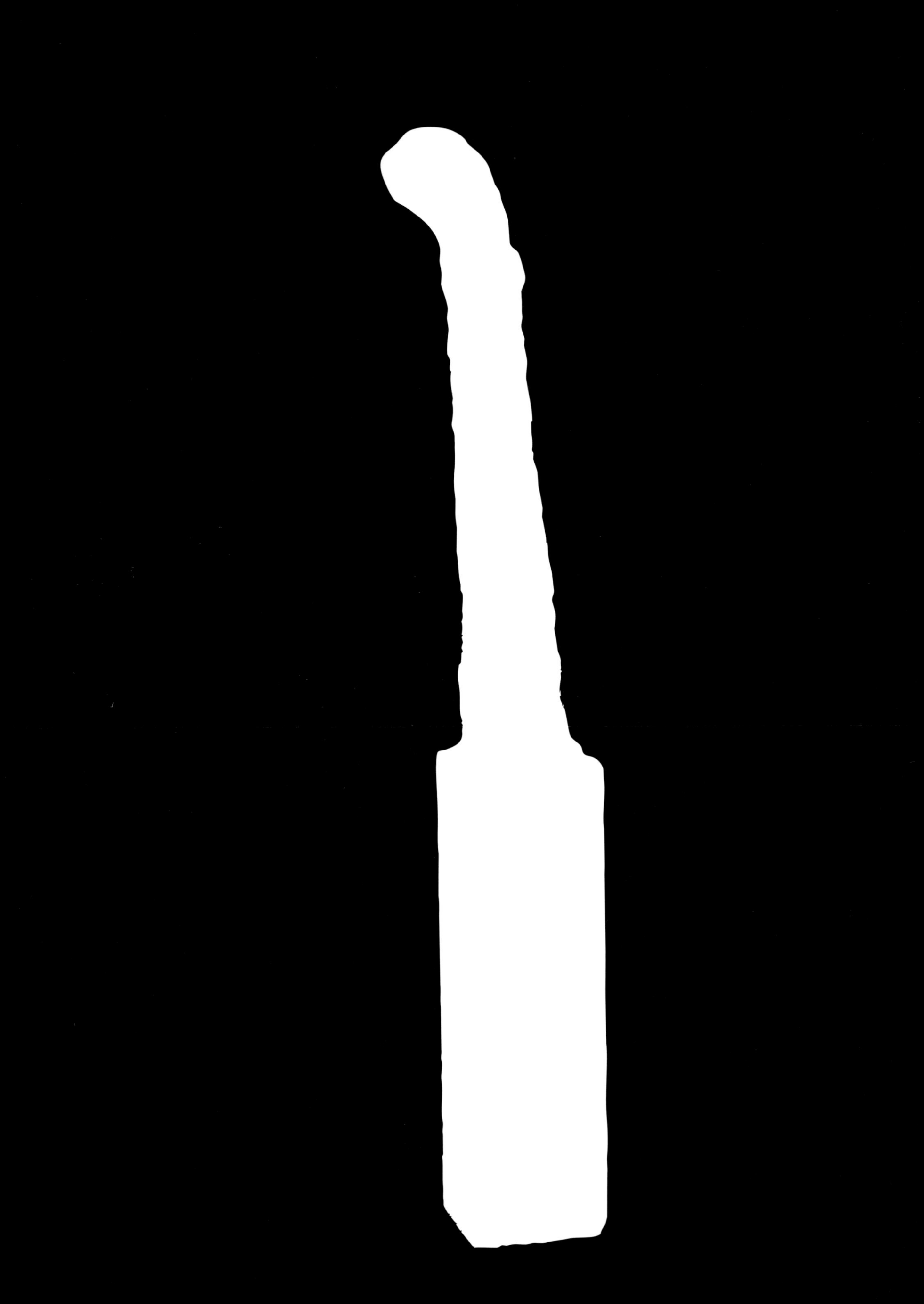

NESSIE AND HOW CLAY FOUND ME

Between 2000 and 2002, I discarded most of the pieces I made. After going to London for graduate school, I was back in São Paulo with a head full of principles but empty-handed. The conceptual work I did before no longer made sense. After two years at Goldsmiths looking for truth in my practice, taking risks, trying new things, and collecting assorted failures, I had made work that my tutors found weak. Worse, it was work that I hated myself. There were digital collages saved on Zip drives, printed out on large plotters, mounted on PVC board. The memory of those materials makes me cringe today.

Anyway, my scholarship had ended, and I had returned to Brazil broke and somewhat defeated. I was using my energy to find jobs to earn a living while waiting for my true work to find me. I was employed mostly in production for art exhibitions, surrounded by a lot of paper. So I started making cutouts and "vases" out of paper scraps—that got me excited to transition from two dimensions into three, in quite a literal way.

Then I went looking for clay. The material did not disappoint: a handful of clay had all the truth I needed. Clay carries energy directly from nature. It is reliable and responds to gestures immediately with unique plasticity, offering its own take on the form. No wonder God chose clay to mold the first human.

I wanted to make shapes that were as truthful as the material. Like a toddler, I started by making snakes and balls. The primordial challenge was moving matter upward. I began stretching the clay vertically as much as I could, to make a "neck." Finding a way to bend the neck became my main ambition. *Cisne com Pincel* (*Swan with Brush*, 2003–12) illustrates the difficulty of the process— if it bends too much, the clay neck will fall.

According to the resistance of the material, I nicknamed each type of curve with a figuration, ranging from a dinosaur, with the smallest nose, to a swan, as the longest curve. Between them, a range of cucumbers and birds.

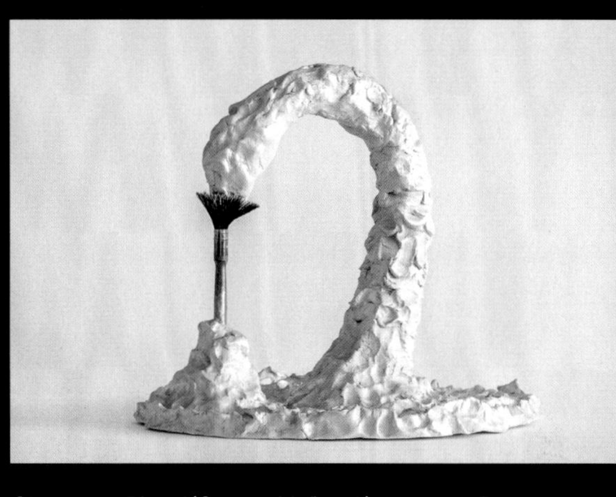

Gato Problema (*Problem Cat*), 2001. Found paper cutout, 16 ½ × 9 ¹⁄₁₆ × 6 ¼ inches (42 × 23 × 16 cm)

Cisne com Pincel (*Swan with Brush*), 2003–12. Bronze, plaster, and paintbrush, 22 ¹⁄₁₆ × 22 ¹⁄₁₆ × 15 ⅜ inches (56 × 56 × 39 cm)

Nessie (2008) is an enlarged version of the dinosaur neck. It's made of chicken wire and self-drying modeling clay. It was the tallest animal in the *Pet Cemetery* exhibition at Galeria Fortes Vilaça, São Paulo, in 2008. Bronze-colored acrylic paint slides down the sculpture as an extra layer. Pouring paint on top of a sculpture is a multifunctional gesture for me. The pouring is performative, and it creates wonder about how it was made (in this case, with a scared me on a scaffolding pouring paint from a plastic Coca-Cola bottle). Attacking a sculpture with paint, and without much control, involves the thrill, or fear, of ruining everything. At that moment, I have a strong feeling of sharing something with the viewer, because I think that part of people's attraction to art comes from reviving the risks taken by the artist. In *Nessie*, the drips reinforce the verticality, calling the eye to the top of the sculpture, then down to the splash marks on the floor. Paint stains the base of the sculpture, too, indicating that the crate that serves as its pedestal is an integral part of the work. The final sculpture seems wet, as if it were emerging from water or mud. I soon associated it with the monster of Loch Ness, adding a narrative that doesn't really interfere with the work's formal journey.

—E.V.

Pavão (*Peacock*), 2008
Bronze and acrylic
35 7/16 × 39 3/8 × 9 7/16 inches (90 × 100 × 24 cm)

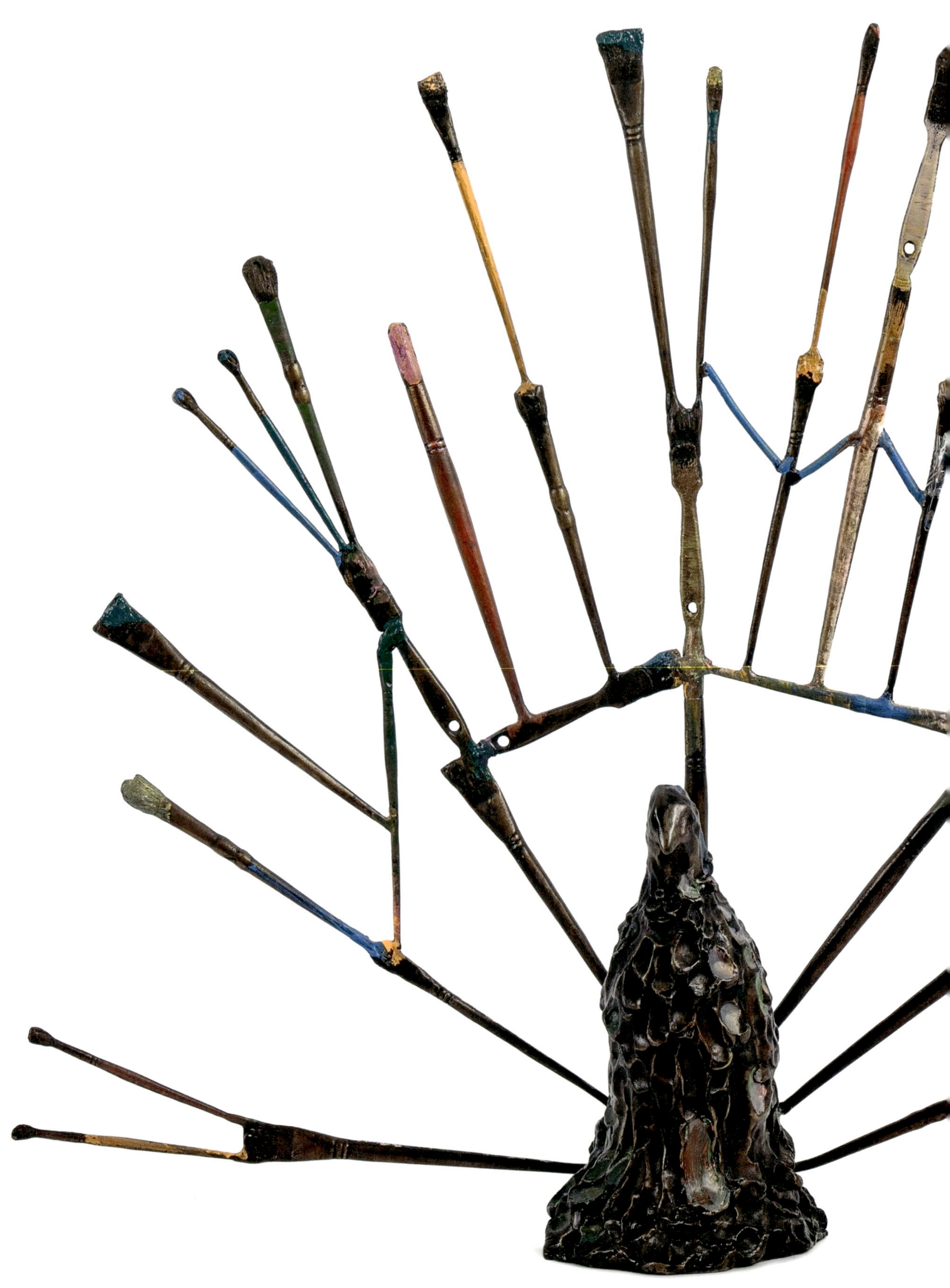

Turtle Modern, 2007
Bronze and plasticine
6 ⅛ × 5 ⅛ × 7 ⅞ inches (15.5 × 13 × 20 cm)

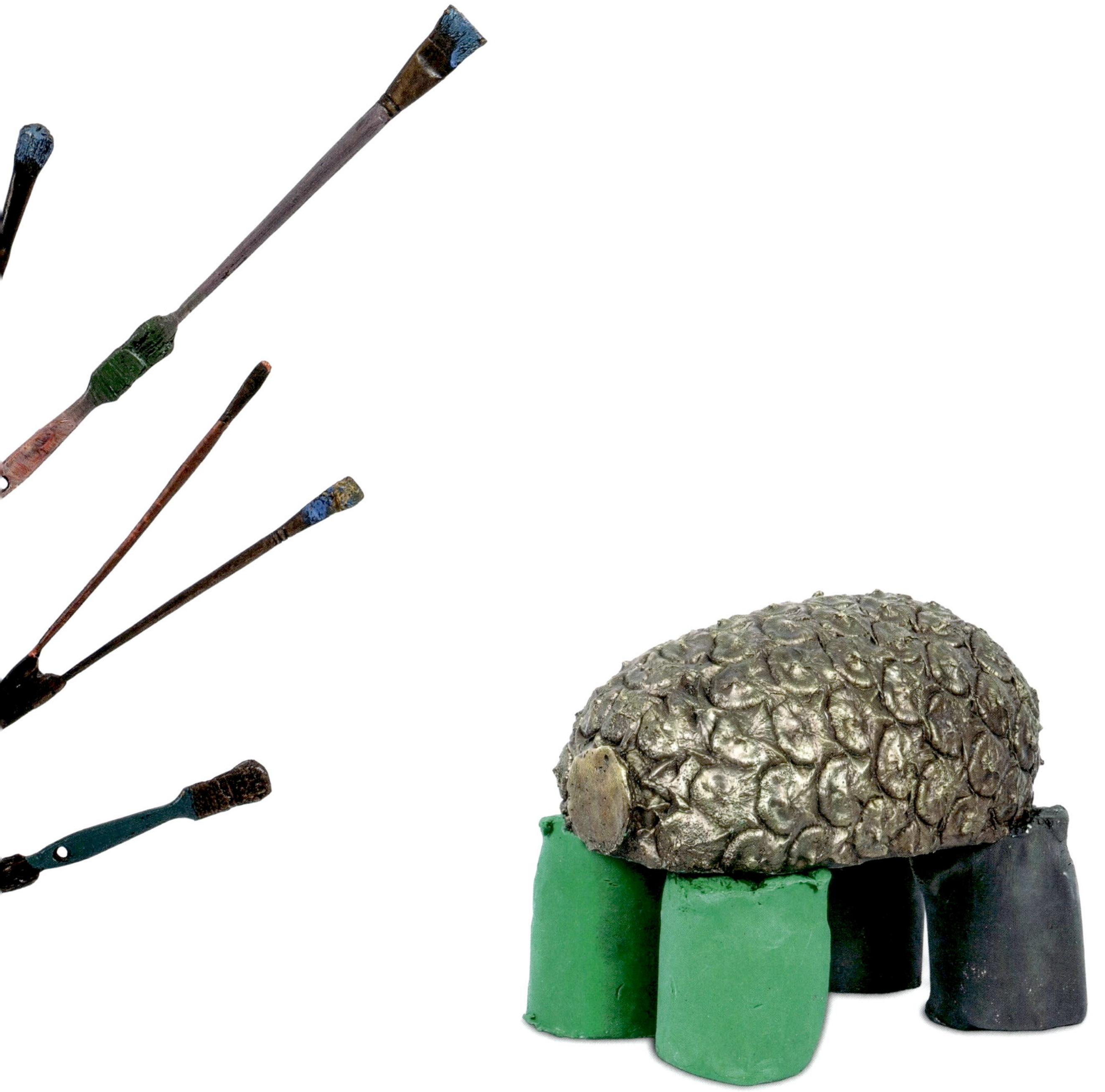

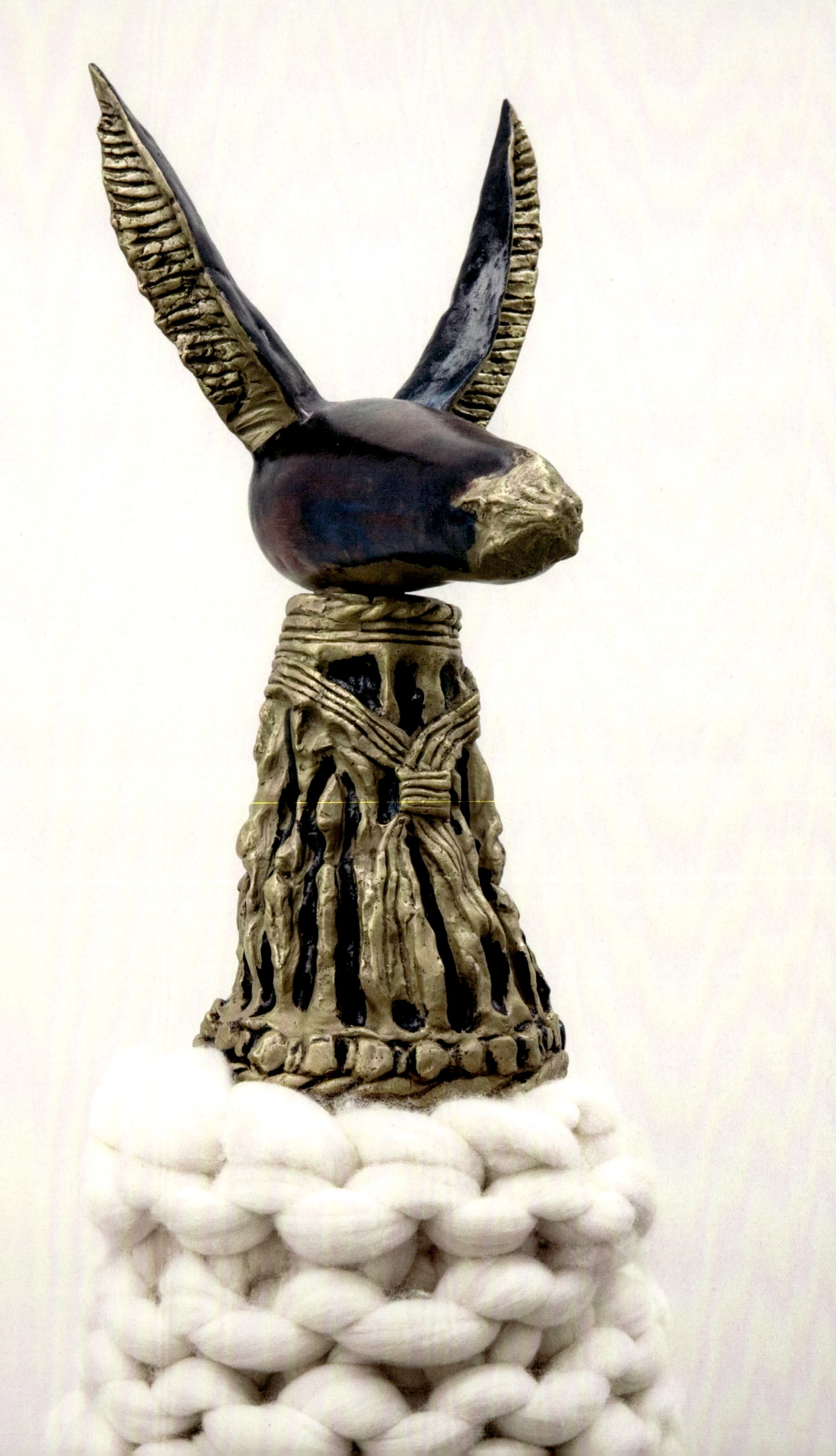

Egito, 2008
Bronze, wood, and wool
72 1/16 × 39 3/8 × 39 3/8 inches (183 × 100 × 100 cm)

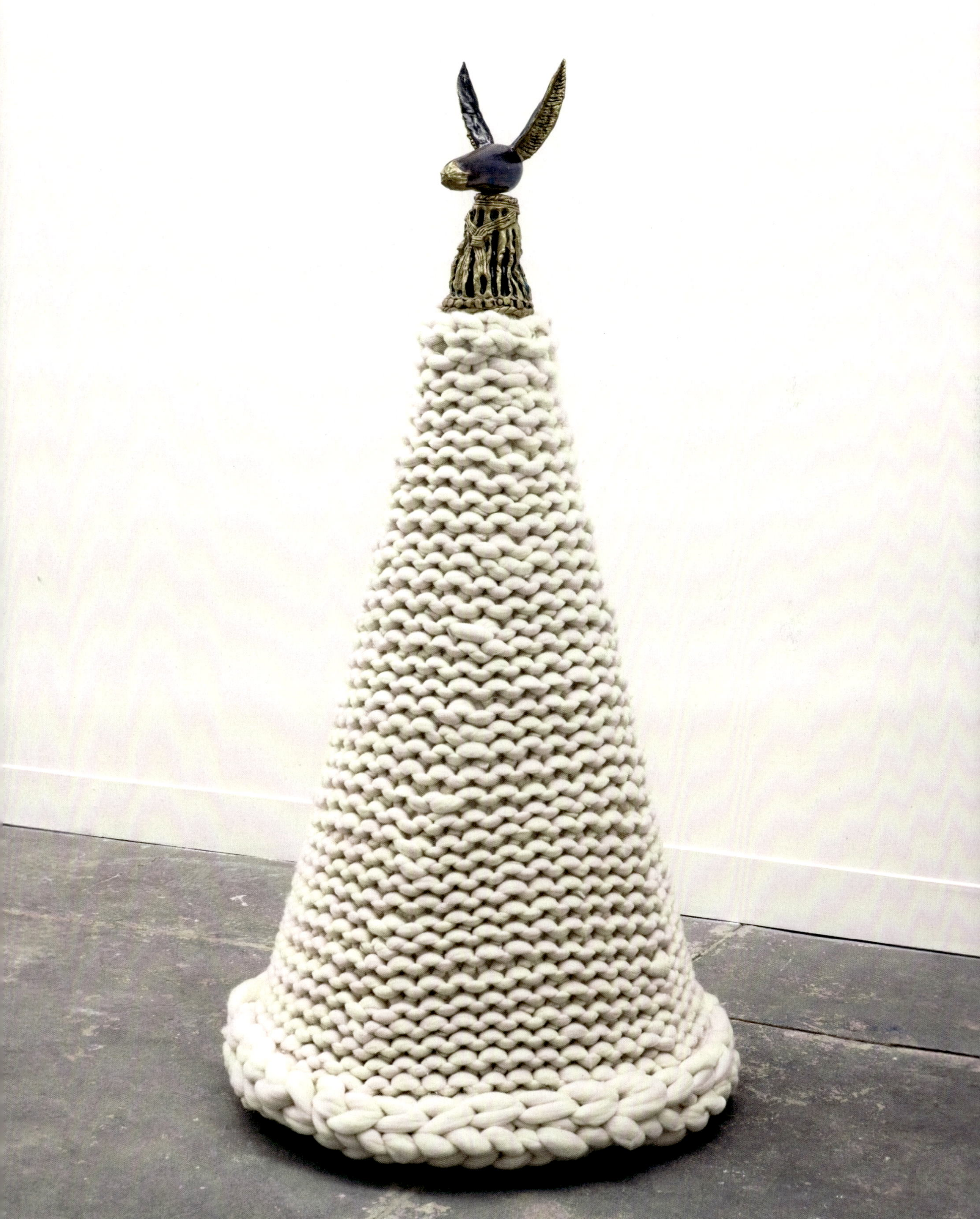

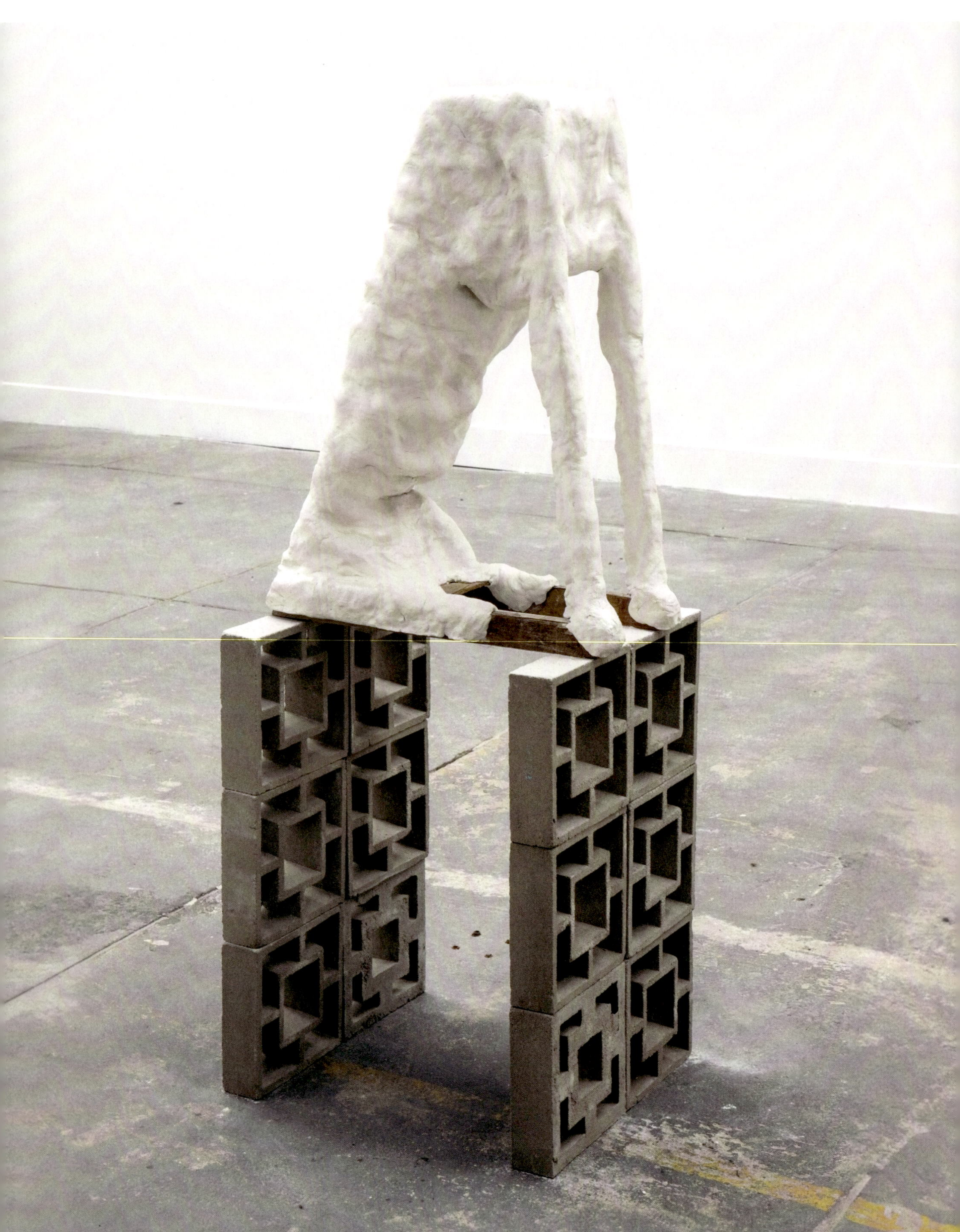

Neo Rex, 2008
Concrete, cold porcelain clay, wood, and acrylic
59 ¹⁄₁₆ × 25 ³⁄₁₆ × 18 ⁷⁄₈ inches (150 × 64 × 48 cm)

Chicken, 2008/2017
Bronze, cold porcelain clay, and acrylic
Dimensions variable

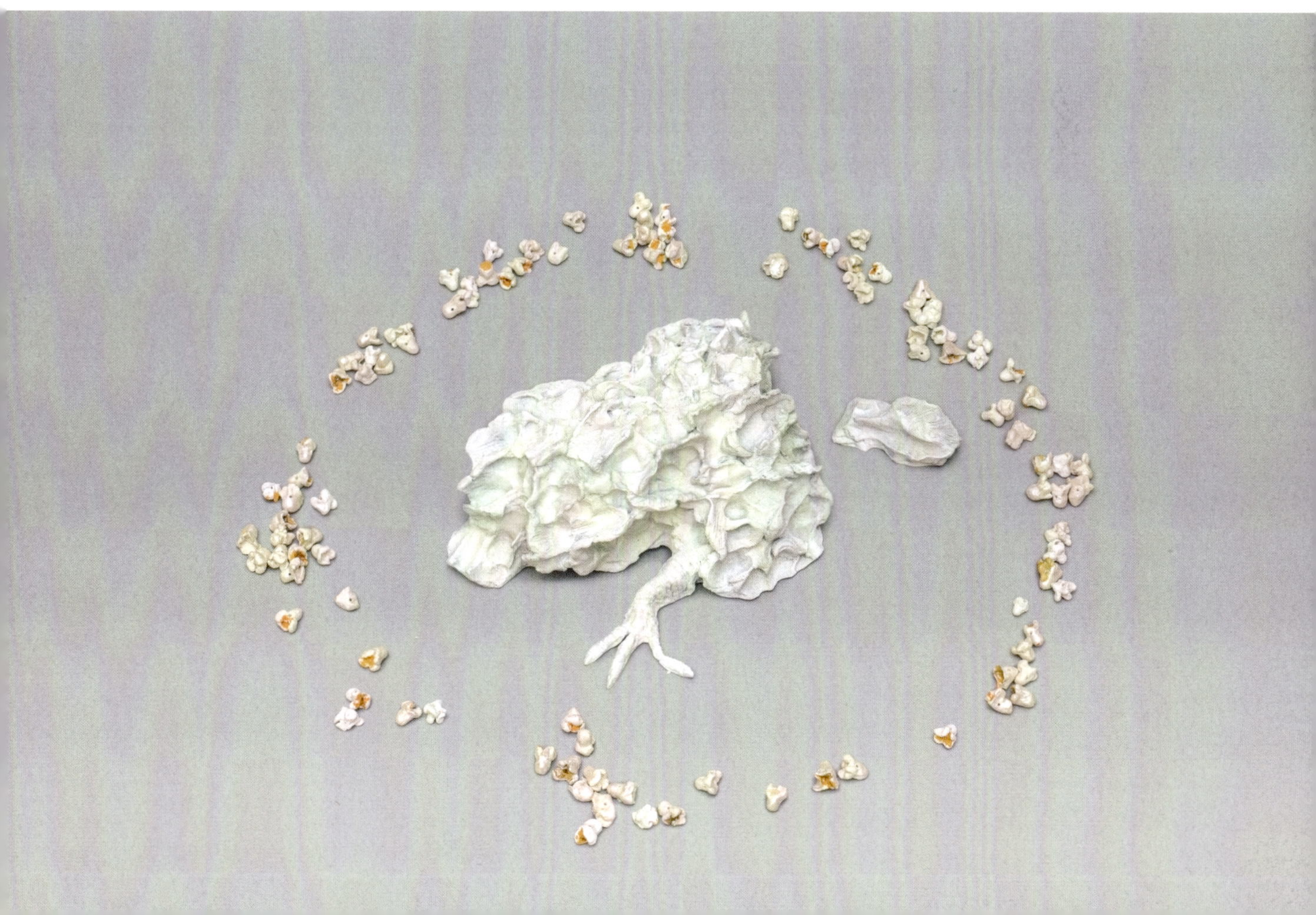

Gato, 2008
Bronze and gravel
25 3/16 × 21 5/8 × 21 5/8 inches (64 × 55 × 55 cm)

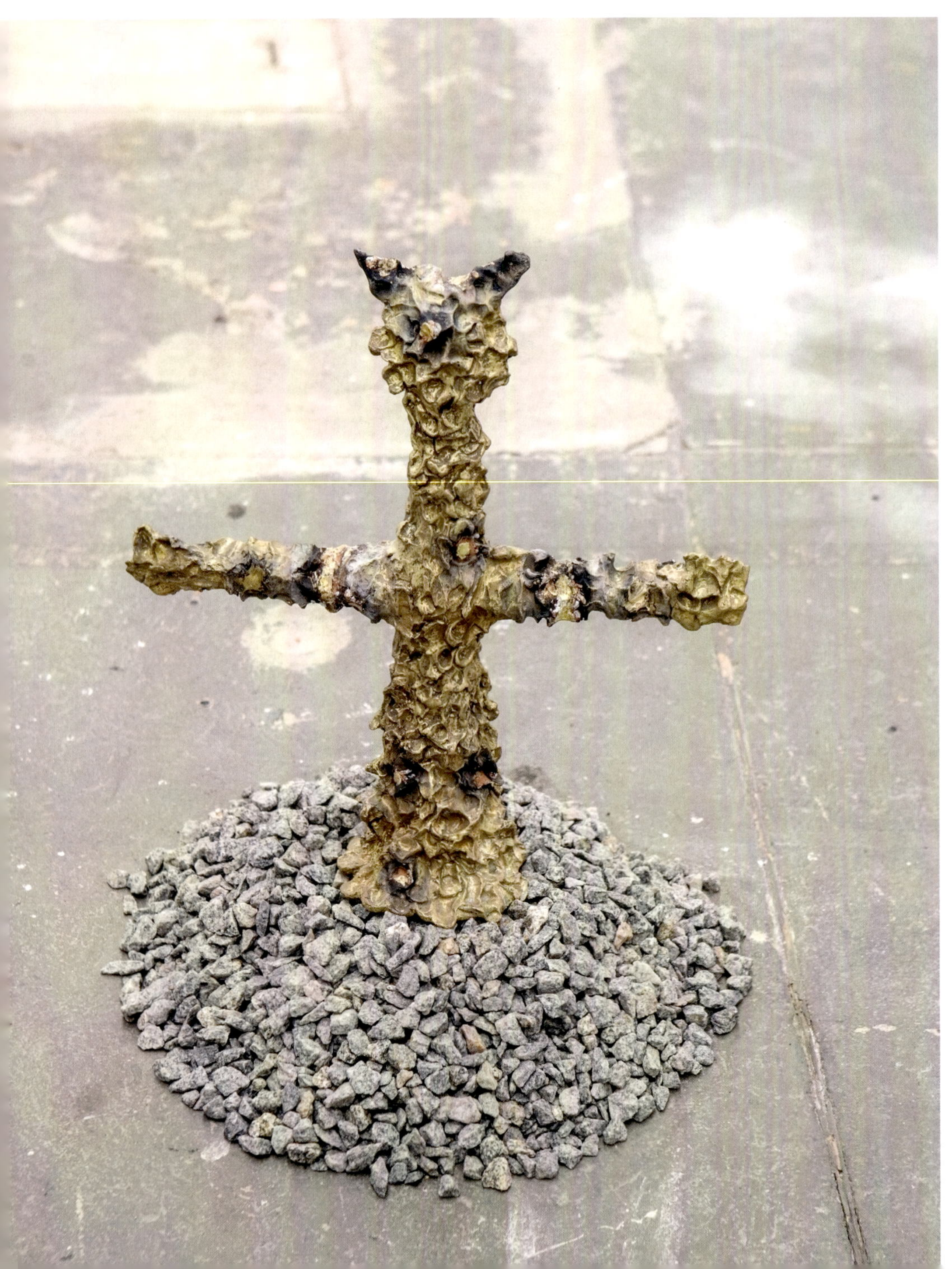

Avestruz (Ostrich), 2008
Bronze and acrylic
51 ³⁄₁₆ × 39 ³⁄₈ × 46 ⁷⁄₁₆ inches (130 × 100 × 118 cm)

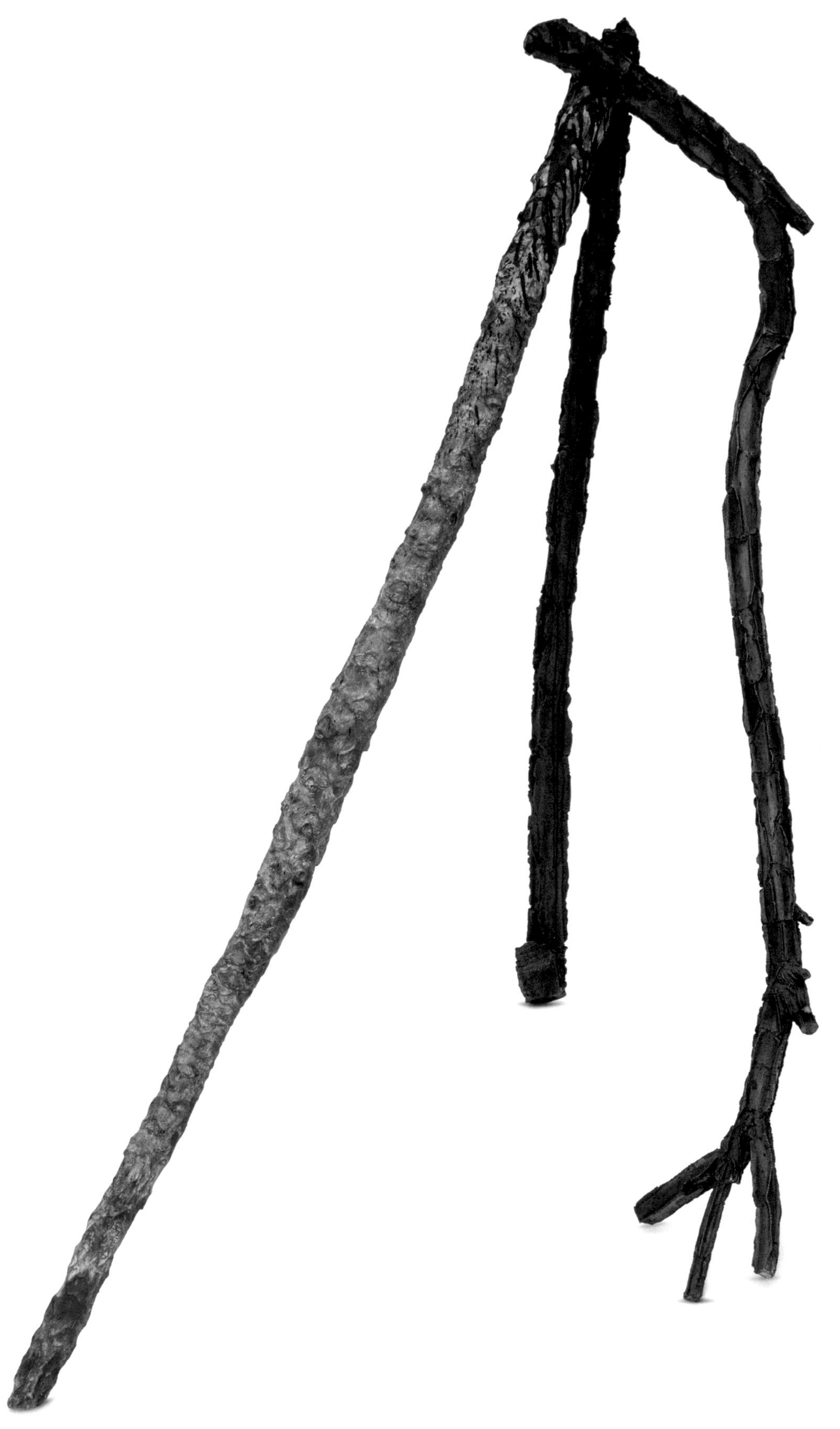

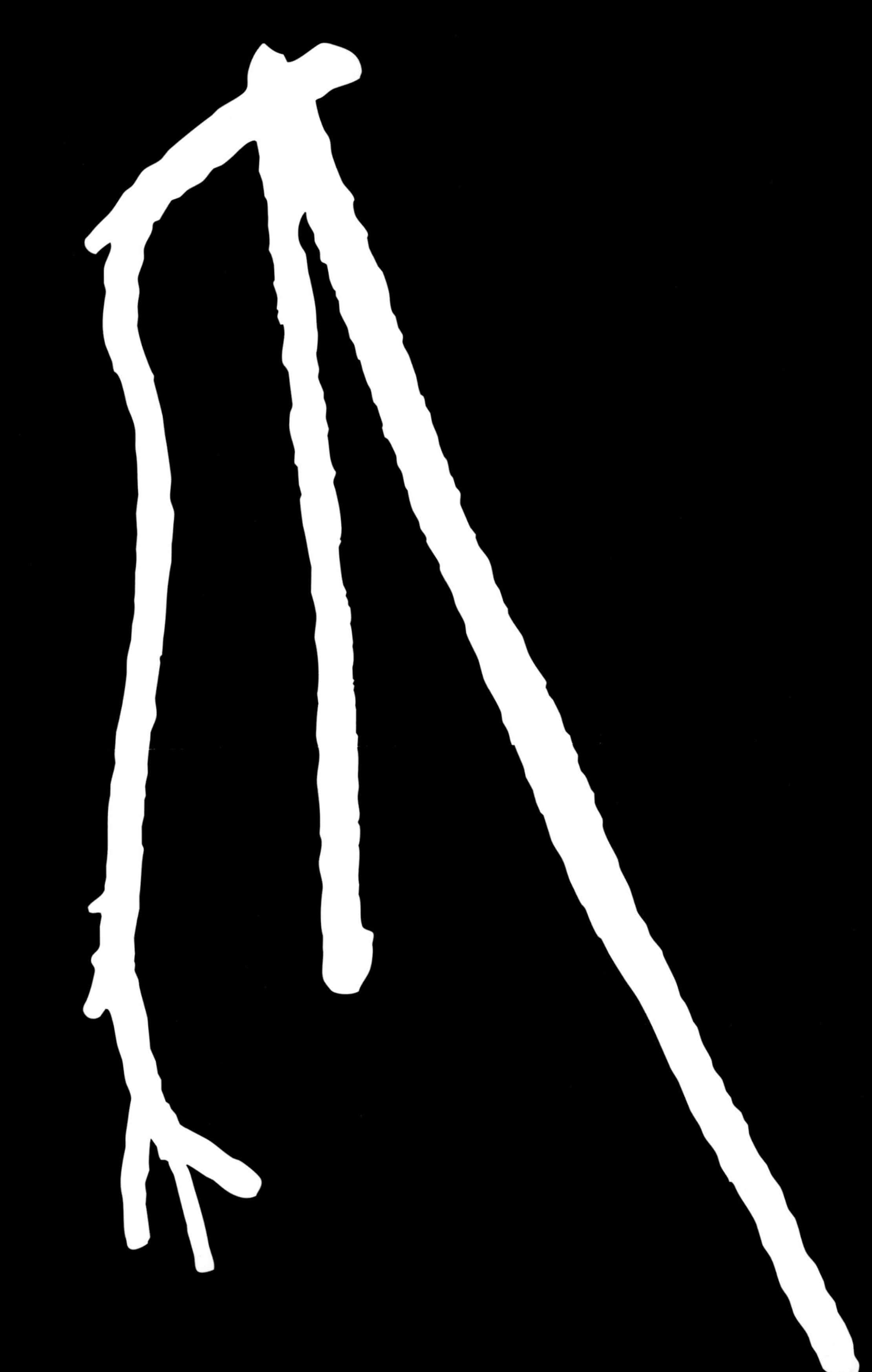

In 2008, I presented an exhibition I called *Pet Cemetery*, at Galeria Fortes Vilaça, in São Paulo. It was a graveyard of sculptures, each dedicated to a different animal—kind of a Noah's ark. I researched cemeteries for pets and saw statues and decorations created in tribute to dogs, cats, birds, even horses. These tributes can be quite artistic, with a great variety of designs, the main materials being bronze, concrete, and ceramics. The leading idea for the *Pet Cemetery* exhibition was to create an opportunity for me to make sculptures of different styles in an investigation of sculpture genres. There are materials and techniques I feel attracted to, but I don't always find a reason or a decent-enough connection with a material to use it. For *Pet Cemetery*, I decided to vary the forms freely and experiment with strange things such as wool, plastic, and lamps.

Avestruz (*Ostrich*, 2008) was the most abstract sculpture in the show. My brother had found fallen branches from a papaya tree and an "alligator tree" (*pau-jacaré*), and one ended in a trident that could act like a tripod. That branch "generated" a bigger tripod. It looked as if the branches could germinate and create an infinite chain of tripods. There are moments when I am just observing the work develop itself. A tripod is the minimum gesture to sustain upright legs. *Avestruz*, with its triple bird feet, carries that power of being essential. Along with that principle, there is also the bonus of figuration in the piece: one can see an ostrich with its head buried in the sand. It doesn't happen all the time, but that is the ideal balance between form and figuration. I do not make formal sculpture that is not connected to the emotions of the known world, nor do I make sculpture for the sake of representation.

—E.V.

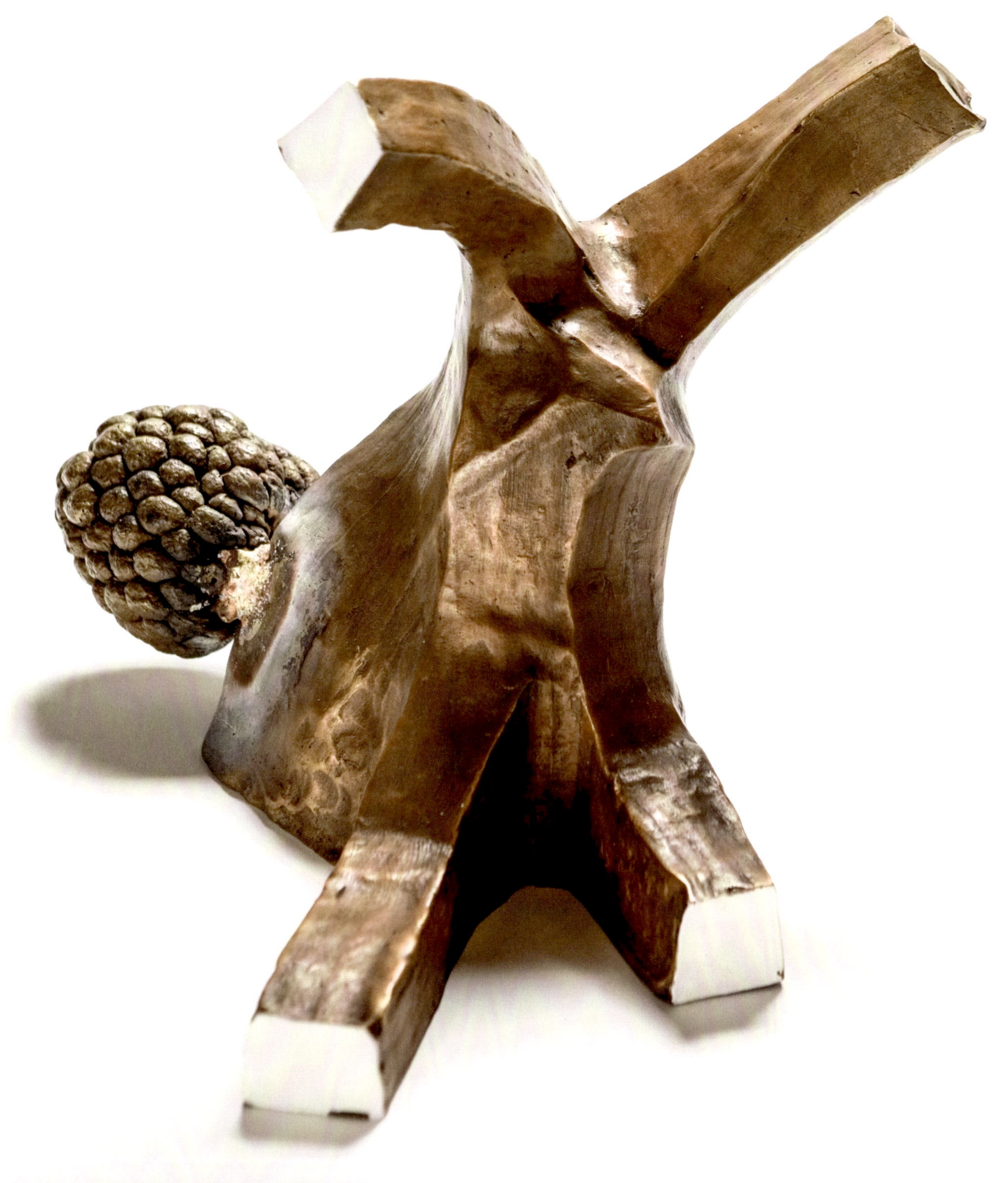

Henry Branco, 2010
Bronze and acrylic
12 ⅝ × 14 ⁹⁄₁₆ × 15 ¾ inches (32 × 37 × 40 cm)

Brasília Quitanda, 2010
Bronze and acrylic
11 ¹³⁄₁₆ × 7 ¹⁄₁₆ × 7 ¹⁄₁₆ inches
(30 × 18 × 18 cm)

Brasília Jóia (Jewel Brasília), 2011
Bronze and acrylic
11 ¹³⁄₁₆ × 7 ¹⁄₁₆ × 6 ⁵⁄₁₆ inches
(30 × 18 × 16 cm)

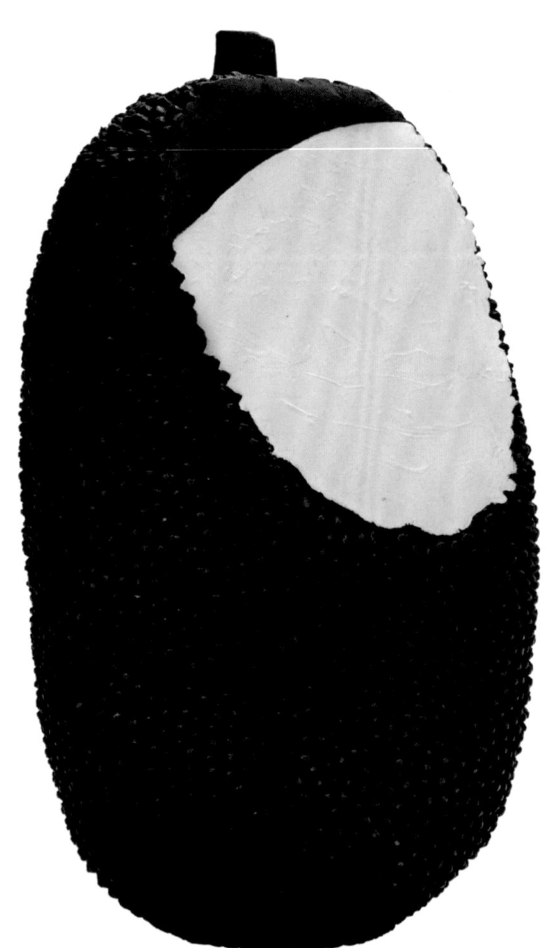

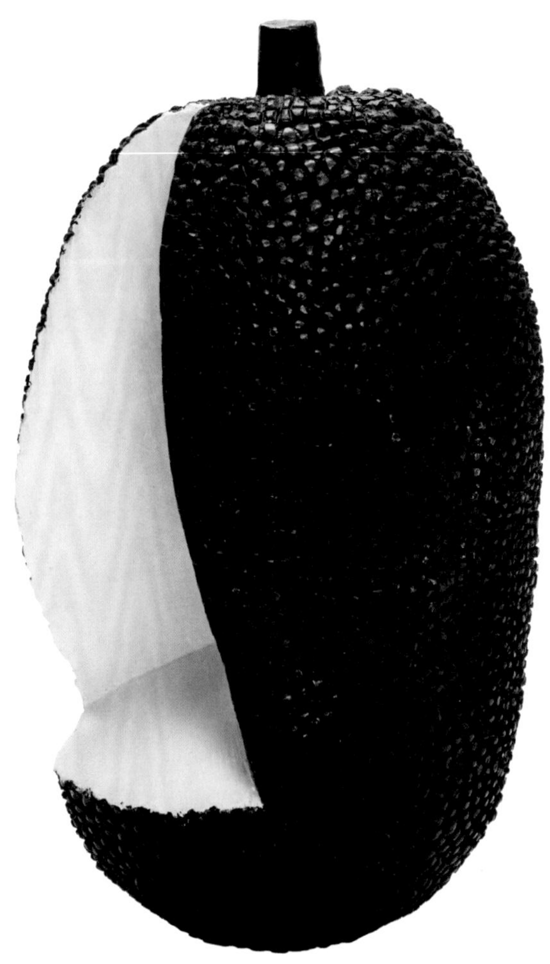

Brasília Acústica (*Acoustic Brasília*), 2011
Bronze and acrylic
11 ¹³⁄₁₆ × 9 ⁷⁄₁₆ × 6 ⁵⁄₁₆ inches (30 × 24 × 16 cm)

Brasília Skate, 2011
Bronze and acrylic
12 ⁵⁄₈ × 8 ¼ × 6 ¹¹⁄₁₆ inches (32 × 21 × 17 cm)

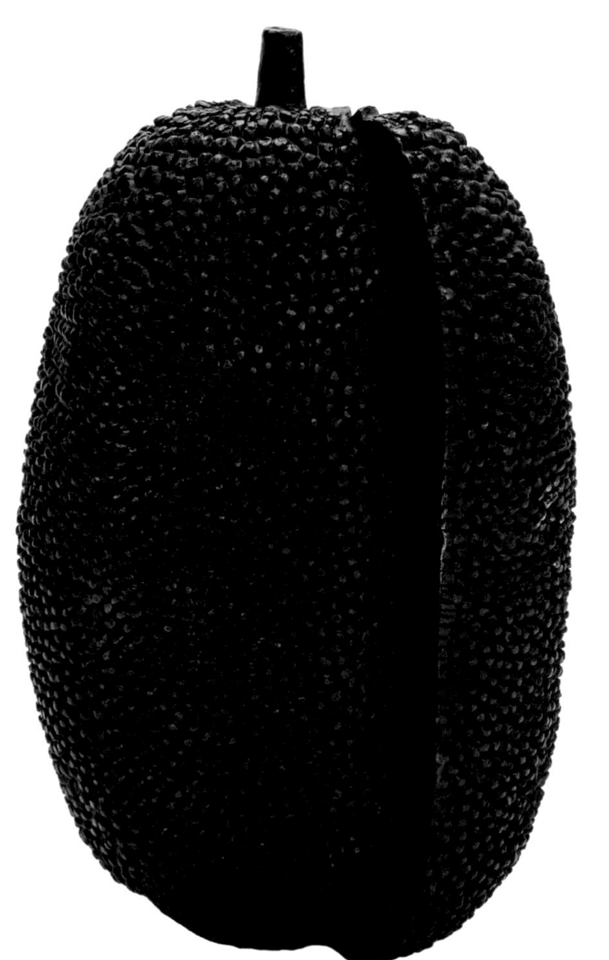

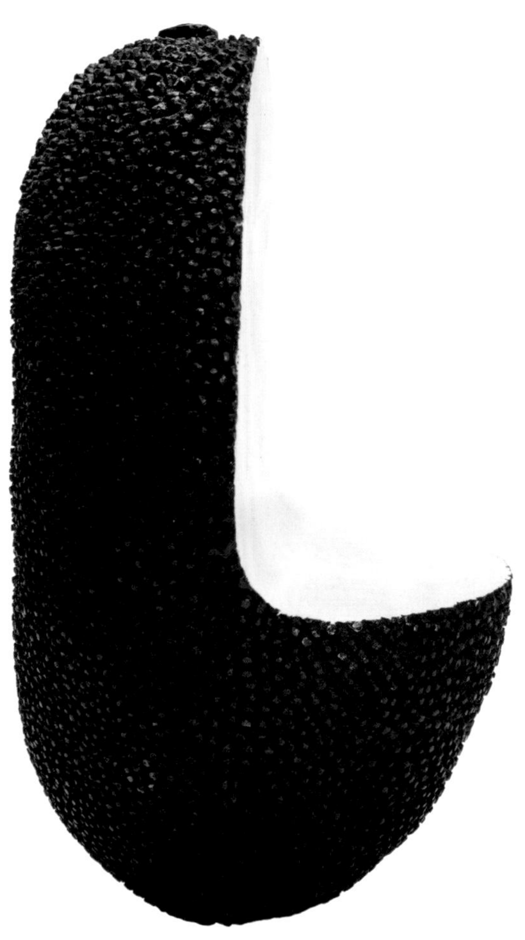

*Brasília Parede (**Brasília Wall**)*, 2011
Bronze and acrylic
12 ⅝ × 8 ¼ × 6 ¹¹⁄₁₆ inches (32 × 21 × 17 cm)

Brasília TV, 2011
Bronze and acrylic
12 ⅝ × 8 ¼ × 6 ¹¹⁄₁₆ inches (32 × 21 × 17 cm)

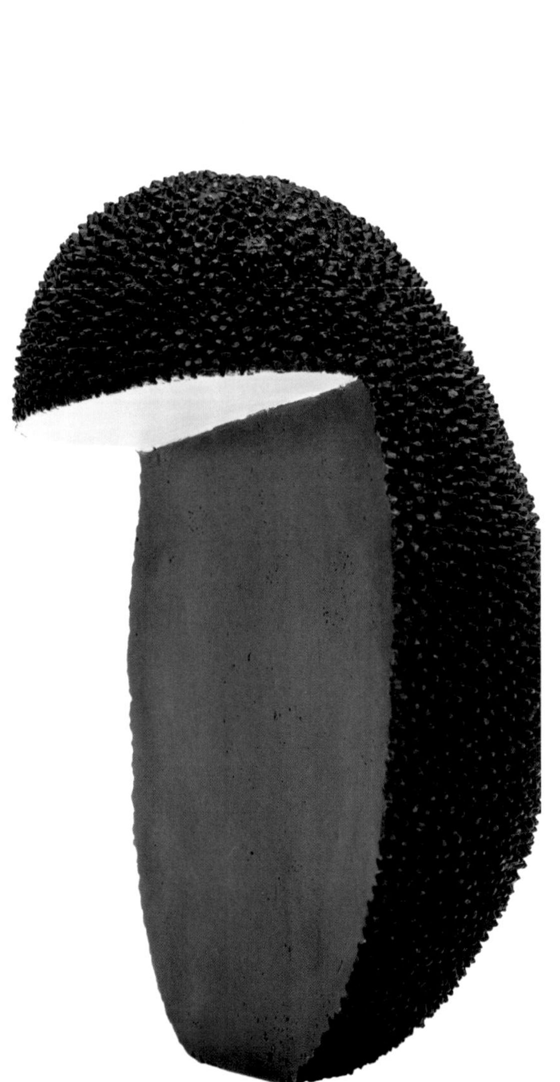

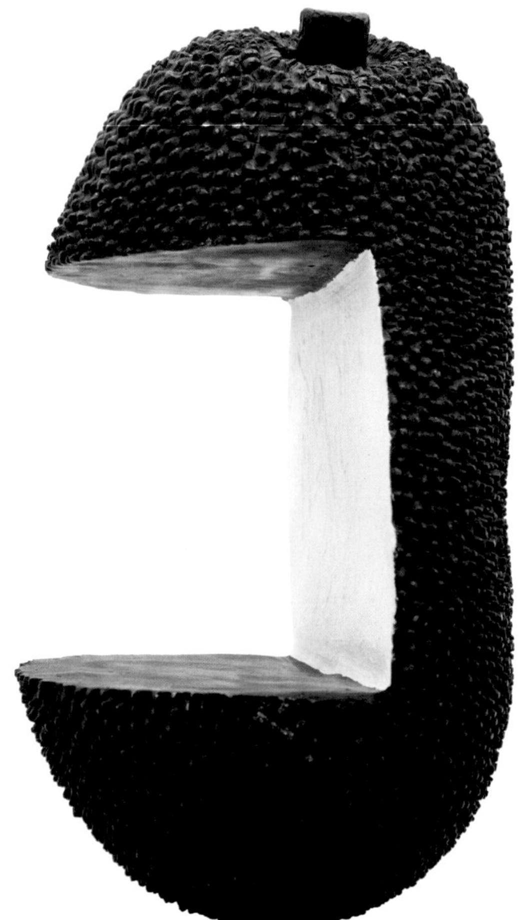

Beijo (*Kiss*), 2011
Bronze and acrylic
14 ¹⁵⁄₁₆ × 14 ³⁄₁₆ × 4 ¾ inches (38 × 36 × 12 cm)

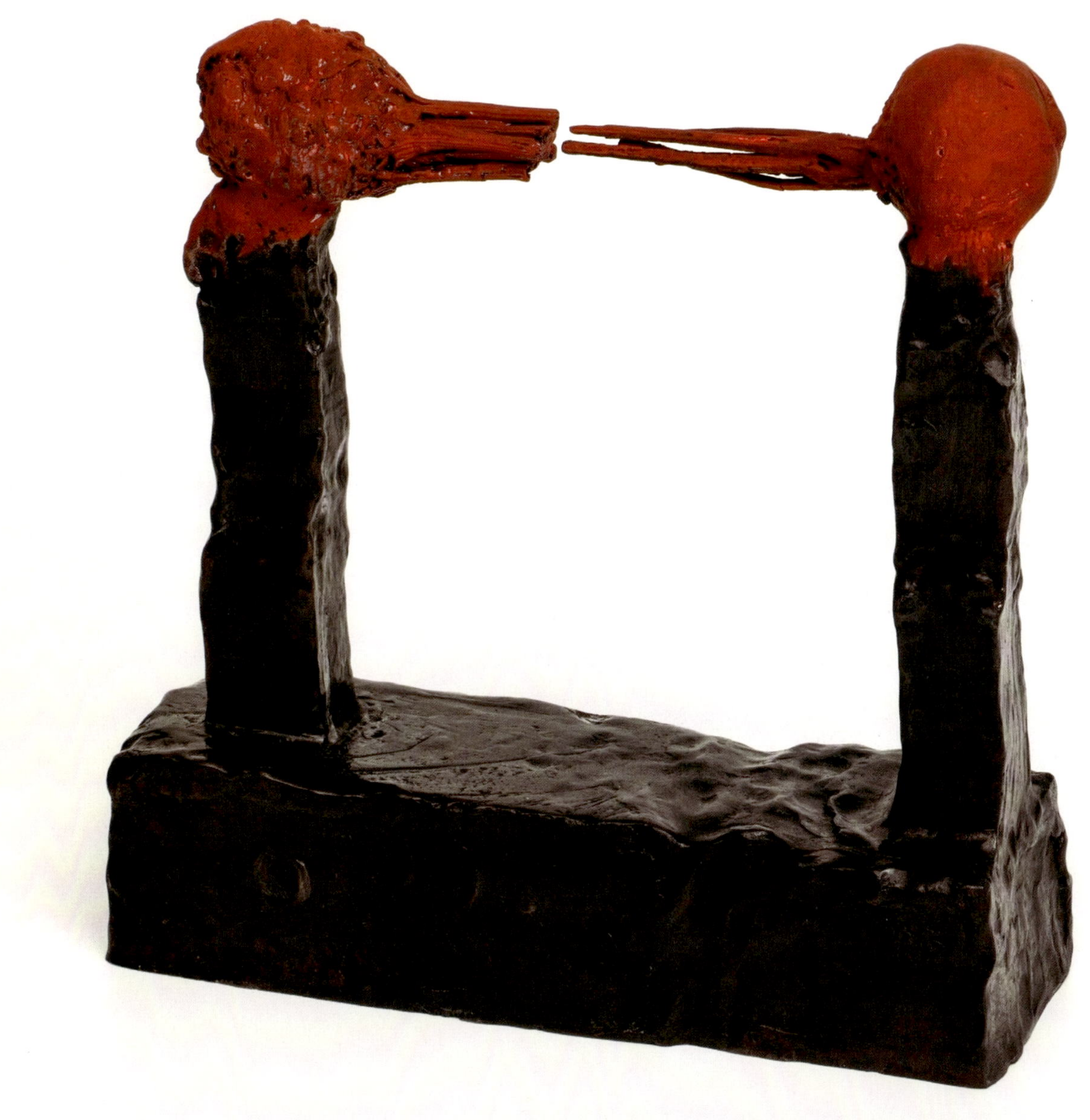

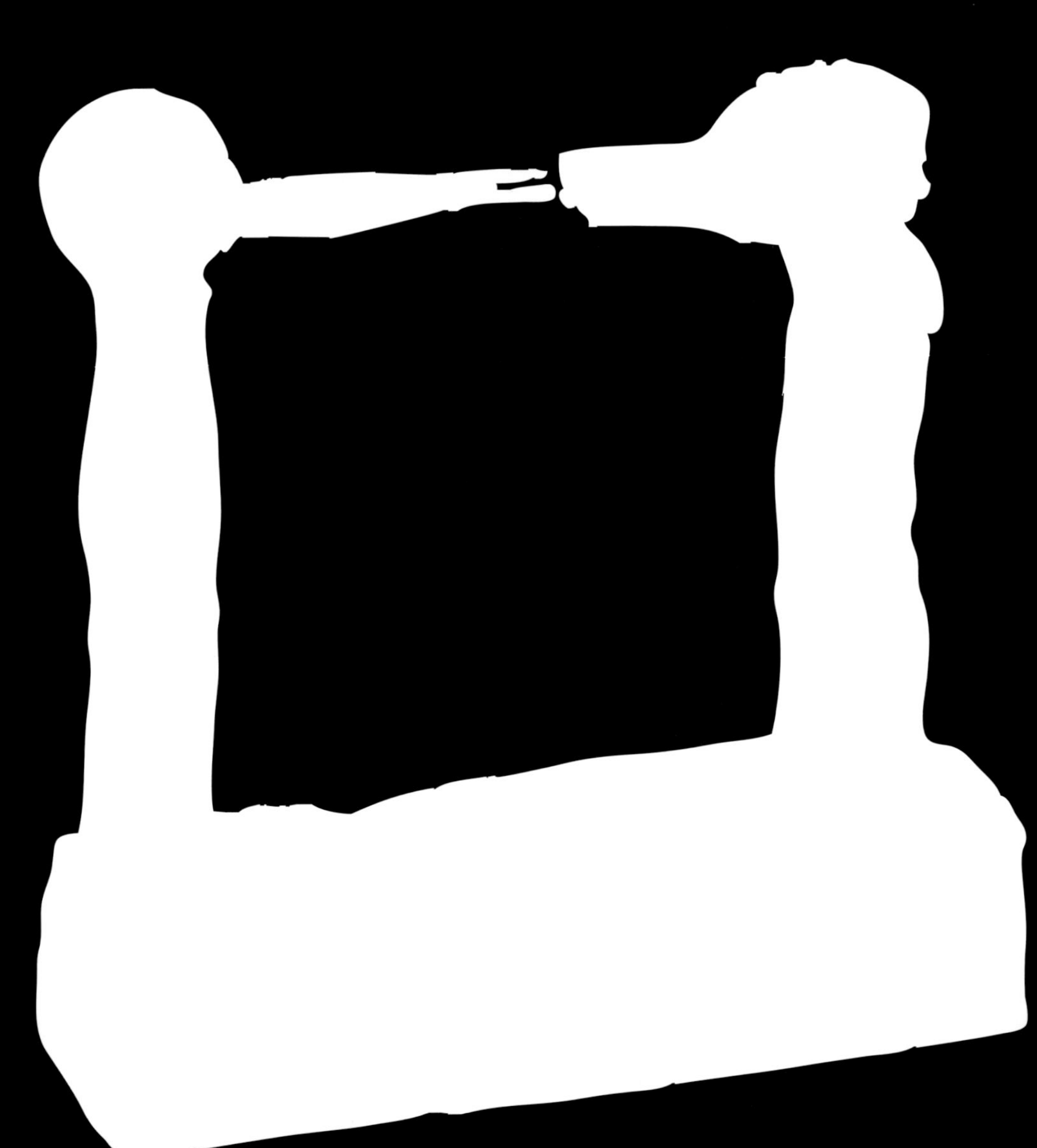

BEIJO

I like to think that there are three
entrances to my process, portals through which I find
the beginnings of work. I might start from an image,
such as a makeup tutorial, a picture of stars, or a
cake decorated with peaches. The second portal is
through an idea. I might decide to paint a newspaper
pattern in a desperate attempt to insert contemporary
issues into my practice, for example. The third is
the material itself. Clay, for one, speaks many ideas
if one listens. Some works reference art history,
but this is rarely the starting motivation. *Beijo* (*Kiss*,
2011) began with the use of vegetables as material.
I had found an expressive piece of beetroot, with its
stalks hydrated and erect, and it quickly reminded
me of Maria Martins's *O Impossível* (*The Impossible*,
1945). In just a minute, a celery root volunteered to
complete the kissing scene.

—E.V.

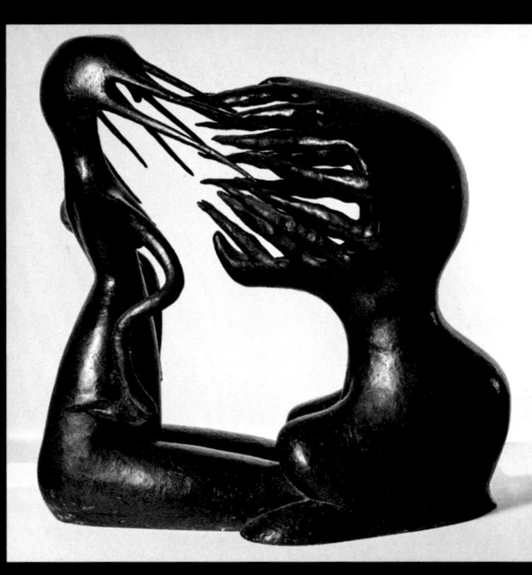

Maria Martins, *O Impossível* (*The Impossible*), 1945.
Bronze, 31 ½ × 31 ¼ × 17 ⅛ inches (80 × 79.5 ×
43.5 cm), Museu de Arte Moderna,
Río de Janeiro

Desenho (*Drawing*), 2011
Bronze and acrylic
12 ⅝ × 17 ⁵⁄₁₆ × 12 ³⁄₁₆ inches (32 × 44 × 31 cm)

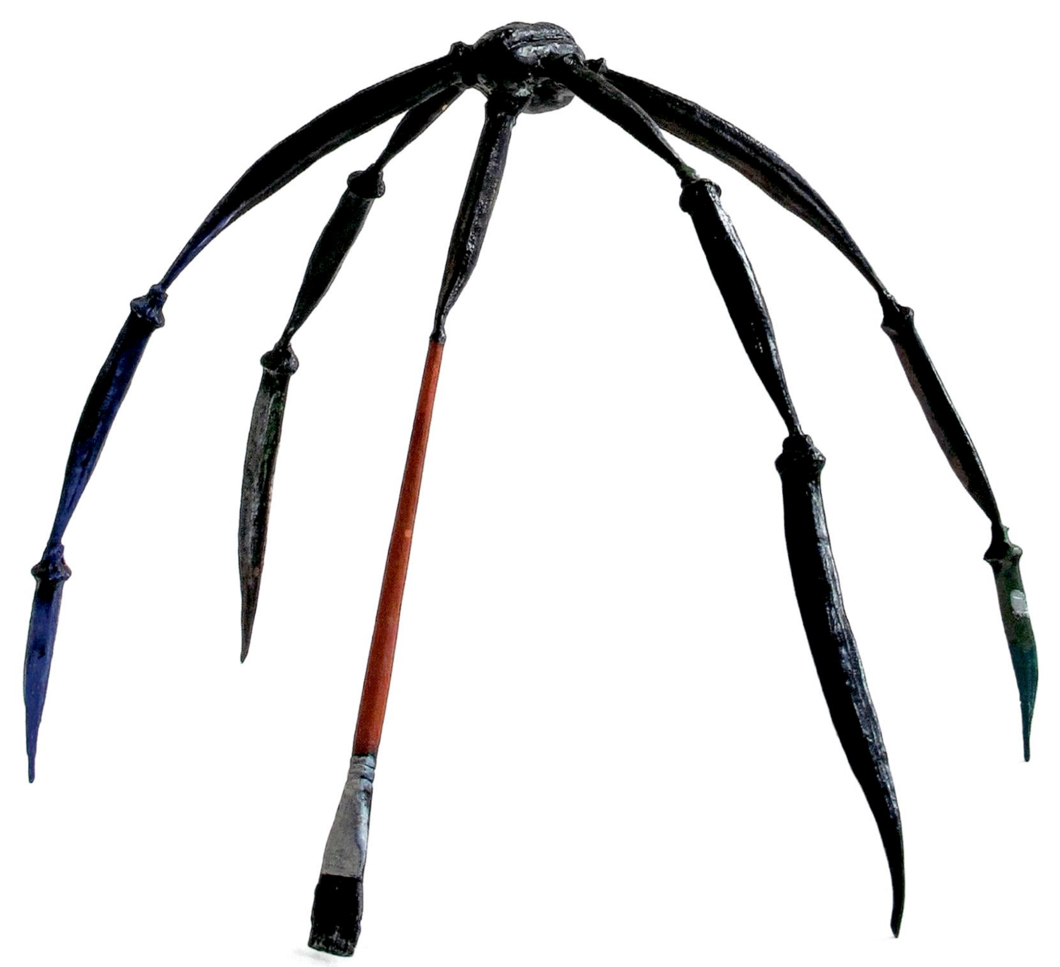

Romana (Blue), 2011
Concrete
30 ⁵⁄₁₆ × 7 ¹⁄₁₆ × 7 ¹⁄₁₆ inches (77 × 18 × 18 cm)

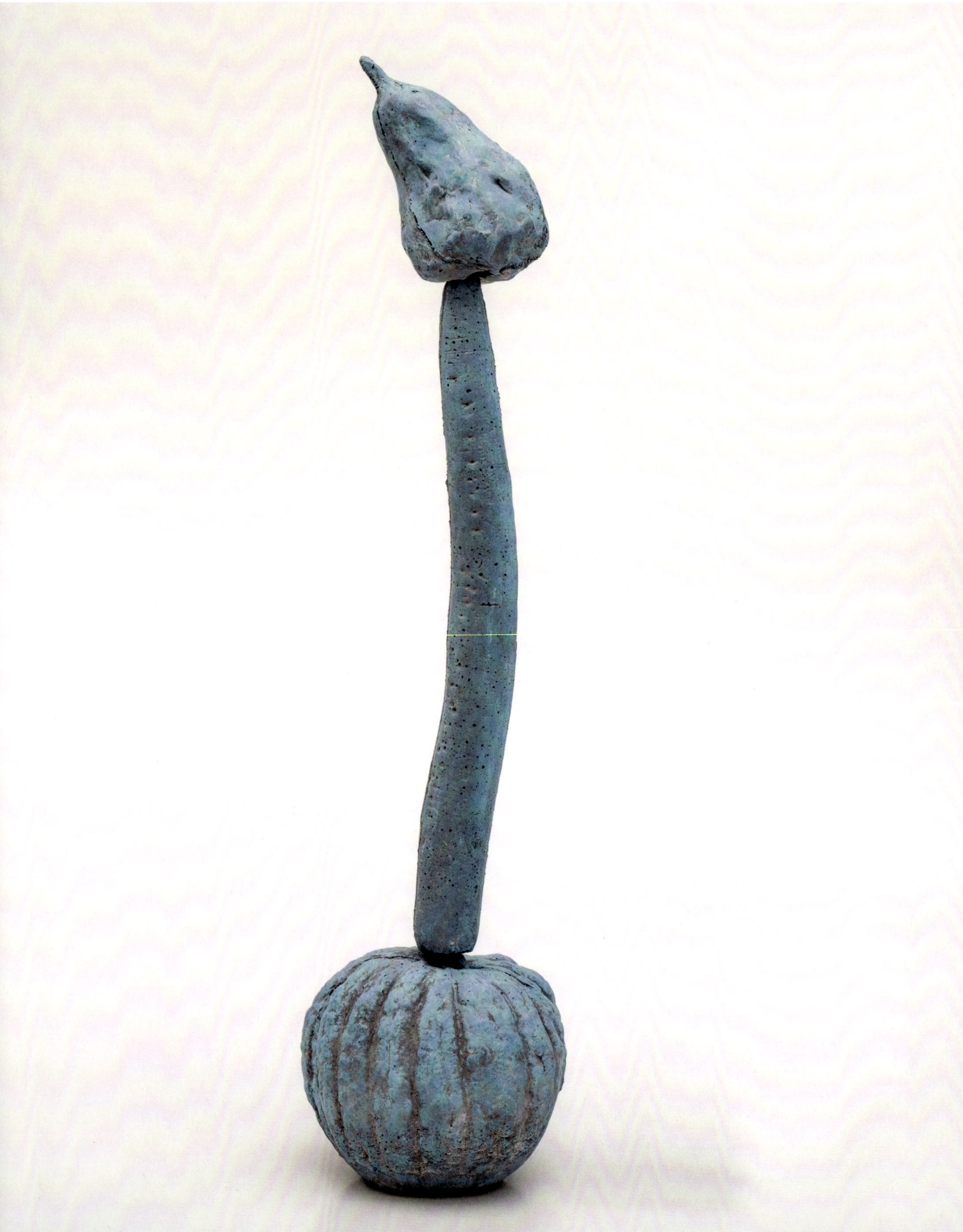

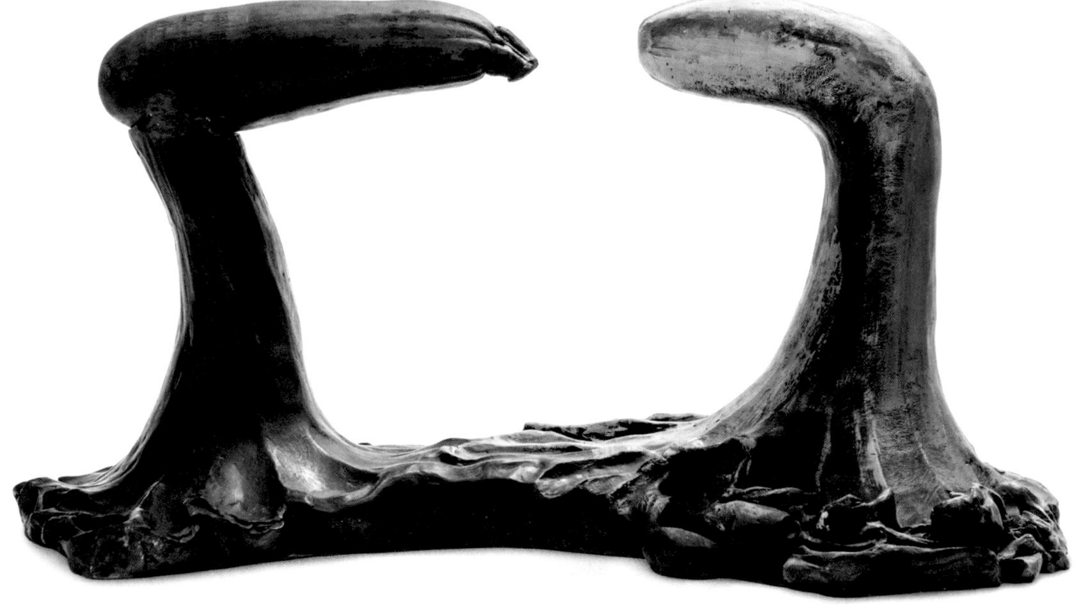

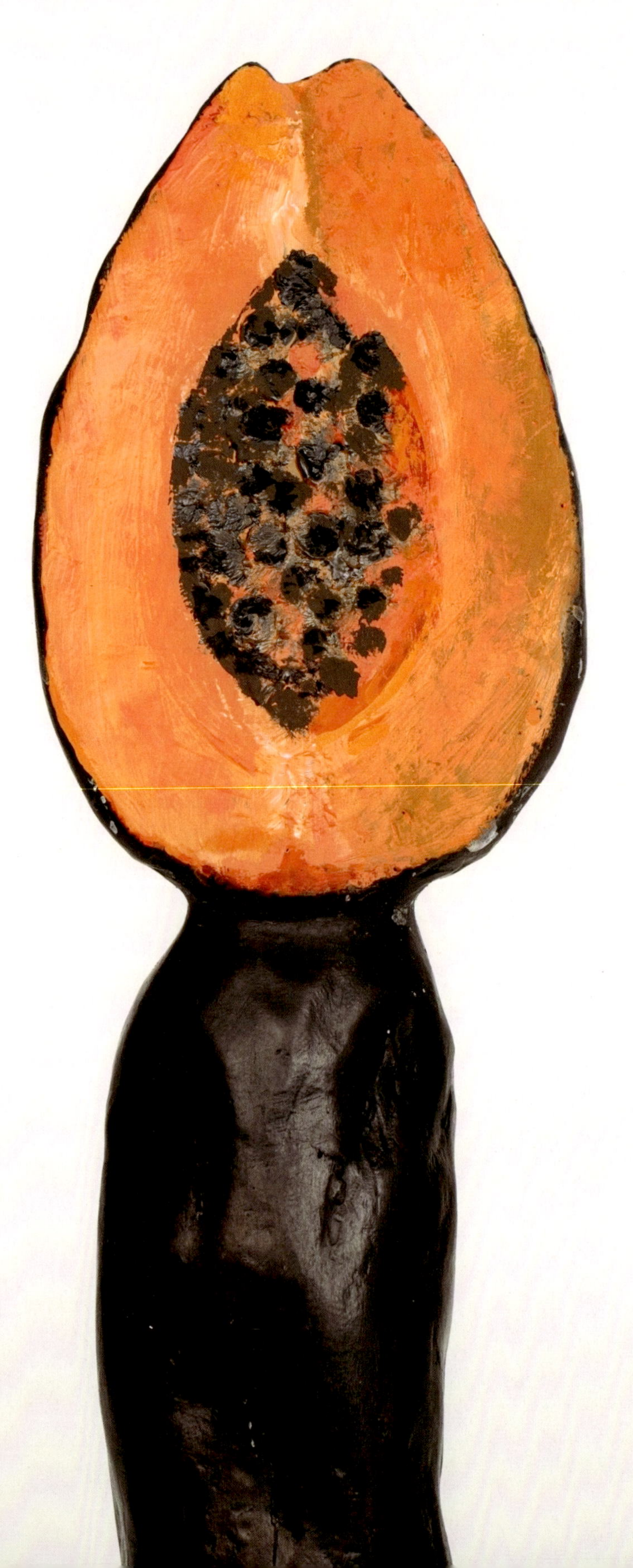

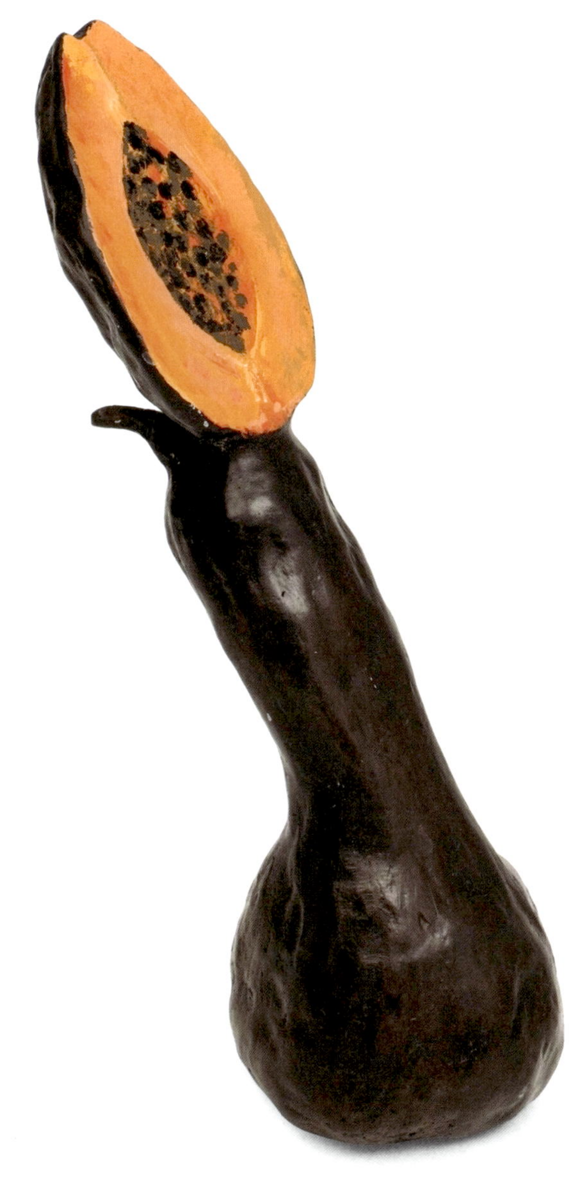

Scale Drawing (*Escala Desenho*), 2011
Bronze, concrete, and oil pastel
9 1/16 × 7 7/8 × 3 15/16 inches (23 × 20 × 10 cm)

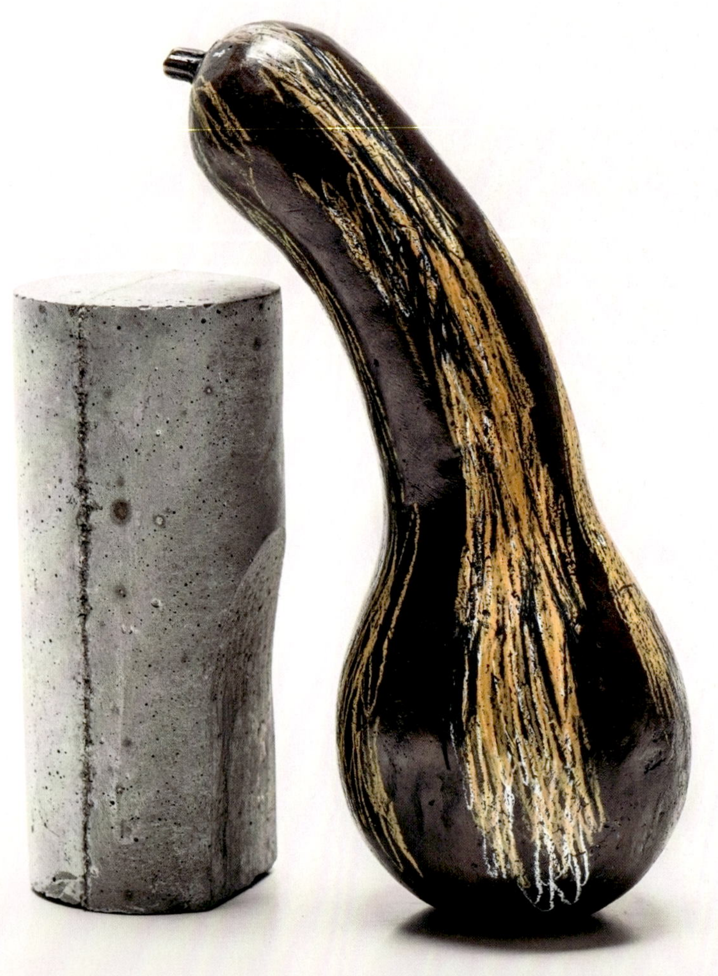

Dino Pot, 2012
Concrete and wax
59 ¹⁄₁₆ × 17 ¹¹⁄₁₆ × 17 ¹¹⁄₁₆ inches (150 × 45 × 45 cm)

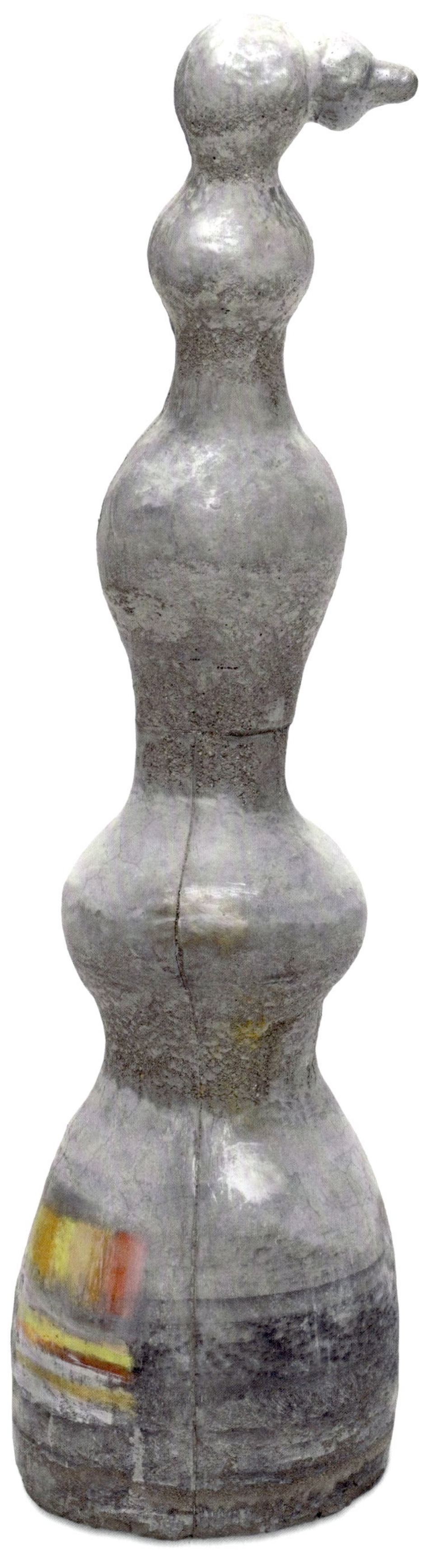

Turner, 2014
Concrete and acrylic
14 $\frac{3}{16}$ × 9 $\frac{13}{16}$ × 5 $\frac{1}{8}$ inches (36 × 25 × 13 cm)

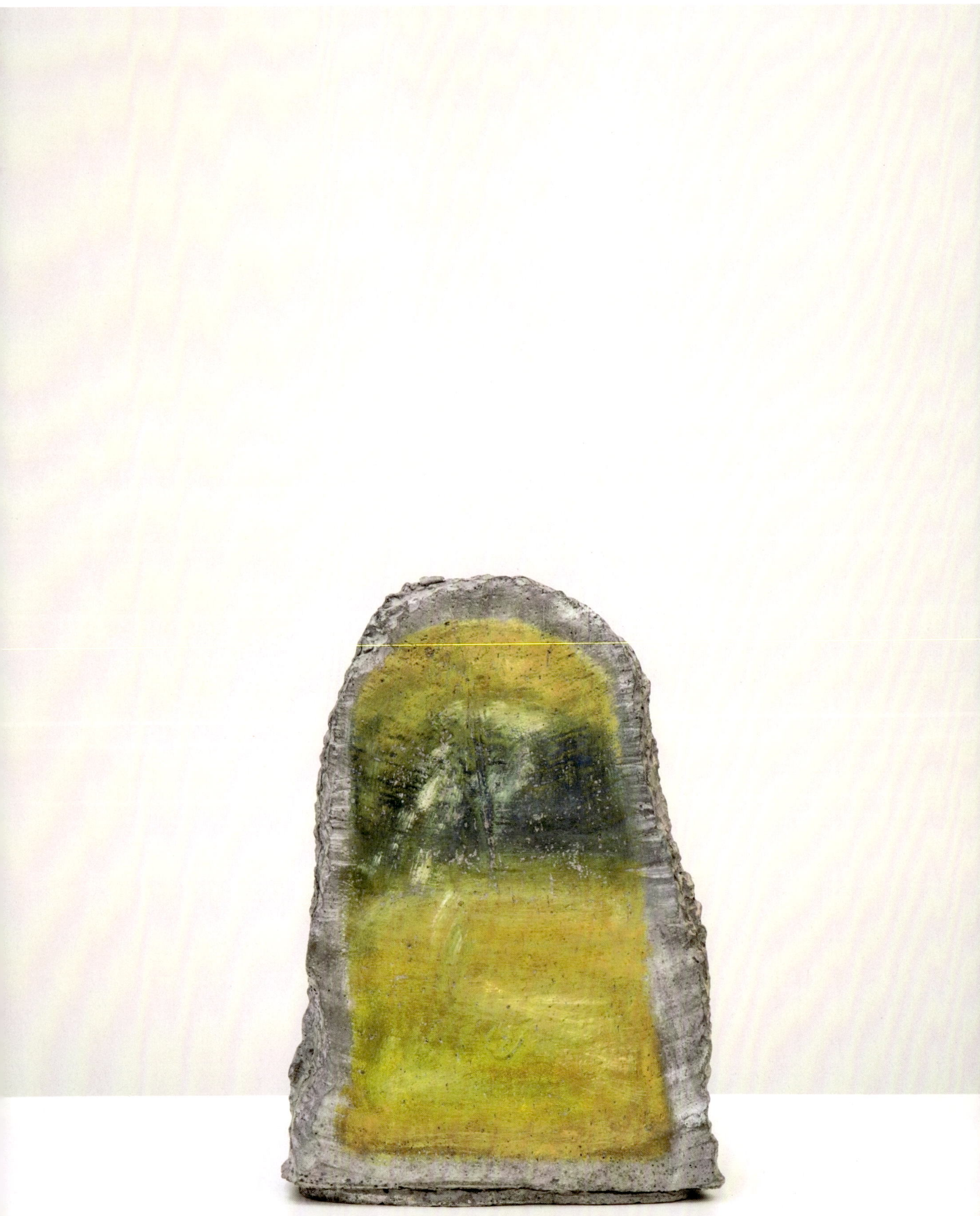

Cisne com Martelo (*Swan with Hammer*), 2013
Bronze and sledgehammer
25 9/16 × 27 9/16 × 27 9/16 inches (65 × 70 × 70 cm)

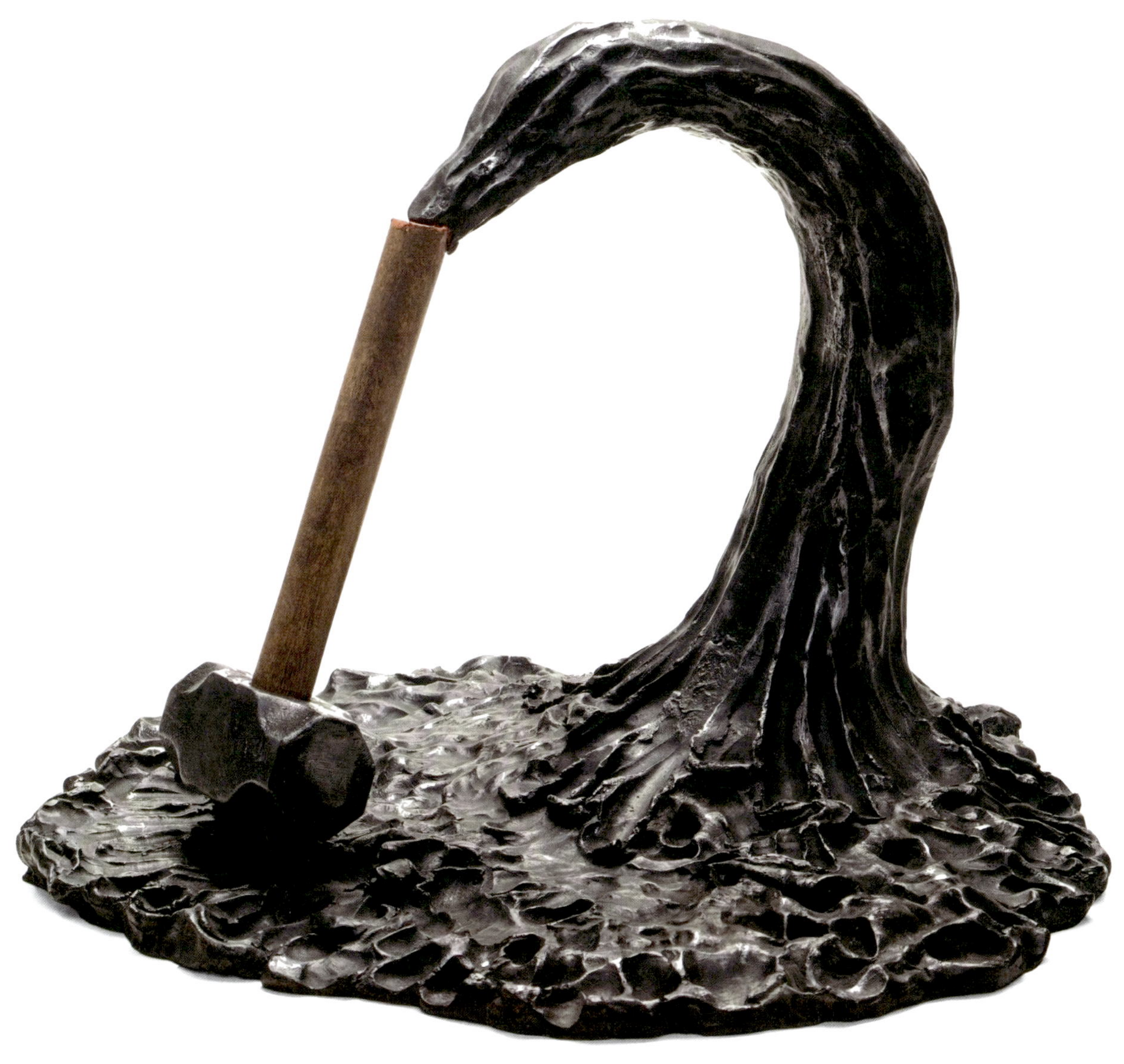

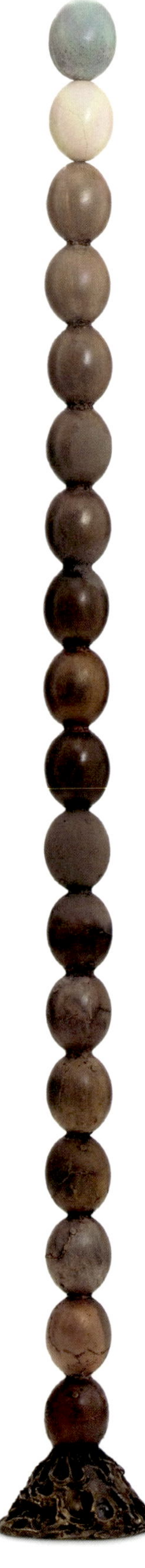

Egg Tower, 2013
Bronze, ostrich eggshell, concrete, and wax
110 ¼ × 15 ¾ × 15 ¾ inches (280 × 40 × 40 cm)

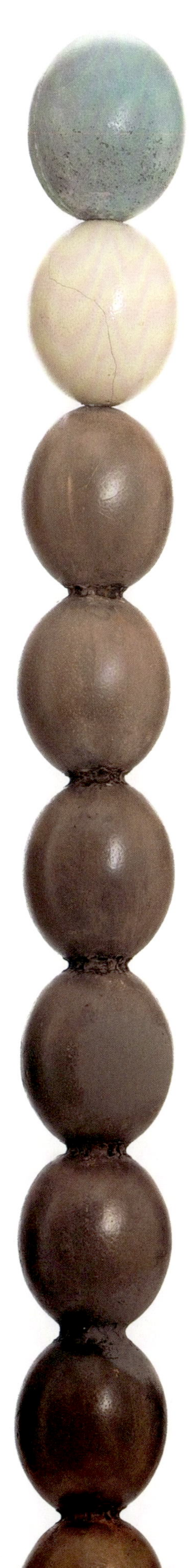

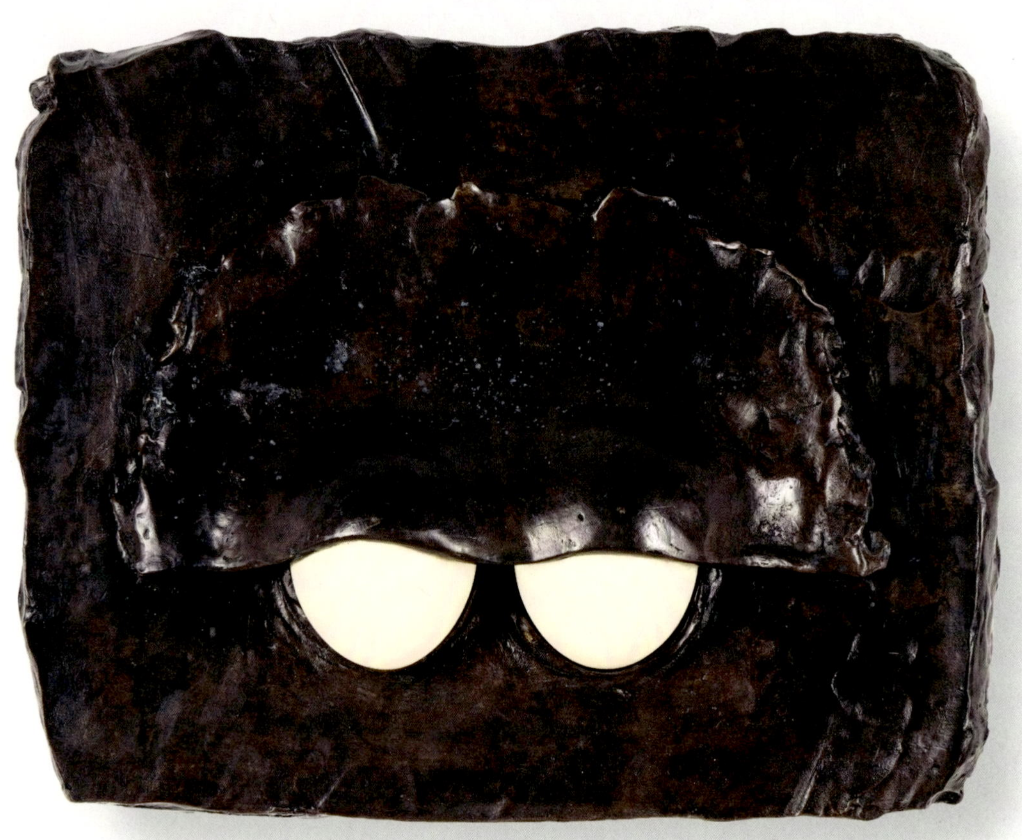

Boyfriend, 2014
Bronze and ostrich eggshell
19 ¹¹⁄₁₆ × 24 × 5 ½ inches (50 × 61 × 14 cm)

Lápis, 2014
Bronze and wax
112 ³⁄₁₆ × 7 ⁷⁄₈ × 7 ¹⁄₁₆ inches (285 × 20 × 18 cm)

Torre Lápis (*Pencil Tower*), 2014
Bronze and wax
74 ¹³⁄₁₆ × 7 ⁷⁄₈ × 6 ¹¹⁄₁₆ inches (190 × 20 × 17 cm)

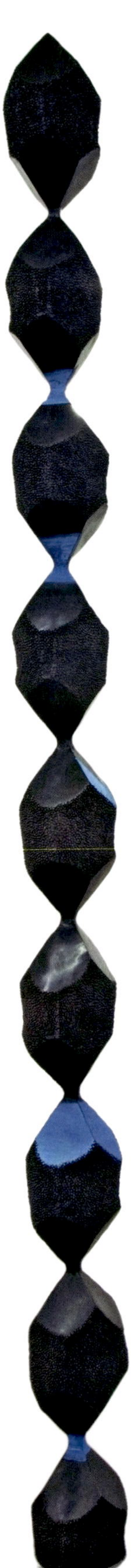

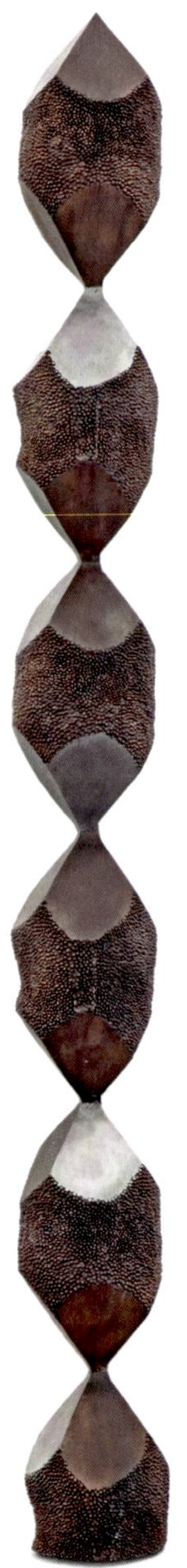

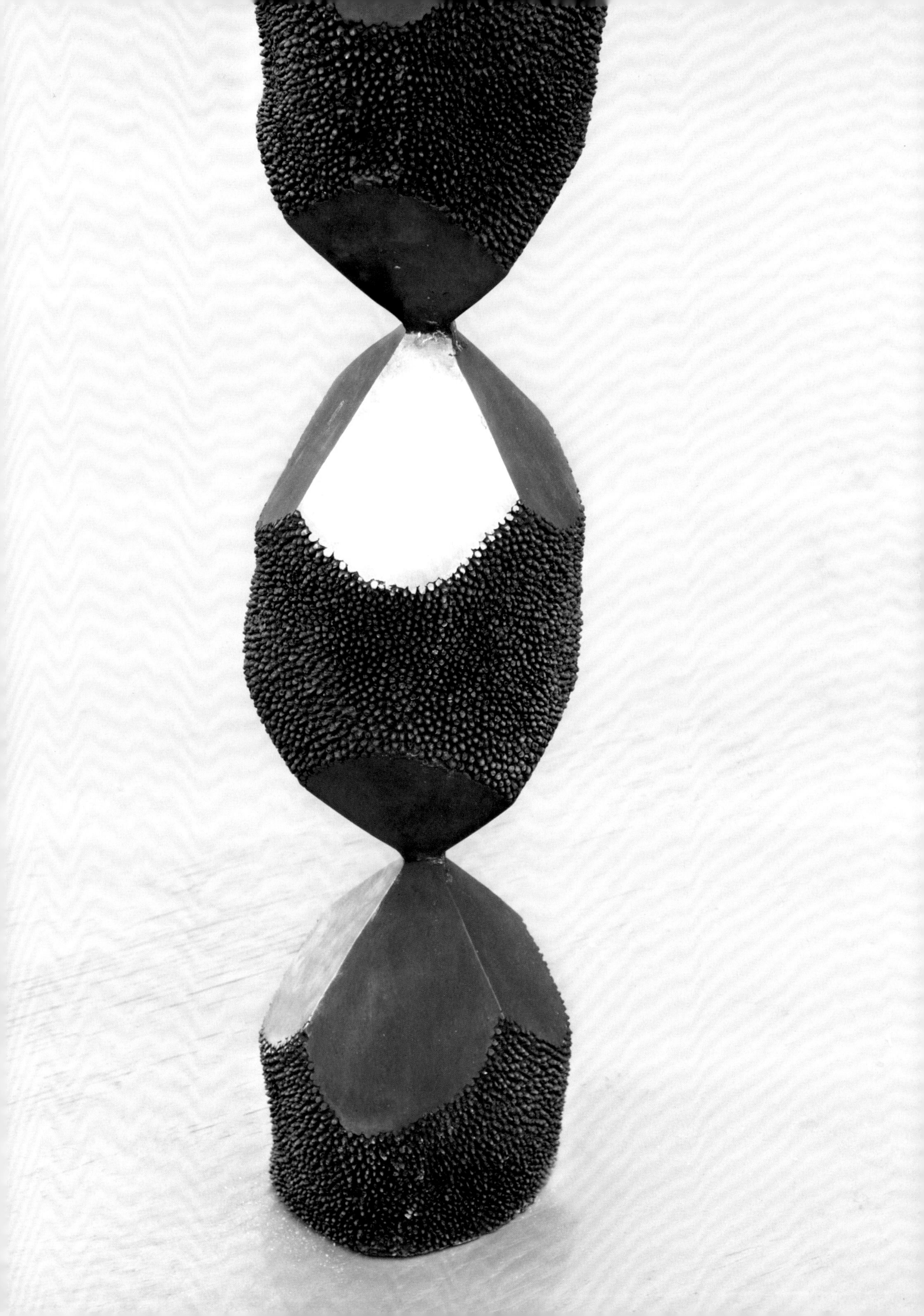

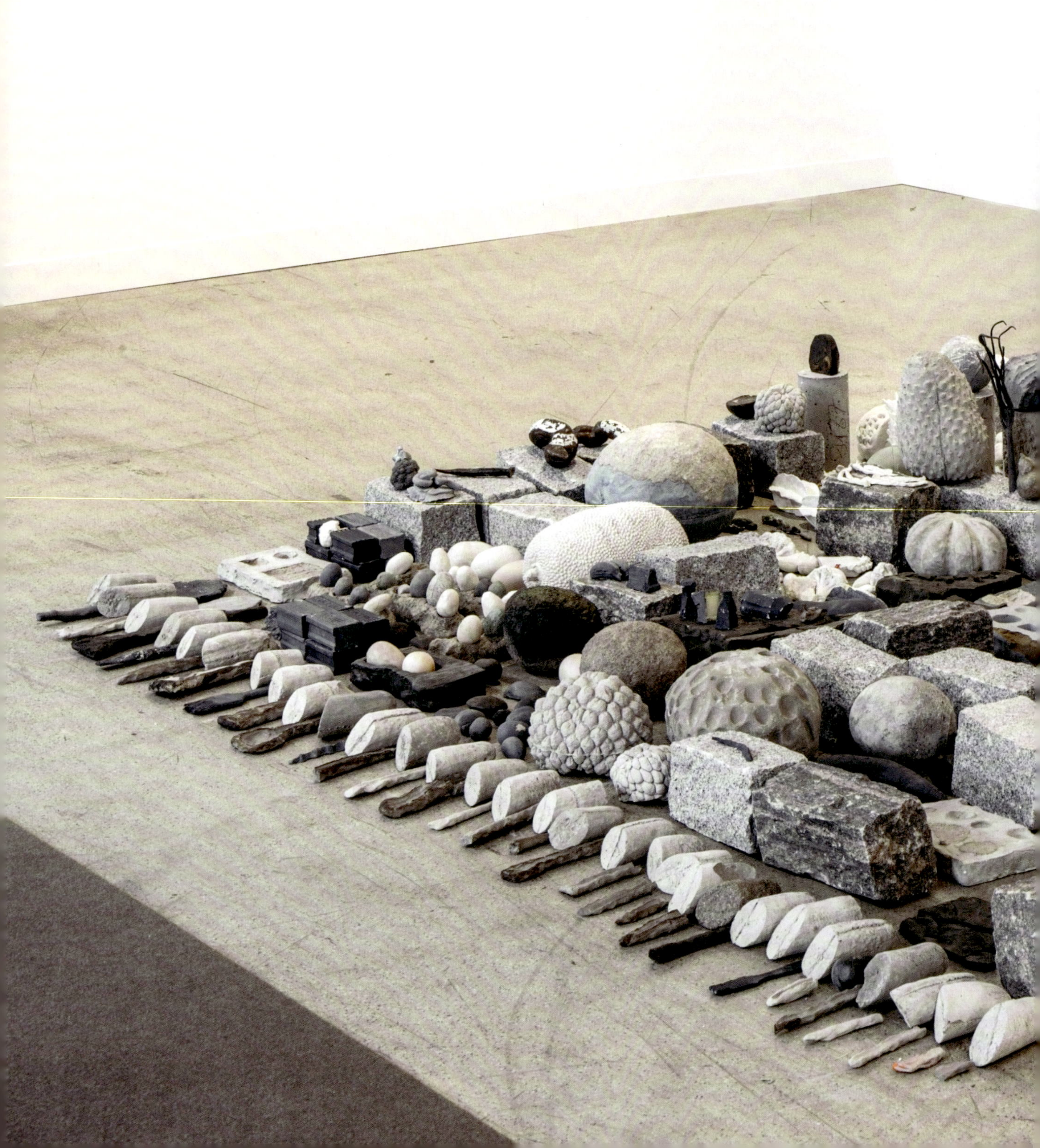

Cemitério com Franja (*Cemetery with Fringe*), 2014
Studio remains: bronze, concrete, clay, cold porcelain clay, and stone
632 pieces: 11 ¹³⁄₁₆ × 86 ⁵⁄₈ × 94 ½ inches (30 × 220 × 240 cm) overall

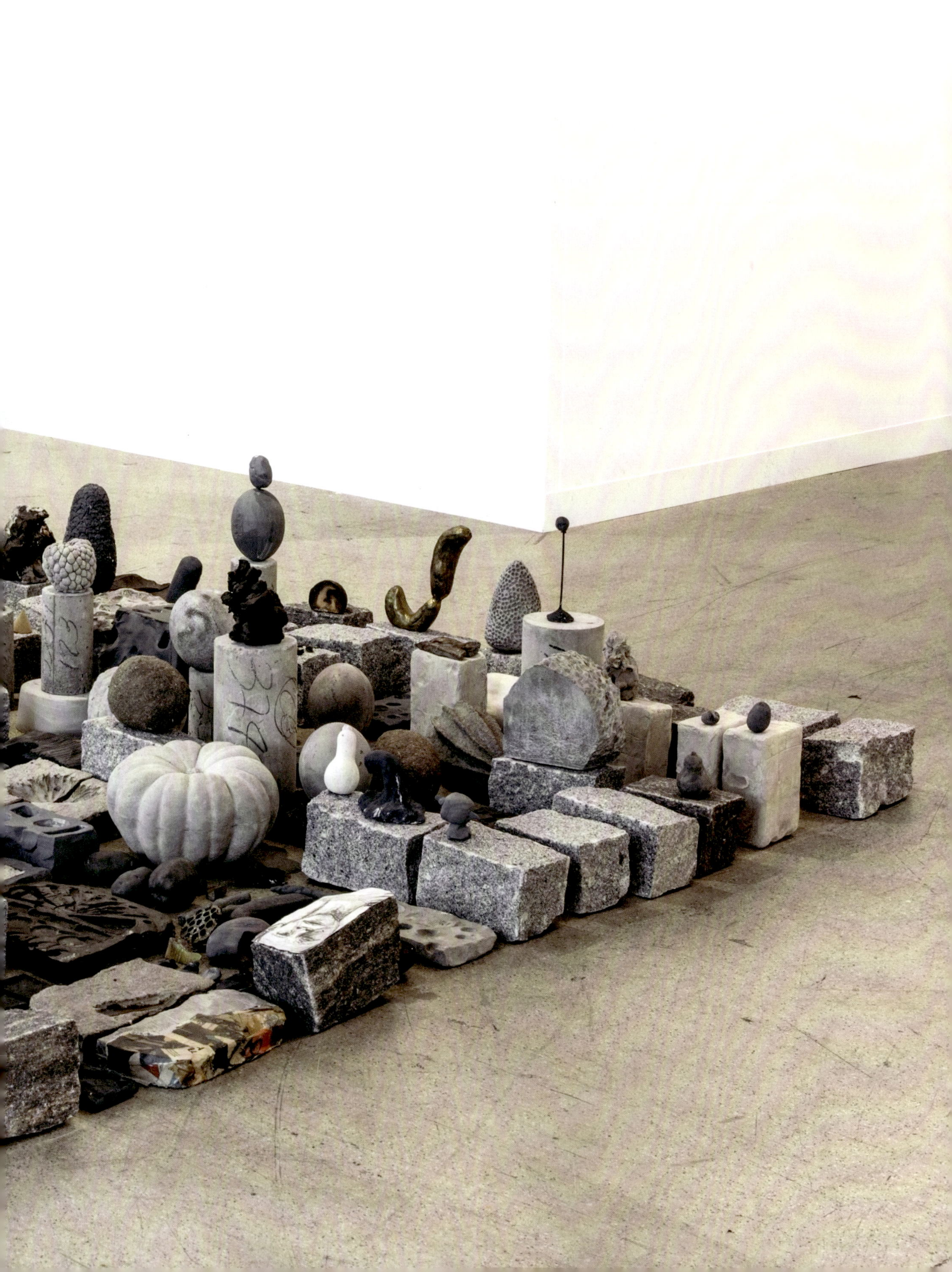

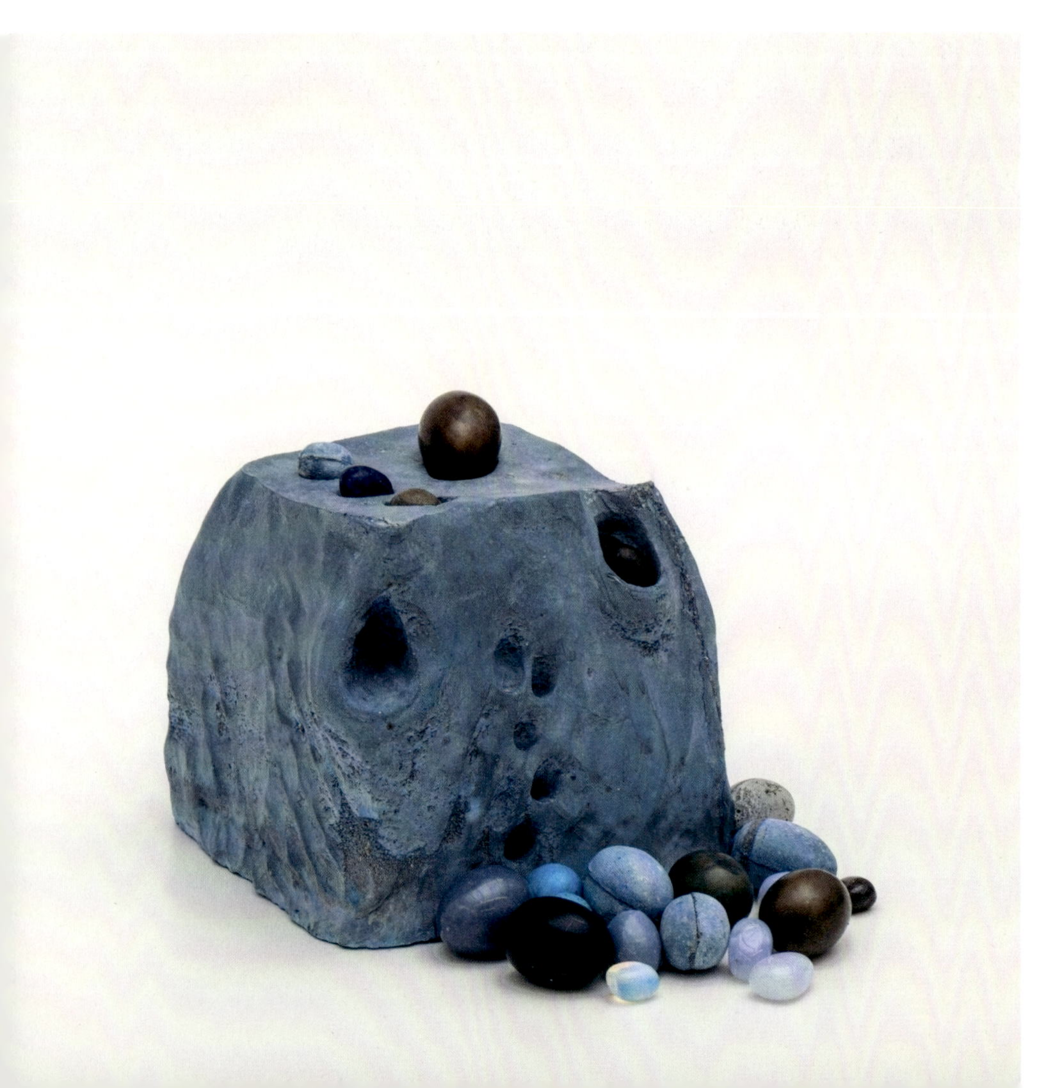

Black Sun, 2015
Bronze and wax
25 ⁹⁄₁₆ × 26 × 1 ¹⁵⁄₁₆ inches (65 × 66 × 5 cm)

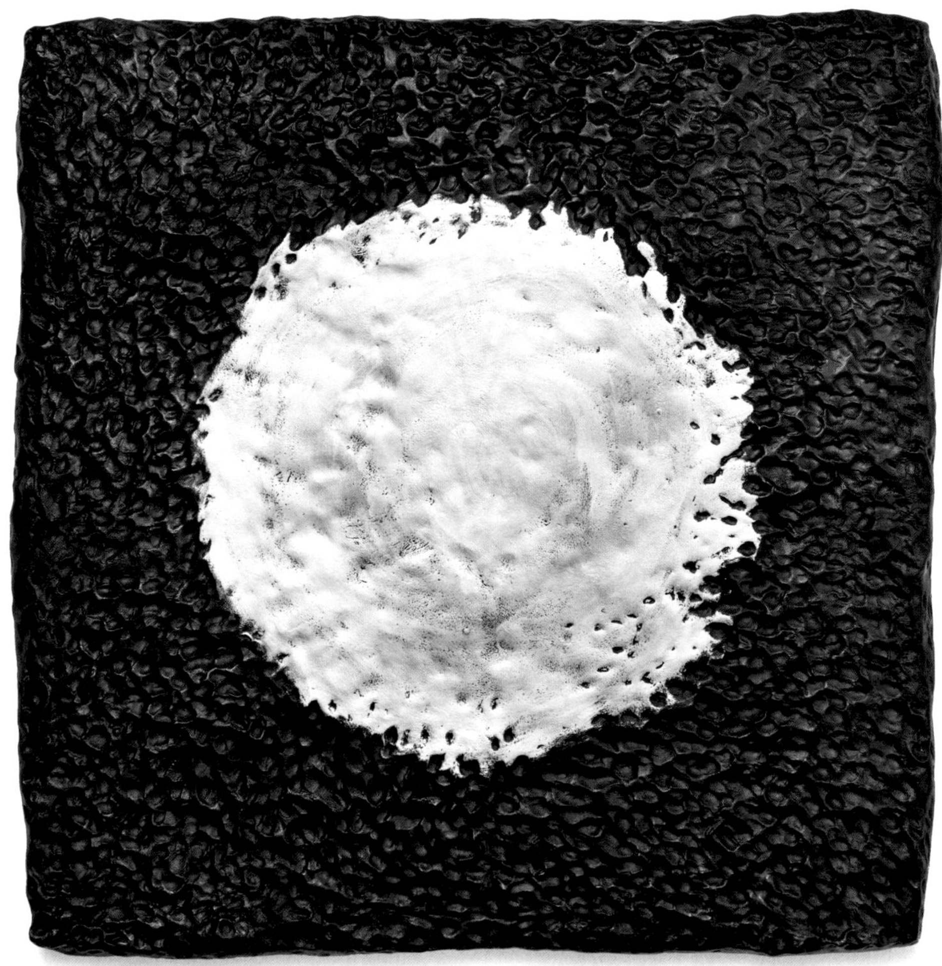

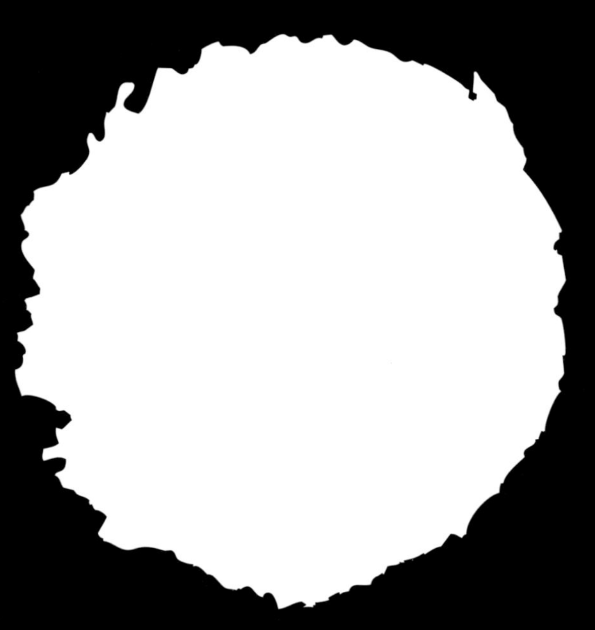

BLACK SUN AND THE NIGHT SCULPTURE CLIMBED THE WALL

If I were to describe *Black Sun* (2015) in one word, it would be "placid." Making bronze reliefs has not always been a serene process.

I worked at home for many years and made most of my fruit sculptures on the kitchen table by assembling real vegetables. In 2013, eggs entered the menu. As a pristine, symmetrical object, the egg brought new possibilities, in contrast to the irregular textures of vegetables. I began modeling clay cubes with intricate caves and depressions to cradle the eggs. I made and collected eggs of bronze, clay, stone, Fimo, and concrete.

I felt intrigued that each side of *Cubo* (*Cube*, 2013) afforded a complete composition in and of itself, and I wanted to experience this more directly. So I cut another cube into slabs and ended up with plates as chunky as books. The "books" would be seen from above, at first with loose eggs deposited on their surfaces. Afterward, I would glue the eggs to make the compositions more assertive.

One night, as I held a plate vertically to check if the eggs had adhered properly, I felt the urge to hang the plate on the wall. I was so excited; it felt as if I had invented the relief in art history. At the same time, it felt somewhat inappropriate, as though I was engaging in a forbidden game. There is a certain sanctity associated with wall works—the legacy of painting—but I was driven by the impact of the eggs defying gravity. It was as if I could sense them reverberating in my teeth.

Two years and numerous reliefs later, the formats had expanded, the gestures were bolder and more diverse. Stimulus didn't come just from eggs but from any source in which I detected tactility (makeup cases, decorated fish plates, Lorenzato's paintings . . .). Amid the frenzy of imagery that ignited these wall works, there was a common principle: they all began with a slab of clay.

When I was making *Black Sun*, that rush of images paused momentarily, allowing the material to take center stage. There were various possible finishes to the clay base, from smooth to crunchy toppings, beaten up by fingertips. *Black Sun* casts a contemplative eye on the "blank" plane, valuing its autonomy. I felt truly present when shaping it; I wanted to caress the bumpy surface until it smoothed out. I cleaned a circle in the center of the field, a space of emptiness safe from the agitated energy of the finger marks, a respite from the

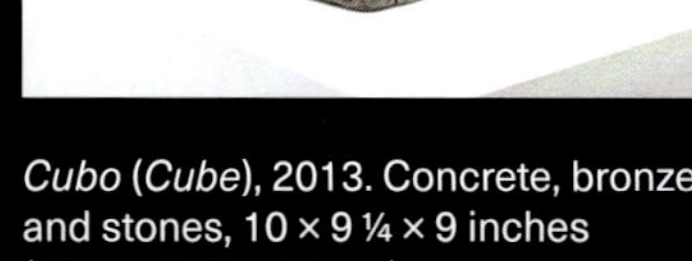

Cubo (*Cube*), 2013. Concrete, bronze, and stones, 10 × 9 ¼ × 9 inches (25.5 × 23.5 × 23 cm)

constant "work, work, work" mentality. The material talked back, shaping the irregular contours of the circle, like a wave licking the sand, the edges melting and merging. Its uneven contour evoked the image of a sun with flames—not the conventional rays but rather the magnificent eruptions that form solar flares. At the same time, I associated the black patina of the bronze with the dark shadow of an eclipse, with the silver acting not as color but as reflection.

—E.V.

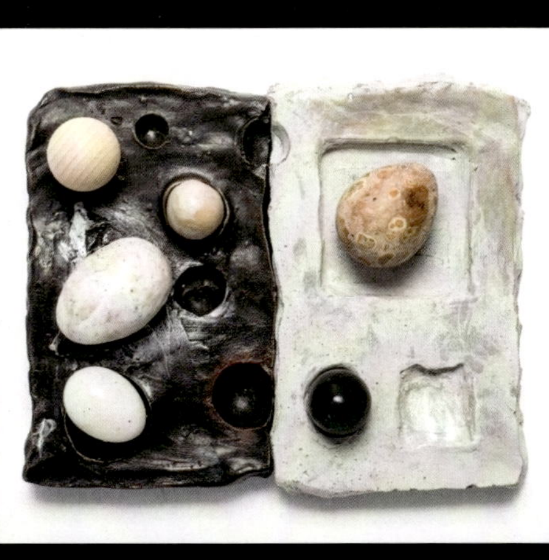

Coffee Table Book, 2013. Bronze, concrete, wood, polymer clay, stones, and wax, 9 × 11 ⁷⁄₁₆ × 3 ⅜ inches (23 × 29 × 3.5 cm)

Turtle, 2015
Bronze, concrete, raku ceramics, wax, and acrylic
18 ⅞ × 39 ⅜ × 26 ⅜ inches (48 × 100 × 67 cm)

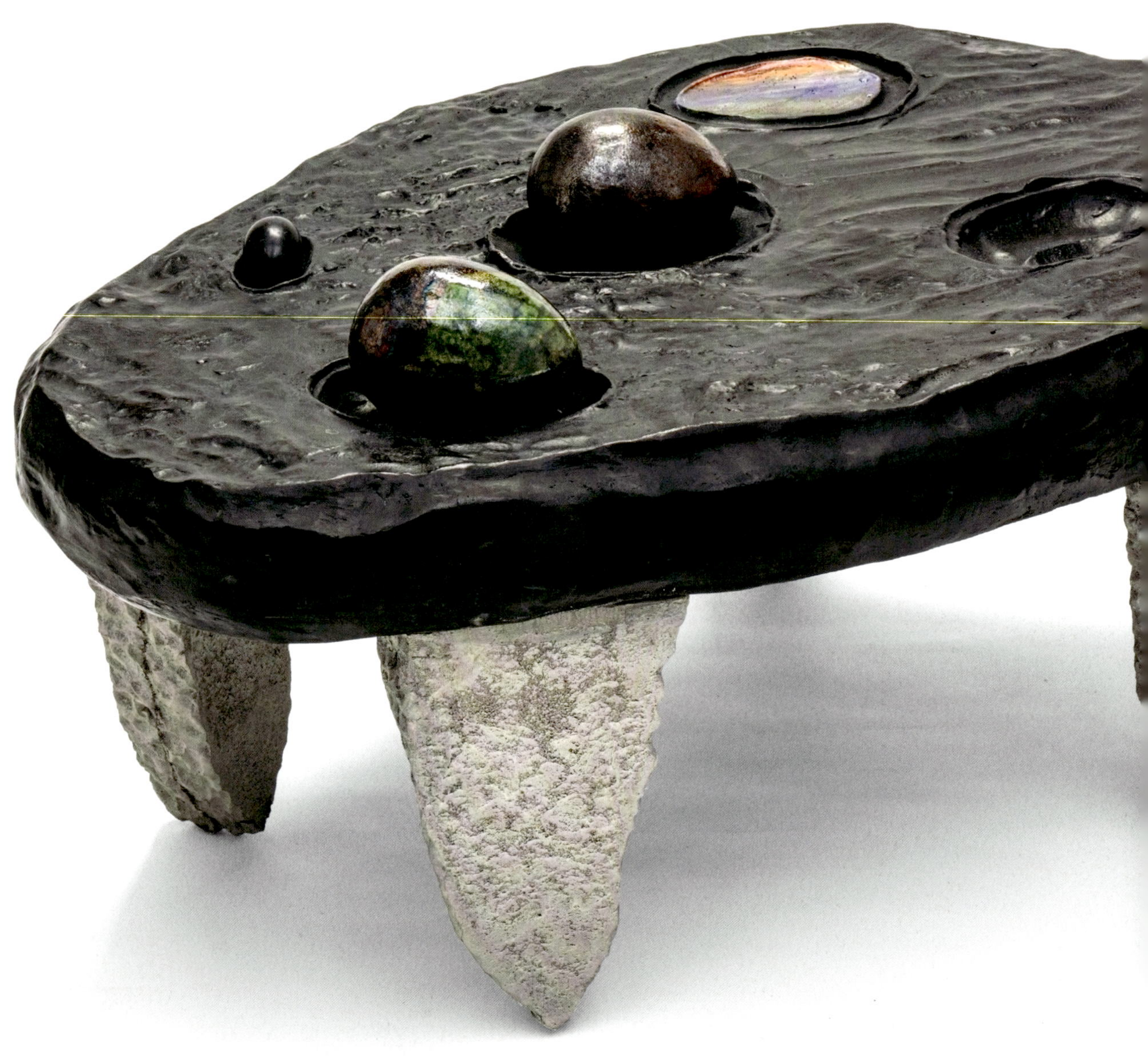

Tarsila com Koons, 2015
Bronze and acrylic
10 ⅝ × 10 ⅝ × 12 ³⁄₁₆ inches (27 × 27 × 31 cm)

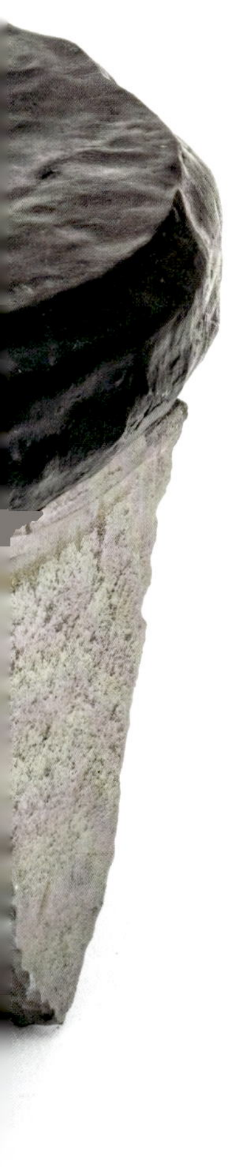

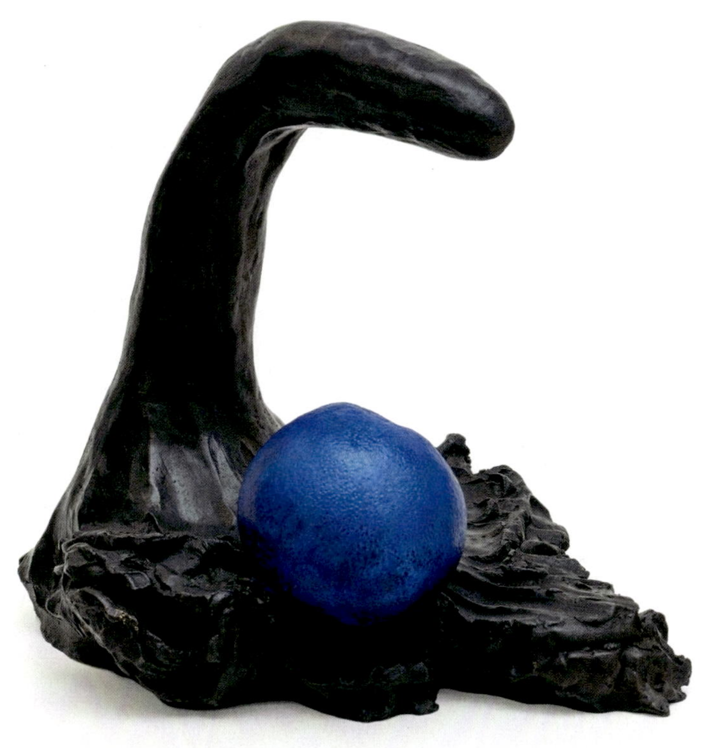

ERIKA VERZUTTI: PAINTBRUSHES AND NEWSPAPER

Ruba Katrib

The reaction to folk and outsider art is perhaps one of the most defining features of twentieth-century Western art.[1] The push and pull of attraction and repulsion toward practices connected to everyday life and the stuff that comprises it has prompted avant-garde movements to either embrace the taboos of prosaic art or make gestures against it. The work of Brazilian artist Erika Verzutti summons high-art references while pulling from more far-reaching annals and everyday life to evolve her objects into critical, witty, and contemporary manifestations of lived experience. Much of her work harkens to moments in which other artists absorbed and transformed what was around them into relatable works, even if surprisingly so. Working primarily in sculpture, Verzutti synthesizes notions of the familiar as extending from objects both ordinary and venerated, as what is familiar includes art itself.

Verzutti references and recodes through material means, deploying doppelgängers, alter egos, and stand-ins as she pursues strategies of subterfuge tied to her exploration of and commentary on the role of the artist and how materials can effectively operate as doubles, playing themselves while containing the possibility of being transformed.[2] This self-reflexive process reanimates certain canonical artists' borrowings from folk traditions, notably Jasper Johns's early collage works, emblematic of 1960s New York, and Tarsila do Amaral's faux-naive style, which draws on pre-Columbian motifs and the cosmovisions of Indigenous peoples in Brazil. Other references include European modernists such as Constantin Brancusi and Alberto Giacometti. The mode of provisionality evident across Verzutti's work of assemblage can also be seen in the sculpture of more contemporary artists including Abraham Cruzvillegas, Isa Genzken, and Rachel Harrison—their provocative combinations of both found and studio-fabricated objects generating a conceptual and narrative thrust in their work. Yet the objects Verzutti creates have a more restrained and even formal appearance than is typical of these peers. For her, the distance between what is found and what is made is much shorter.

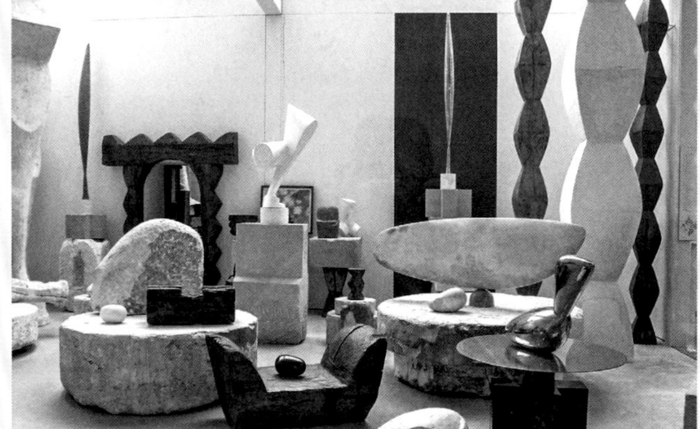

Reconstruction of Constantin Brancusi's studio, Centre Pompidou, Paris, 1997

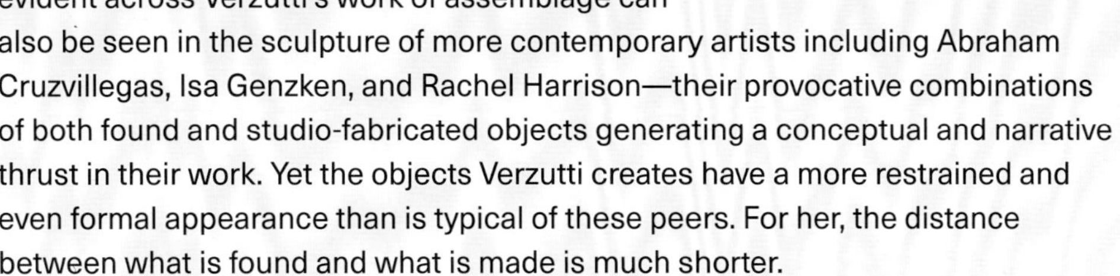

1   New York's Museum of Modern Art was built on such debates, as its founders embraced and reacted against folk and outsider art in its collections and galleries.

2   On the concept of the doppelgänger and live performance in Verzutti's work, see my essay "Swan Song," in *Erika Verzutti: The Indiscipline of Sculpture* (São Paulo: Museu de arte de São Paulo Assis Chateaubriand, 2021), 222–35.

An early work that exemplifies Verzutti's approach is *Jaspera na Escola* (*Jaspera at School*, 2006–8; page 16), a near-literal visualization of influence and study that merges two of Jasper Johns's motifs—the Ballantine Ale can and the paintbrush-filled Savarin coffee can—into a pineapple shape sitting on a notebook. In Verzutti's rendering, the paintbrushes are flamboyantly presented so as to resemble the pineapple's leaves, with their bristles projecting upward from the painted-bronze body of the fruit, instead of being hidden within, as in the original. The Ballantine Ale label is legible on the face of the pineapple, though splotches of blue paint interrupt its veracity; the notebook, meanwhile, is perhaps Verzutti's own. In the work's title, the femininization of Johns's name, "Jaspera," could be read as a stand-in for Verzutti herself, while "at School" suggests processes of learning, unlearning, and considering legacy. In Verzutti's hands, the ordinariness of a male artist's beer can in midcentury New York turns tropical. For Johns and Verzutti, the act of making an artwork about making art is a key modality, and the paintbrush a recurring motif. As an actual object, it offers a finishing touch—quite literally, the inclusion of a brush, or a bunch of brushes, physically completes many of Verzutti's painted constructions. Yet while the representation of the tool representing itself in her sculptures seems straightforward, how it completes the image or thing she is representing feels unexpected, like the scalpel the surgeon forgot to remove from the body of a patient. Her use of actual paintbrushes, along with other studio materials, points to various recent histories of art, and she is explicit about her interest in "making sculptures out of sculptures."[3]

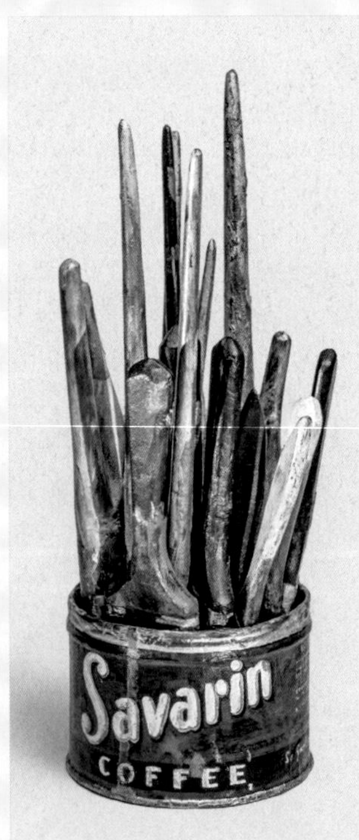

Jasper Johns, *Painted Bronze*, 1960. Oil on bronze, 13 ½ × 8 × 8 inches (34.3 × 20.3 × 20.3 cm). The Museum of Modern Art, New York; Promised gift of Marie-Josée and Henry R. Kravis in honor of David Rockfeller

3   Erika Verzutti, quoted in *Erika Verzutti*, ed. Christine Macel (Paris: Editions Centre Pompidou, 2019), 87.

Of Johns's emergence on the New York art scene in the late 1950s and early 1960s, art historian Thomas Crow writes, "No other contemporary figure was fashioning objects with so many homologies to folk forms, that is, to their modesty and restraint; to their tendencies toward symmetry and embellishment of entire surfaces; to their masking of obsessive and private meanings in self-imposed disciplines of work."[4] Johns's and, likewise, his contemporary Robert Rauschenberg's incorporation of the objects and tools of the studio in discrete artworks was an innovation that broke illusions around the processes of art making, craft, and labor. This act at once revealed the artists' blue-collar upbringings and propelled subsequent generations of the avant-garde. The biographical aspects that are embedded in such objects are tied to ideas around the persona and presence of the artist, as well as to the importance of studio practice. These concerns find their way into Verzutti's trajectory as she works between the lines of how an artwork is realized—by whom and how. She not only includes tools, mundane objects, and a range of materials, but she also blurs the lines between materials already extant and entities she has formed herself. The status of a natural rock versus one that she has made is the crux of *Mineral* (2013), which uses bronze, concrete, clay, and acrylic paint as well as papier-mâché, polystyrene, steel, and oil to represent amethyst and quartz geodes. On the other hand, her poignant and restrained sculpture *Poodle* (2008) comprises an upright pile of smooth, white, actual pebbles. Quietly present, *Poodle* comes to life in profound—and humorous—ways through language.

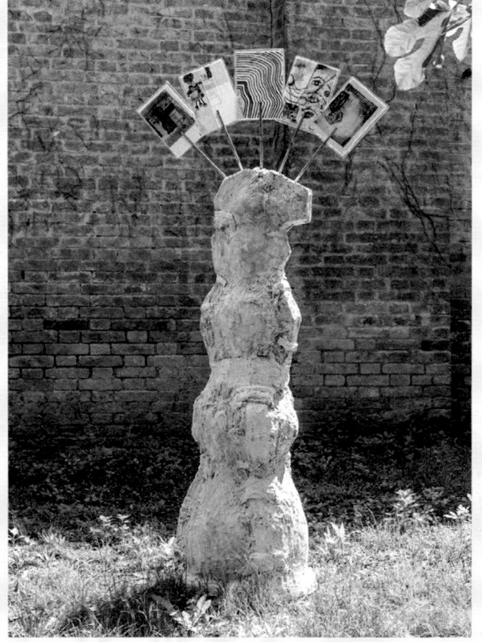

Erika Verzutti, *Dinosaur with Helmet*, 2017. Concrete, bronze, and laminated drawings, 72 13/16 × 22 7/16 × 22 7/16 inches (185 × 57 × 57 cm)

While Verzutti often uses highly traditional materials to make her work, such as bronze, plaster, and papier-mâché, going against the grain of much contemporary art, she also investigates the ad hoc and banal. Such a merger of art and life can be seen in the work *Dinosaur with Helmet* (2017), which features a column made of bronze coated with lumpy concrete and topped with five sticks, each holding a colorful laminated drawing. The sculpture is indeed suggestive of a dinosaur standing erect and helmeted like a gladiator. The work has been shown outdoors, where the bronze and concrete can withstand the elements, though the playful addition of the drawings complicates matters. Even laminated, the paper is vulnerable to wind, sun exposure, and even heavy rain. Verzutti is poking at the idea of longevity that bronze and concrete imply. She makes a dinosaur helmet that is beautiful, expressive, and ultimately fragile.

4   Thomas Crow, *The Long March of Pop: Art, Music, and Design* (New Haven: Yale University Press, 2015), 37–38.

Newspapers, and paper ephemera generally, appear as archetypal stuff throughout Verzutti's oeuvre. About her daily practice, she has talked of pursuing "autonomy" in the production of work, "knowing that I can do practically anything in a day using only shredded newspaper and glue."[5] A very early series, made in the early 2000s, consists of paper vases that she crafted out of discarded receipts, bills, and notebook pages. In the 2010s, after she had started exploring denser sculptural materials such as bronze and clay, Verzutti brought papier-mâché into works such as *Peacock* (2014), explaining, "I thought I was becoming too serious with bronze."[6] *Peacock*, like *Jaspera na Escola*, has paintbrushes sticking out from its molded-paper body; fanlike, this time they suggest plumage. For another early piece, whose title translates to "sickly," *Dodói* (2003), Verzutti modeled unfired clay into a pillar with an acute bend at its top and affixed it to a base covered in newspaper. The two paintbrushes that prop up the clay pillar right below its curve were also presumably used to paint the sculpture. The metaphor of the surgeon leaving his instruments behind becomes more obvious here, for the title implies the sculpture is not doing well. Verzutti tends to it by incorporating supports. Her brushes can be leaves, feathers, and now crutches.

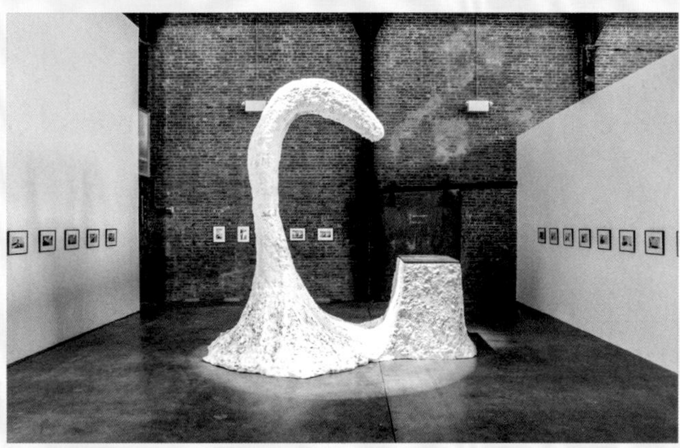

Erika Verzutti, *Cisne com Palco* (*Swan with Stage*), 2015. Polystyrene, iron, polyurethane, fiberglass, and acrylic, 145 ¼ × 137 ¾ × 137 ¾ inches (369 × 350 × 350 cm). Installation view, *Erika Verzutti: Swan with Stage*, SculptureCenter, Long Island City, New York, 2015

The immediacy of the "sickly" object is further amplified by the seemingly incidental placement of the sheet of the newspaper on its base. However, as Verzutti had an actor explain in performing a monologue at the site of another work, *Cisne com Palco* (*Swan with Stage*, 2015), newspaper, as material, can hold social and political significance, conveyed through notions of weight and other physical and conceptual characteristics. This later work, in which the theme of the artist's role reaches a critical juncture, scales up the swan form into a structure that houses a small base and platform for performers on its back, so to speak.[7] During the performance, the actor's monologue described the process of making the work, dramatizing it into a dynamic and complex affair. He announces, "We are talking about materials here, we are talking about masking tape, politics, and love . . . pretty much." At one point, the actor professes that newspapers are the best material, preferring *Folha do São Paulo* because it is "very light" and "dissolves quickly," while stating that a paper like *O Estadao* is too "heavy" and hard to digest, and *Veja* is "couché paper," and "useless."[8] The ubiquity of the newspaper is no longer random but one that takes on particular characteristics.

5   Verzutti, quoted in *Erika Verzutti*, 71.
6   Ibid.
7   See my essay "Swan Song."
8   Ibid., 227.

On the surface of *A Era da Inocência Acabou* (*The Age of Innocence Is Over*, 2020), a wall-based painted bronze with the impression of fingerprints along its rounded rim, is a sort of Cubist mise en abyme that places a section of Pablo Picasso's *Still Life with Chair Caning* (1912) composition at the center of a Brazilian newspaper page from June 2020. The typeface and partial title from the newspaper snippet recall the front page of the "very light" *Folha do São Paulo*. A response to the crisis of the current moment—*A Era da Inocência Acabou* was made a few months into the COVID-19 pandemic— and it bears the fragment "impeachment e vacina" (impeachment and vaccine) in addition to the work's title among its painted headlines. Thus, Verzutti folds a twentieth-century artwork made during a time of crisis into a present-day manifestation of anxiety. The radical shock of the everyday was critical to the Cubists, who famously included newspaper sheets and collage techniques in paintings that merged abstraction with veracity, and likewise Verzutti's contemporary endeavor. Indeed, the age of innocence is over.

Erika Verzutti, *A Era da Inocência Acabou* (*The Age of Innocence Is Over*), 2020. Acrylic and oil on bronze, 12 × 11 ⅝ × 1 ⁹⁄₁₆ inches (30.5 × 29.5 × 4 cm)

In reproducing the June 2020 page in paint on bronze, Verzutti embeds critique and pathos in her art materials, bringing to light the impossibility of neutrality and the ways that citation opens up different times, places, and contexts. "Making sculptures out of sculptures," in her own words, she sandwiches materials and their representational roles together to flatten them. It is in this way that her materials tell stories—in combination with fashioned forms and suggestive titles. Always, and in every aspect, a sculpture by Verzutti works in multiple ways to shift meanings and play with historical assumptions, making the everyday new again.

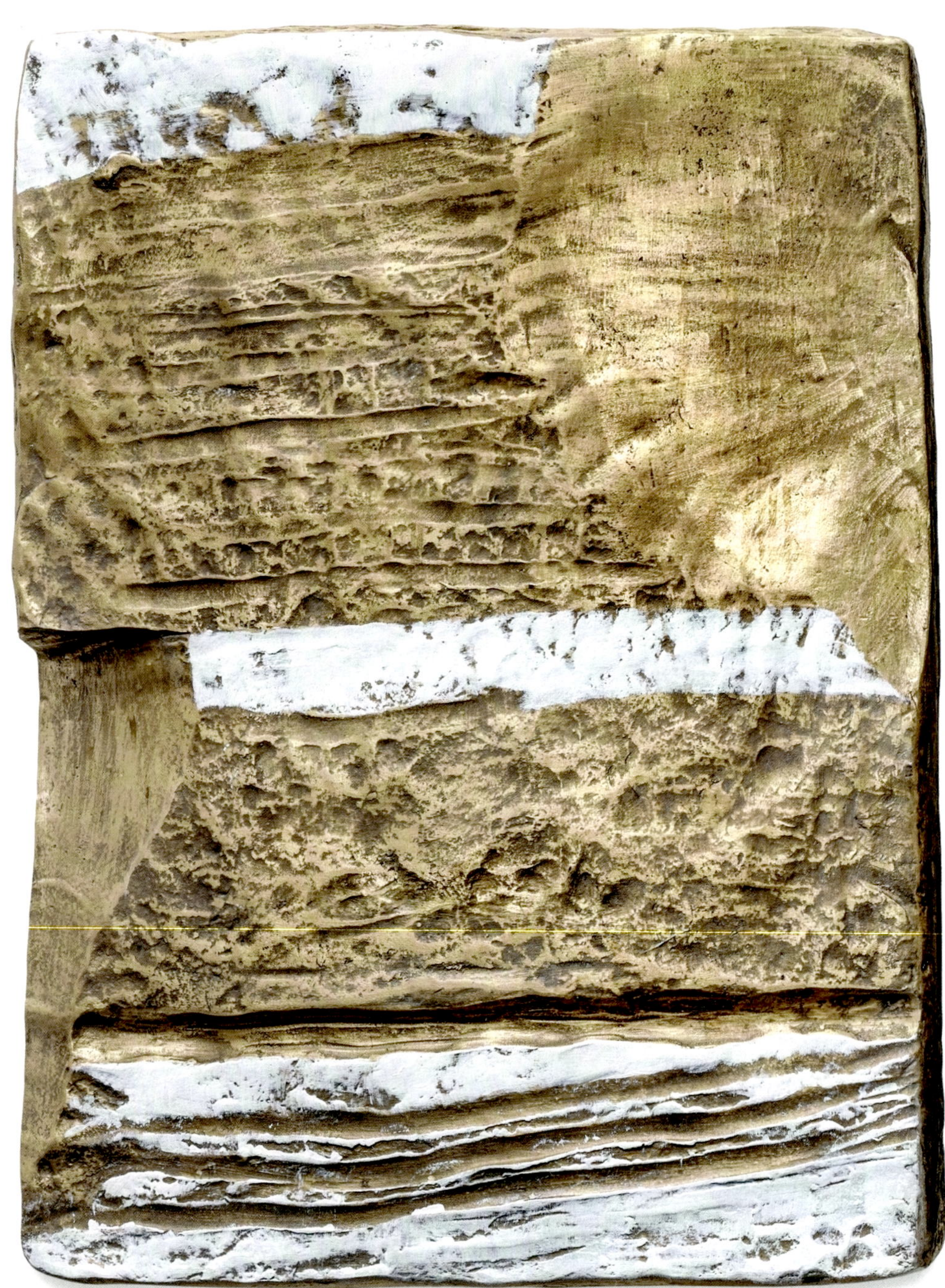

The Dress, 2015
Bronze and acrylic
Two parts: 23 ⅝ × 35 ⁷⁄₁₆ × 3 ⅜ inches (60 × 90 × 8.5 cm) overall

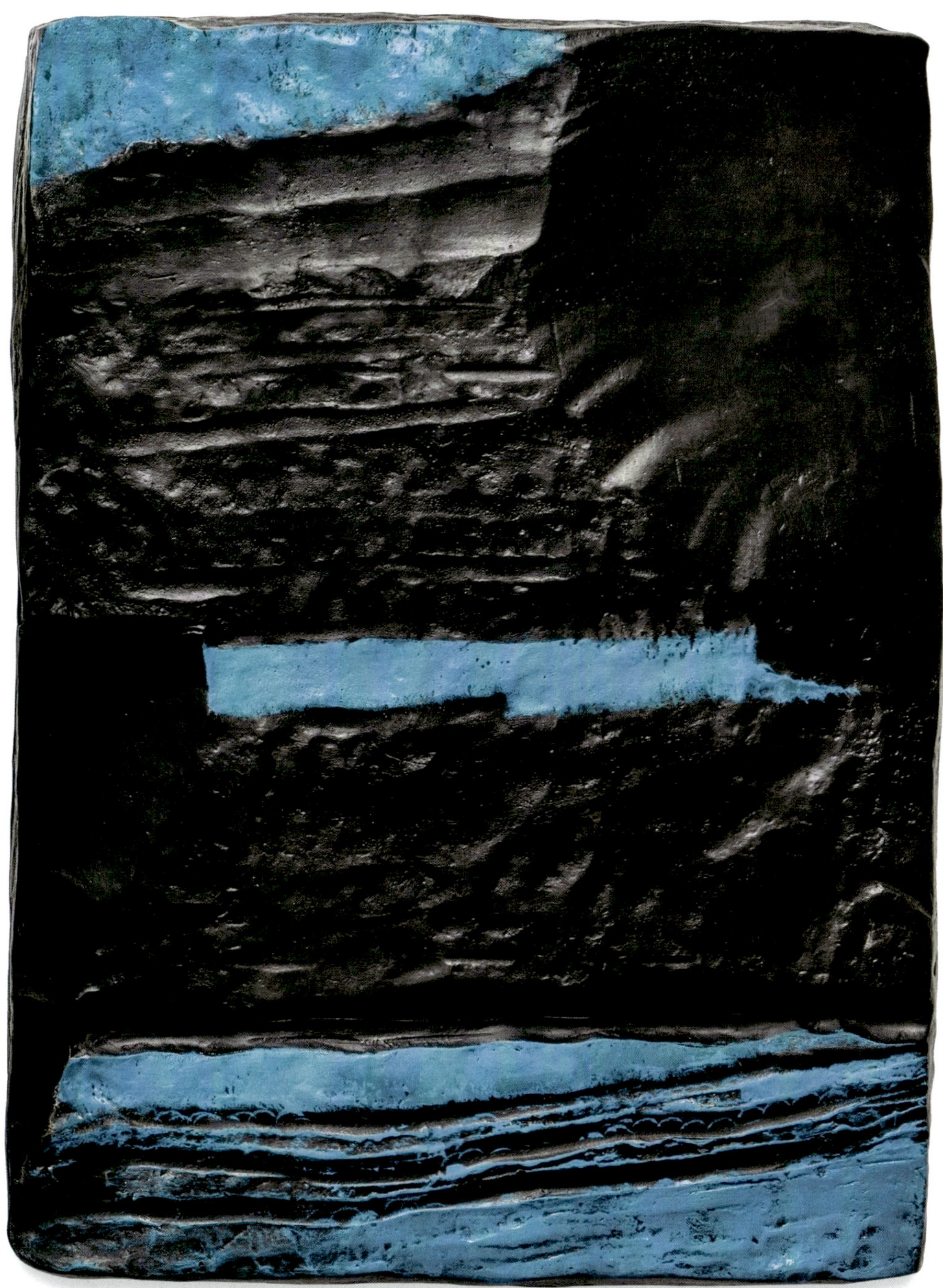

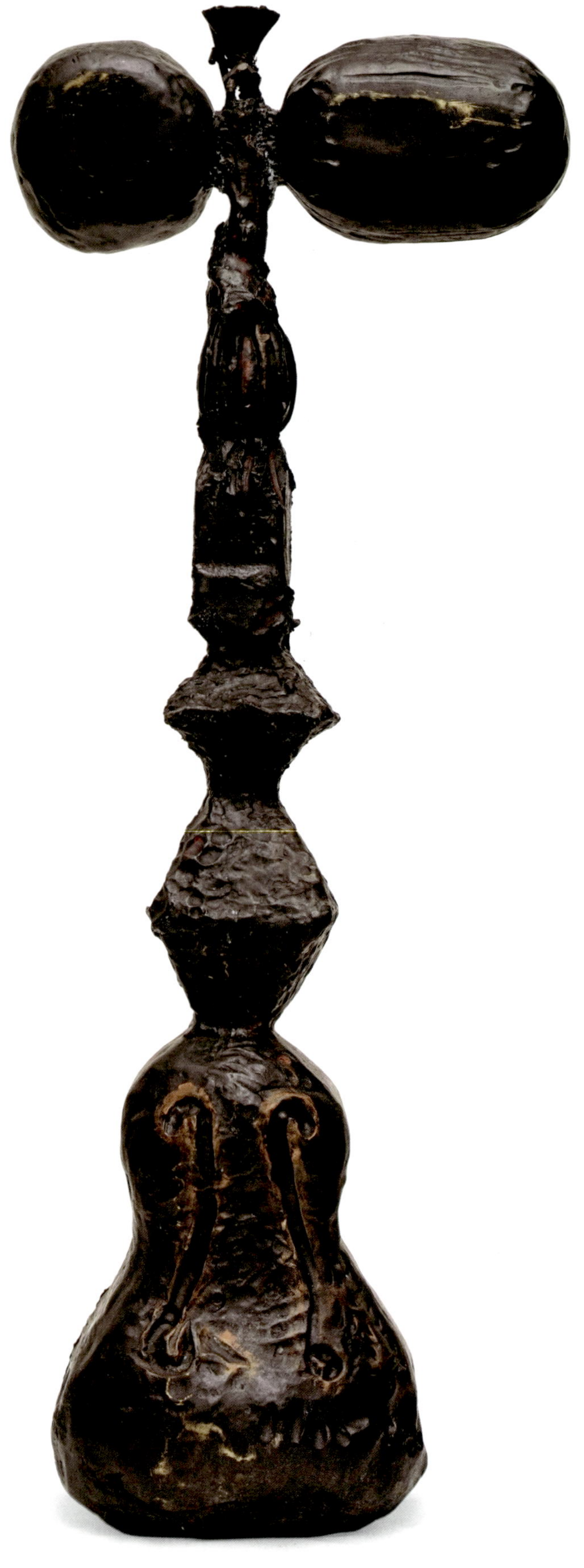

Surrealista, 2015
Bronze, acrylic, and wax
66 ⅛ × 25 ³⁄₁₆ × 17 ¹¹⁄₁₆ inches (168 × 64 × 45 cm)

Mexicana, 2015
Bronze, acrylic, and wax
35 ⁷⁄₁₆ × 19 ¹¹⁄₁₆ × 11 ¹³⁄₁₆ inches (90 × 50 × 30 cm)

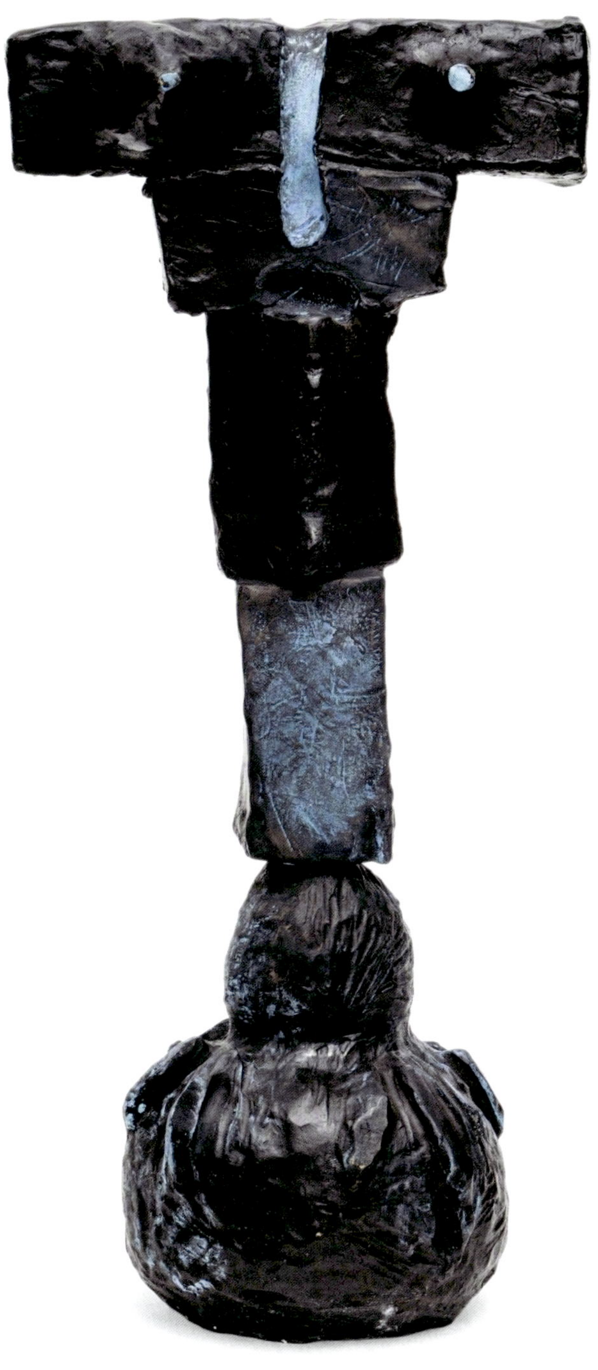

Star Without Makeup, 2015
Bronze and wax
15 ¾ × 15 ¾ × 3 ⁹⁄₁₆ inches (40 × 40 × 9 cm)

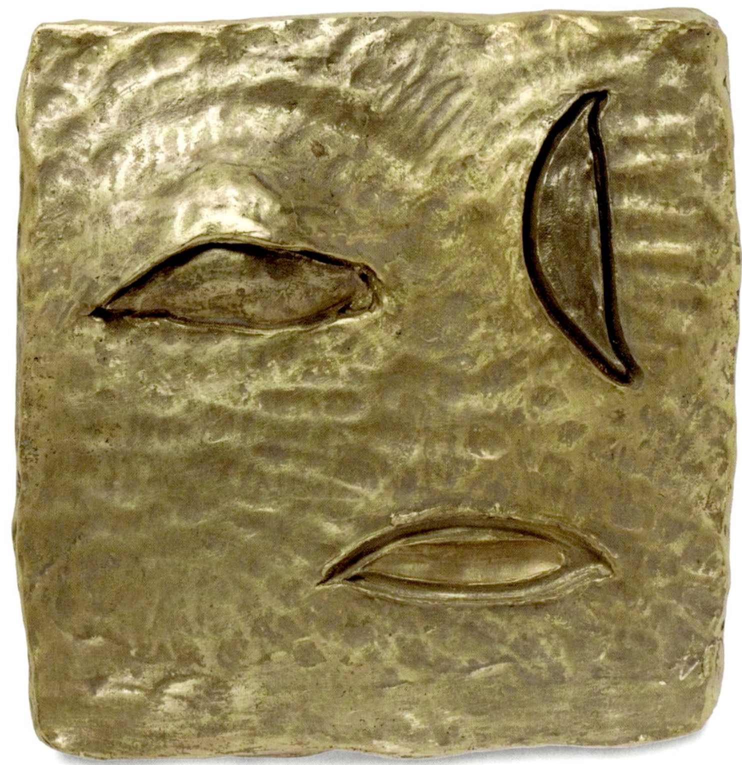

God Flower Brain Flower, 2016
Bronze
98 ⁷⁄₁₆ × 70 ⁷⁄₈ × 2 ¾ inches (250 × 180 × 7 cm)

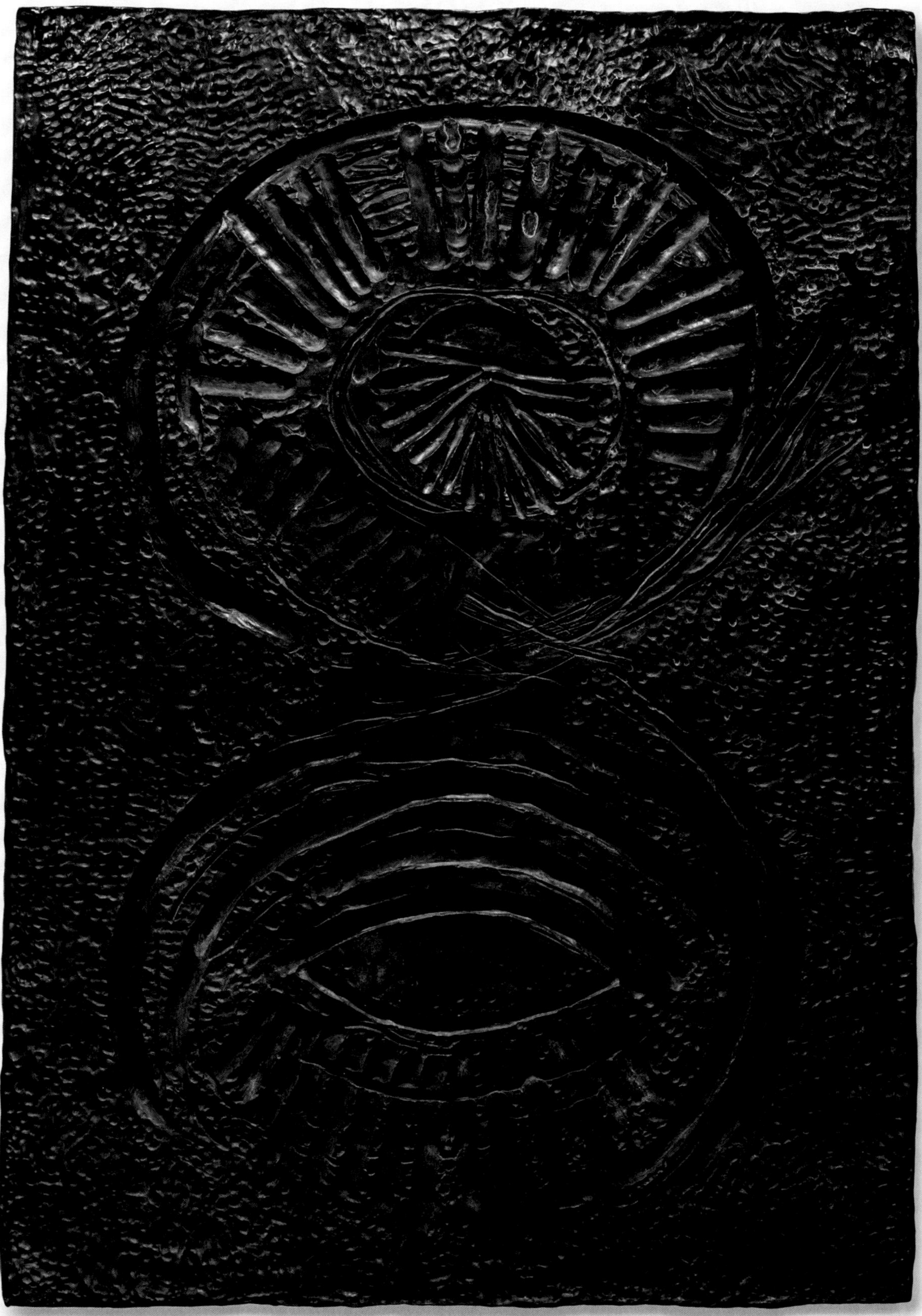

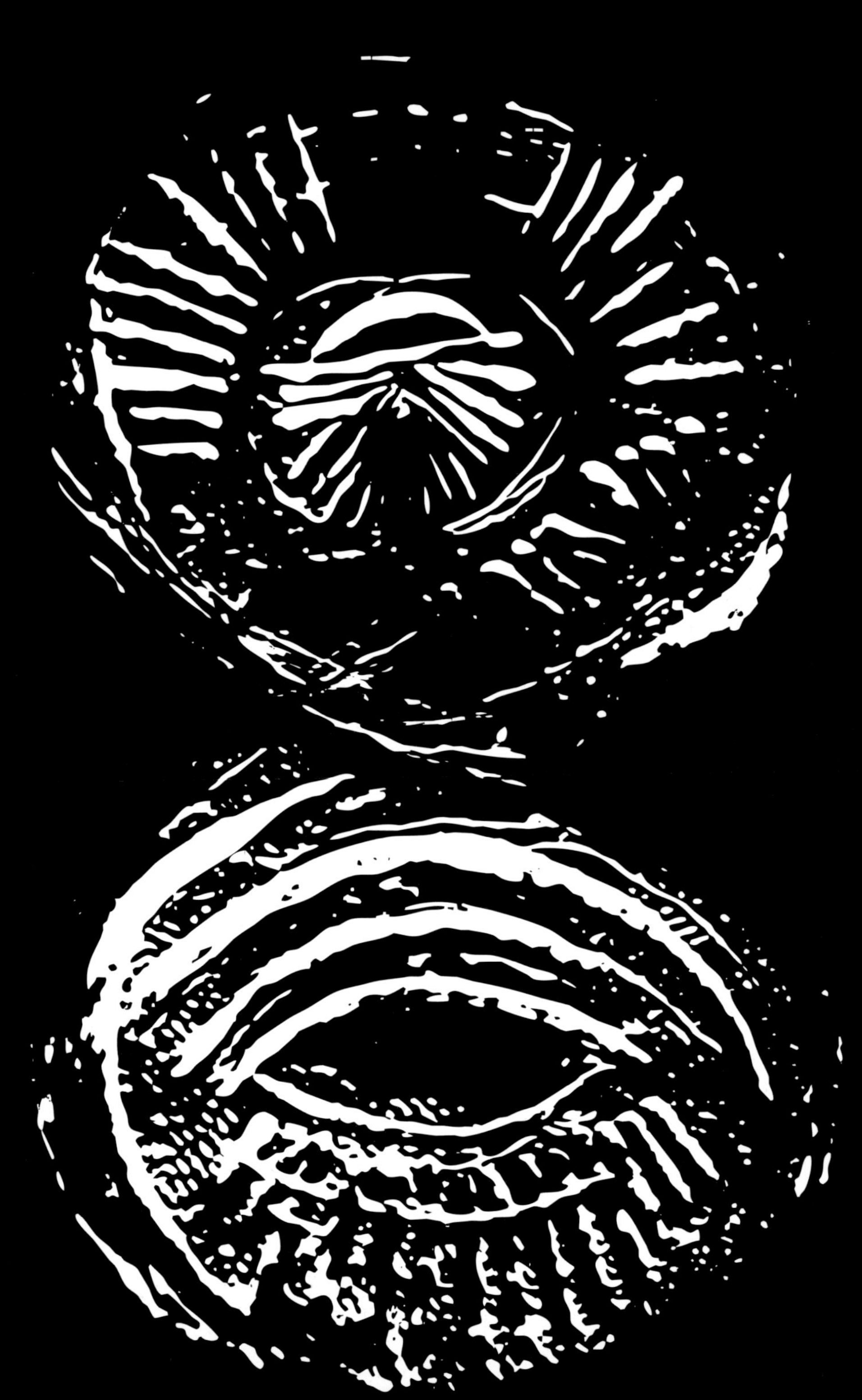

GOD FLOWER BRAIN FLOWER AND TANTRA DRAWINGS

God, Flower, Brain, Flower, Serpent, Eye, Swan, Spiral, Cobra, Eight, Brain, Dance, Infinite, Serpent, Dance, Spiral . . . I wanted this title to be just sound. *God*, as I call it, from 2016 is the largest bronze relief I've made so far: a plank of clay as big as the door of a church and carved using arches of metal and my elbows. I wanted it to be as nonverbal as sex or dance.

Years later, when I got to know tantra drawings, I encountered the emanating power I wanted to evoke while working with clay. Unlike the big bronze relief, these anonymous tantra drawings are often crafted to be carried in the pocket for protection and to attract positive energy. They seem to be empty of ego and report only to spiritual aesthetics. Ovals and spirals are recurring motifs, while the Brahmanda, or Cosmic Egg, is the source of the universe and the subject of many traditional drawings. My spirals don't have fixed meanings, but I want to believe these works converge somewhere in the schemes of geometric devotion.

—E.V.

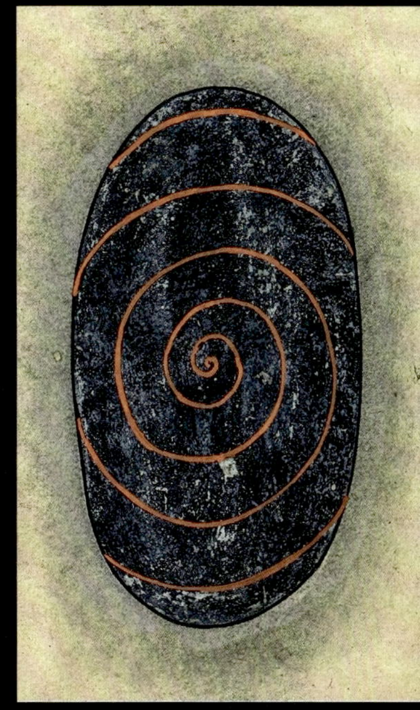

Anonymous, *Brahmanda (Cosmic Egg)*, n.d. Ink on paper, 11 ½ × 6 inches (29 × 15 ¼ cm)

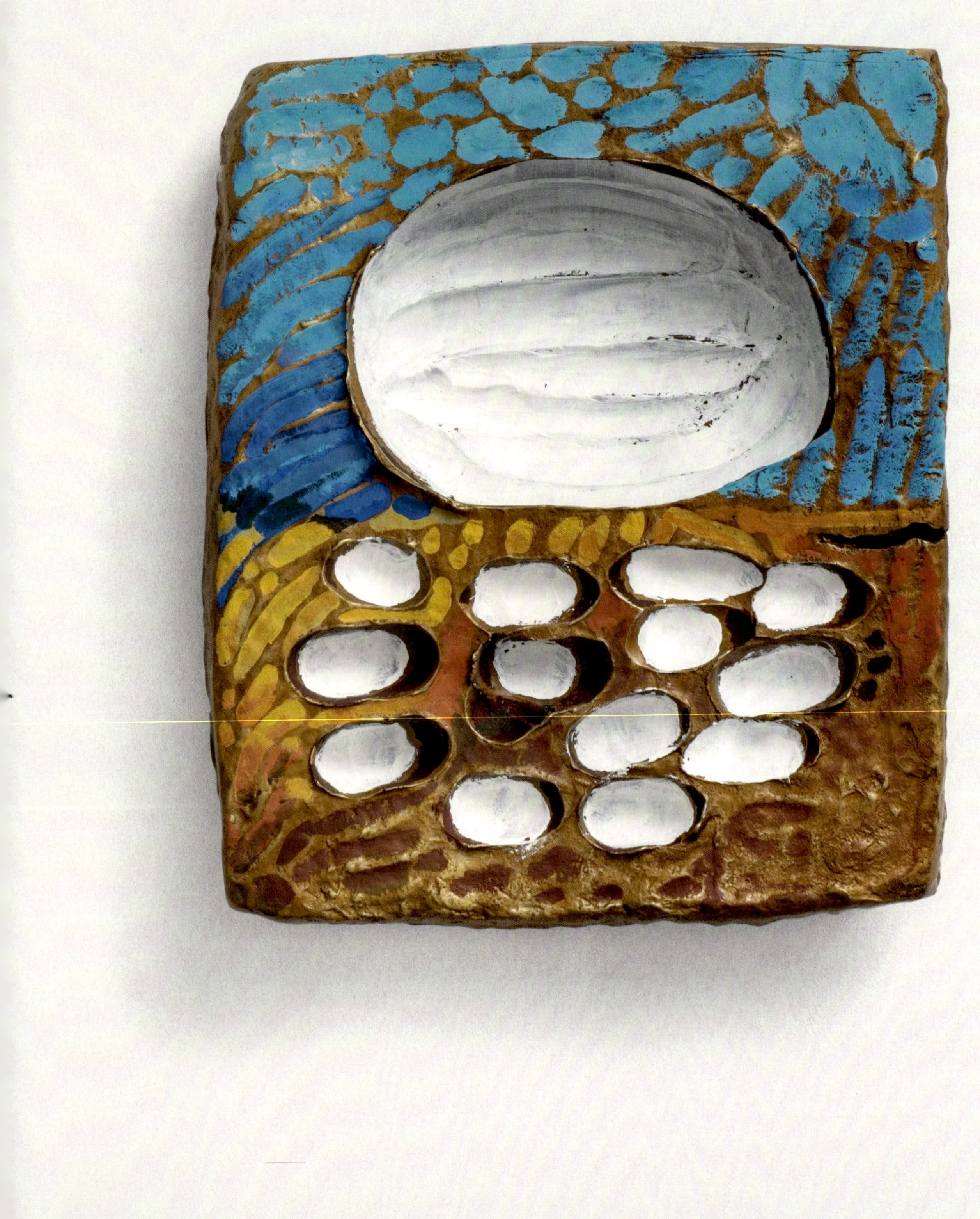

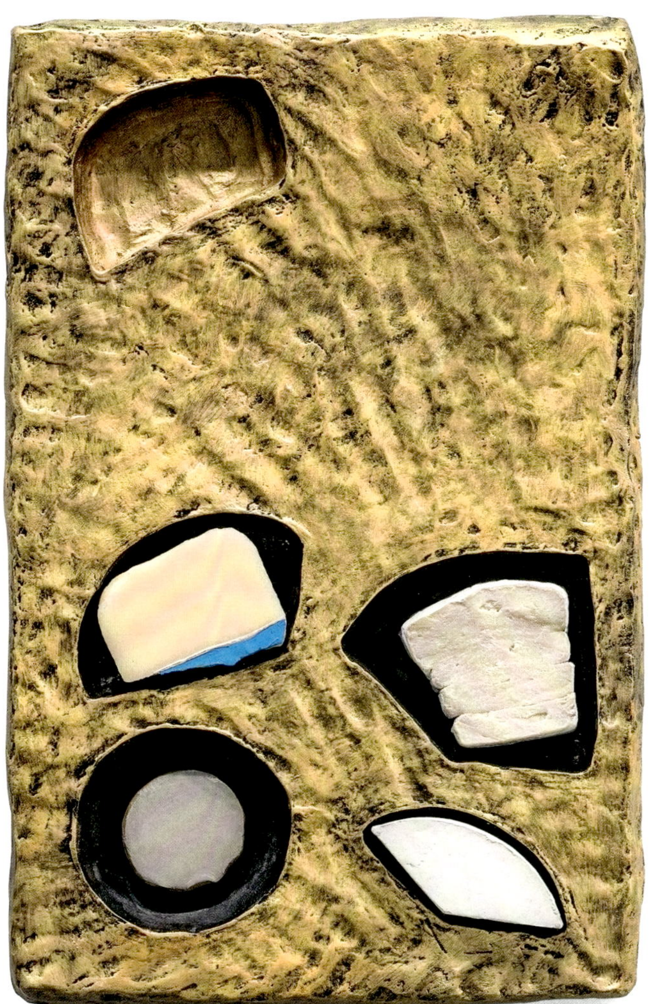

Gober, 2016
Bronze, wax, beeswax, cold porcelain clay, and acrylic
23 ⅝ × 14 ¹⁵⁄₁₆ × 2 ¾ inches (60 × 38 × 7 cm)

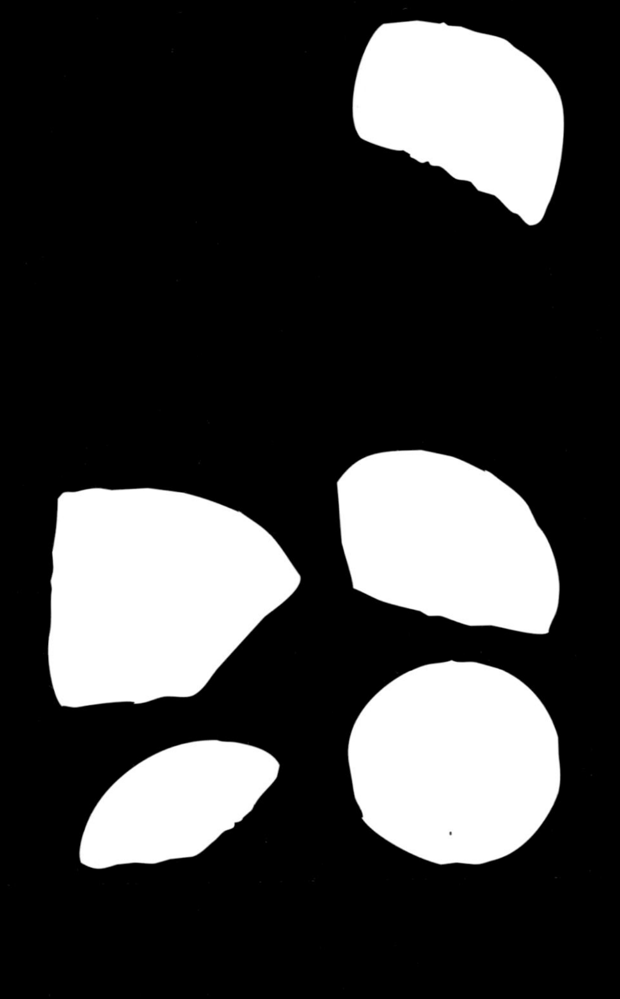

Some works allow me to explore subjects, forms, or materials that are alien to me. My unfamiliarity leaves an imprint on the work itself; my uncertainty manifests in unsteady gestures and indecisions that envelop the piece in a patina of vulnerability. *Gober* (2016) is one such work. Looking at it again today, I see solutions and processes I didn't recognize at the time but from which I now learn.

The work came from a cheese plate that looked like a neo-Concrete composition. Works often come to me through tactile annotations, be they related to food, film, or makeup, or anything with characteristic protrusions, indentations, or elasticity. There was nothing to be changed in the found composition—I could have made the shapes and fixed them to the base in defiance of gravity. But this time I wanted to nest and groove the volumes. Initially, the bronze was to have a black patina. Out of anxiety, however, instead of sending it to be depatinated, I covered the surface with golden wax. Though it was not a noble way to solve the problem, it gifted me with contrast and a greasy feeling that helped define the work as unique.

As each cheese was crafted, it seemed to dictate its ideal material: bisque for Brie, plaster for goat cheese, raw clay for organic cheddar, and beeswax for Parmesan. I wasn't thinking about the artist Robert Gober until I touched the beeswax. Its soft, satiny warmth forged a connection to his surfaces, particularly his urinals and their autonomous shapes. They provided me with a sense of reassurance, as if they were the guardians of my cheese nests.

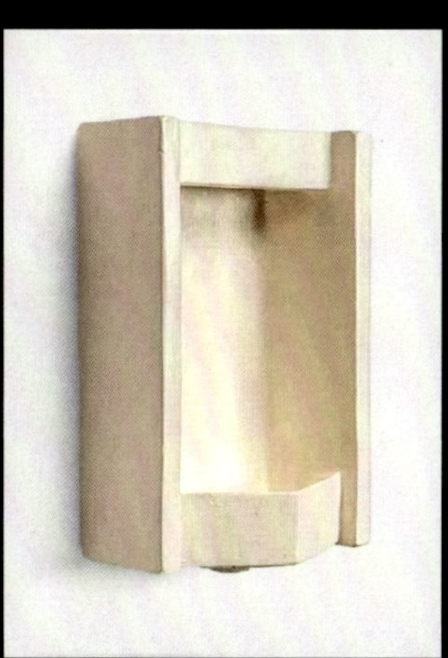

Robert Gober, *Urinal*, 1985. Plaster, wood, and semigloss enamel paint, 28 × 18 ½ × 11 ½ inches (71.1 × 46.9 × 29.2 cm)

—E.V.

Porn Star, 2011
Bronze and acrylic
129 15/16 × 3 9/16 × 3 9/16 inches (330 × 9 × 9 cm)

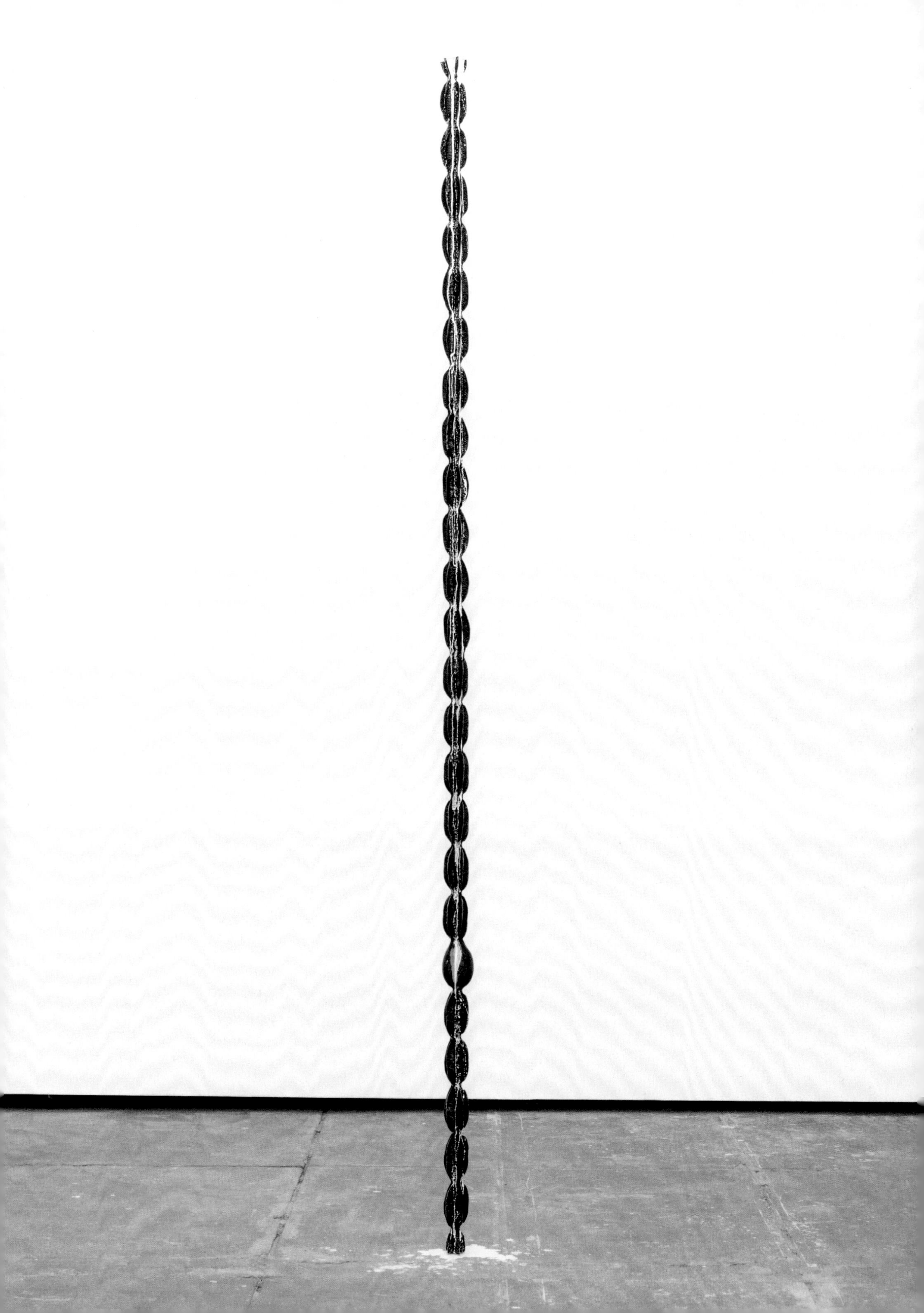

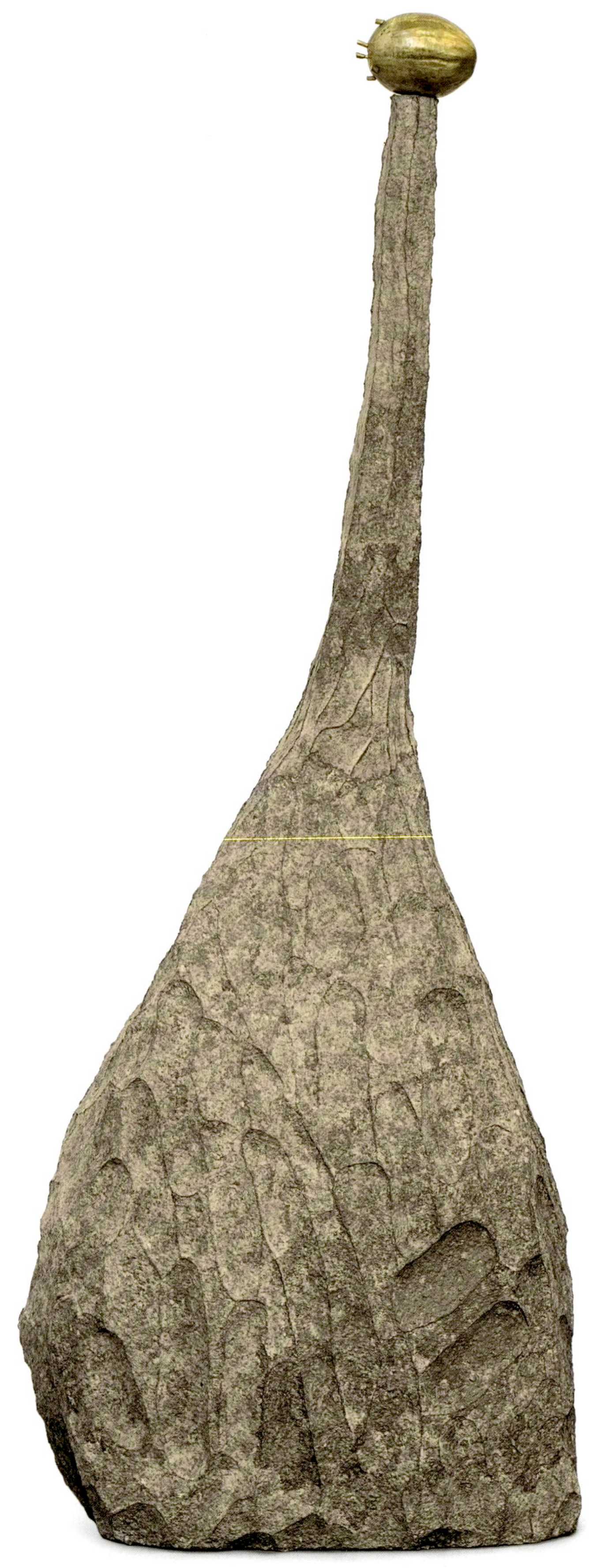

Camelo, 2016
Papier-mâché, polystyrene, bronze, and acrylic
101 $\frac{3}{16}$ × 29 $\frac{1}{2}$ × 33 $\frac{7}{16}$ inches (257 × 75 × 85 cm)

Camel, 2017
Ceramic
36 ¼ × 47 ¼ × 20 ⅞ inches (92 × 120 × 53 cm)

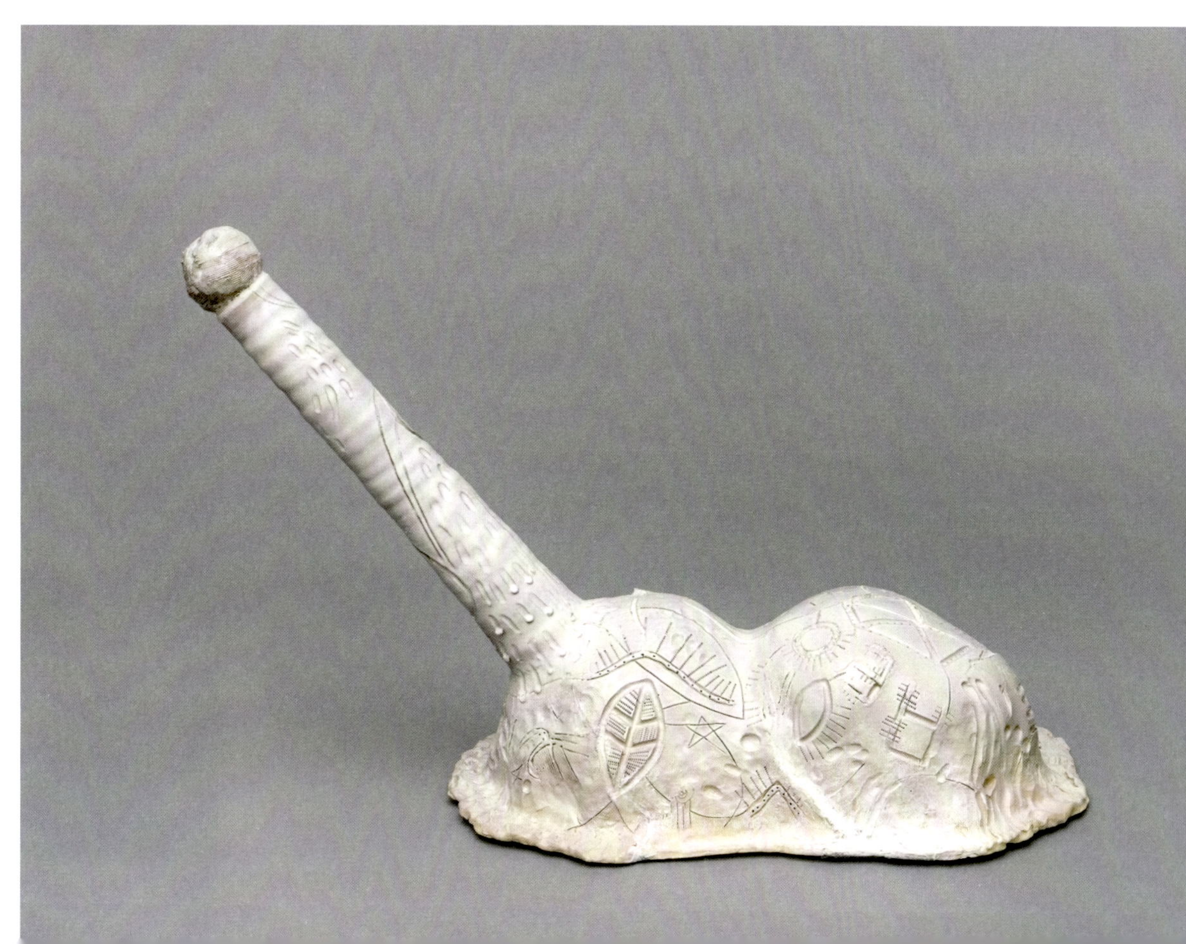

Flat Grandpa, 2017
Papier-mâché, polystyrene, concrete, and oil
27 ¾ × 38 ³⁄₁₆ × 7 ¹¹⁄₁₆ inches (70.5 × 97 × 19.5 cm)

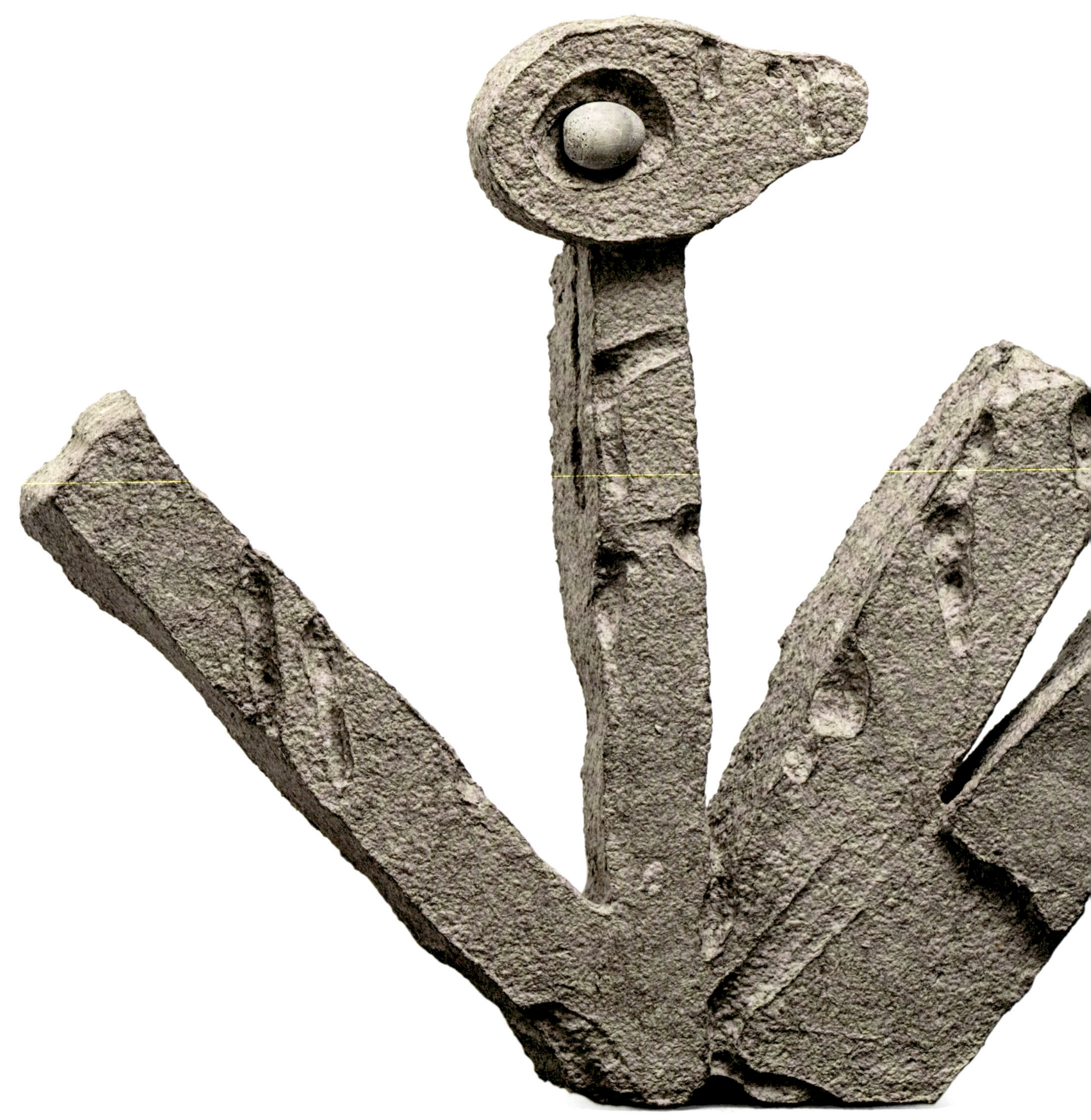

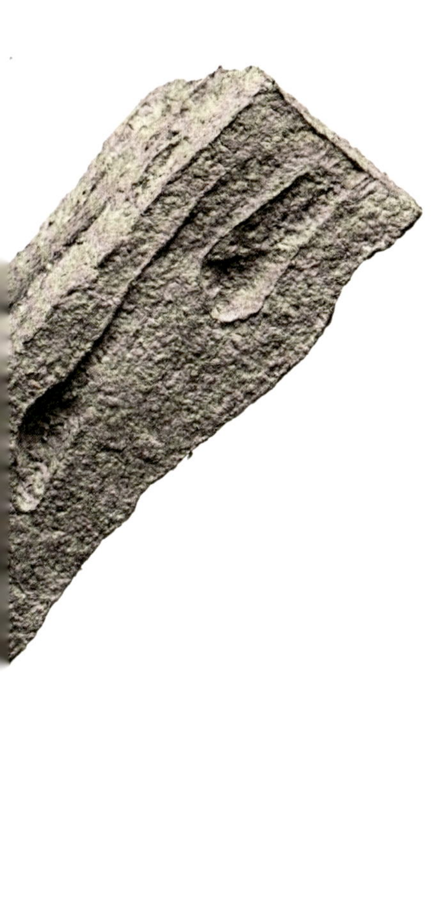

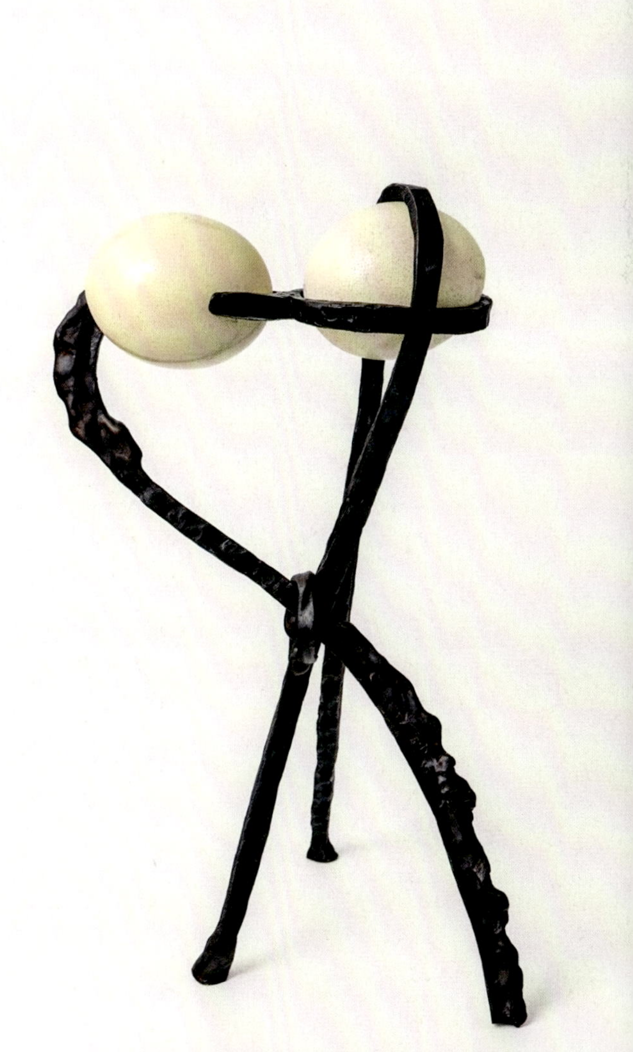

Sex, 2017
Bronze and ostrich eggshell
25 9/16 × 13 3/4 × 13 3/4 inches (65 × 35 × 35 cm)

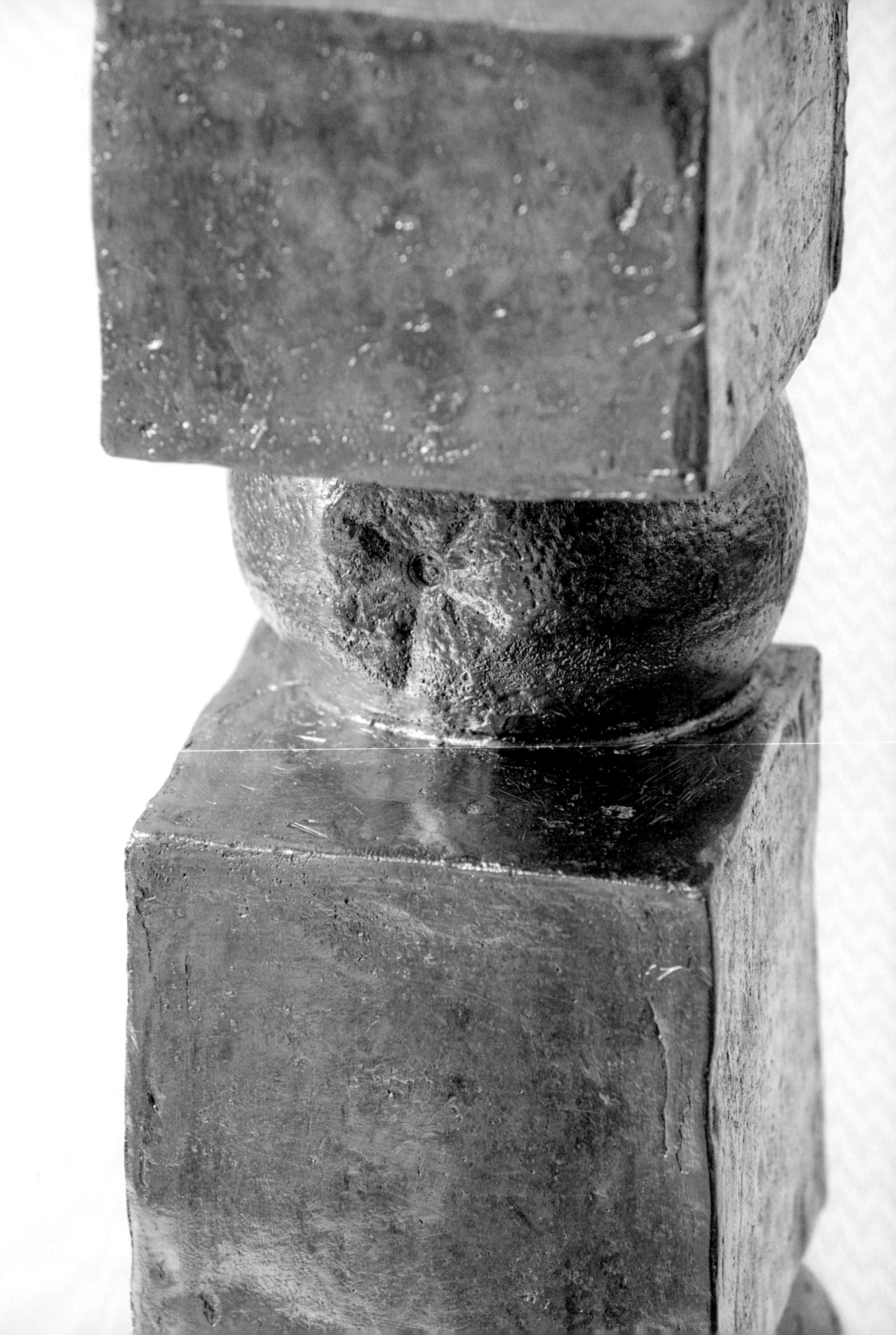

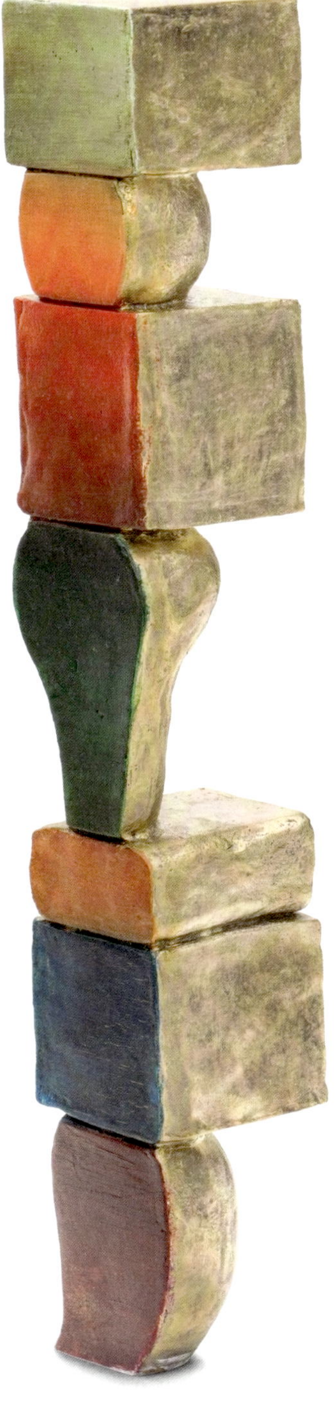

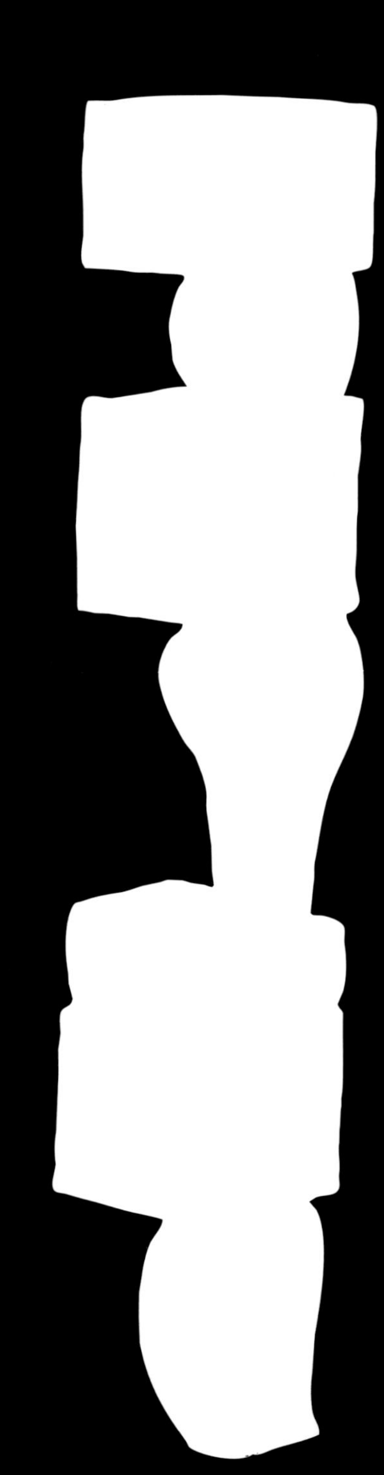

I mentally assign shapes and colors to weekdays, months, and numbers. Grapheme-color synesthesia, where one connects letters and days of the week to colors, may be the most well-known type of synesthesia. As an interplay between the senses, these are "involuntary perceptions." Whenever I think of the number eight, for example, I see it as a deep yellow. *Dias da Semana* (*Days of the Week*, 2017) is about that.

In my mind's eye, the image of the week appears cartoonlike: flat with fine, black-outlined forms filled with colors that are not completely solid. Typically, I don't visualize a single week in isolation. Instead, weeks are represented as vertical strips that connect without end. So if today is Thursday and someone suggests meeting next Wednesday, before putting it in the calendar I visualize something like this:

Workdays were named after planetary bodies, but now are all about productivity. In the capitalist week, Sunday's shape narrows as the day passes, shrinking with anxiety and challenging the stability of the sculpture.

—E.V.

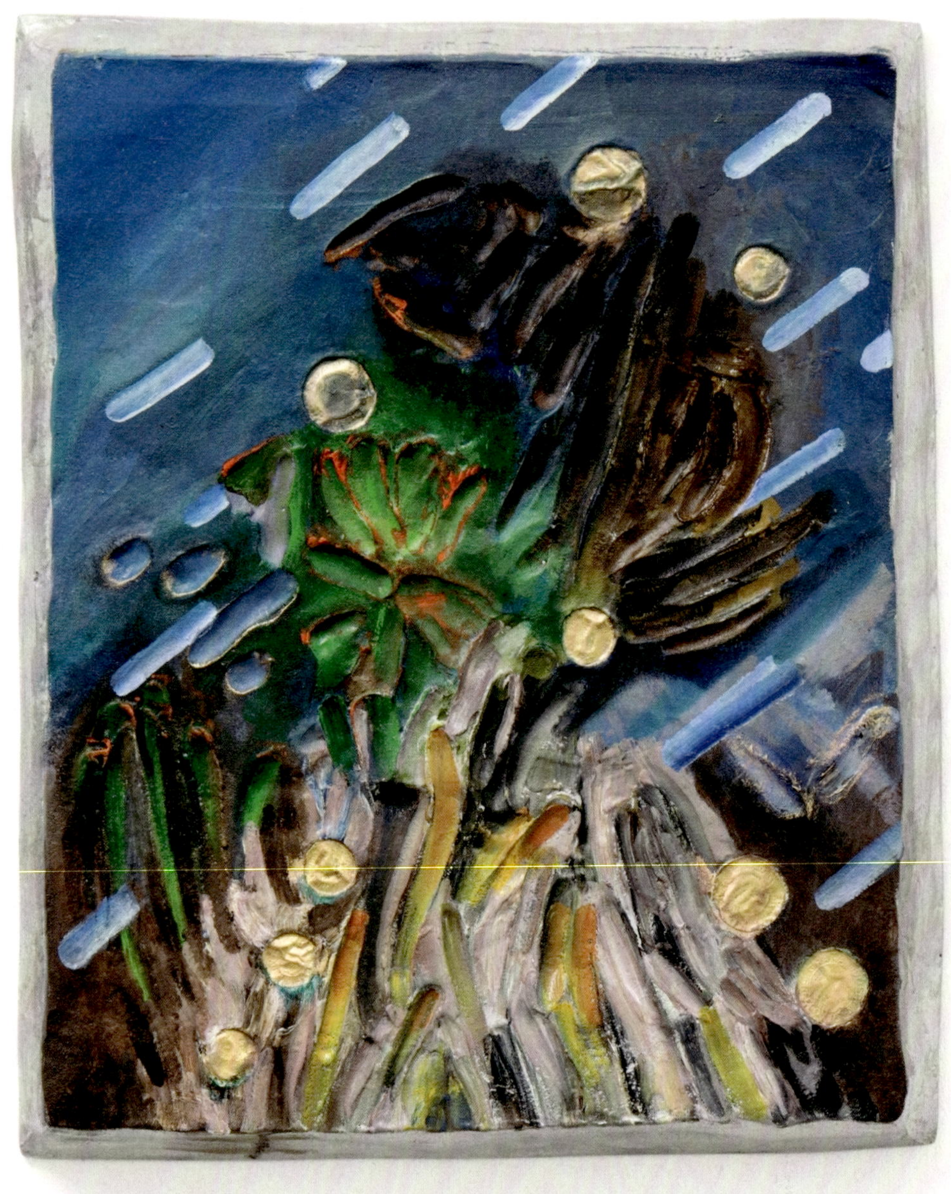

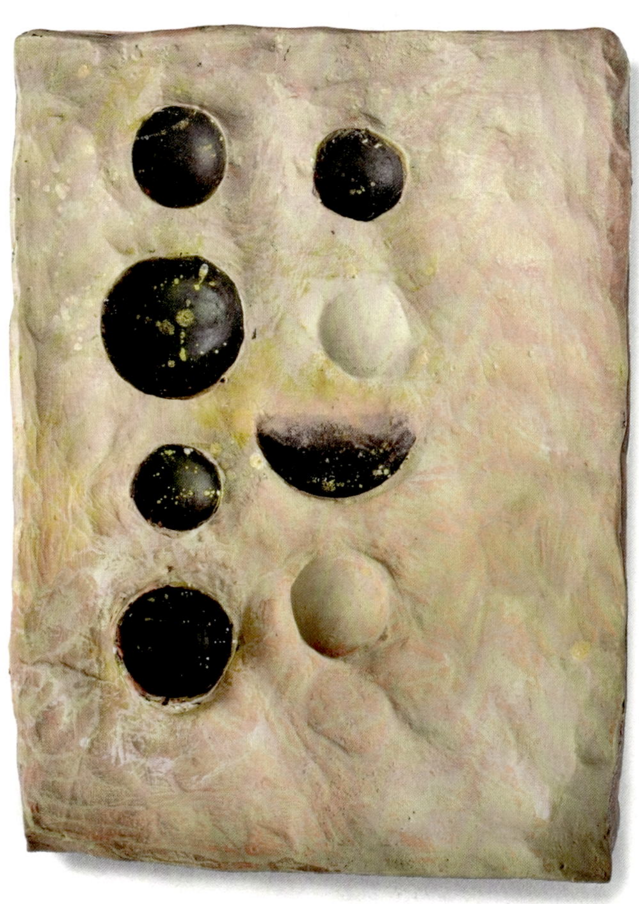

Skin Moon, 2019
Oil and acrylic on bronze
10 ¼ × 7 ½ × 1 ⁹⁄₁₆ inches (26 × 19 × 4 cm)

The Painter's Wife, 2015
Bronze and wax
16 ⅛ × 16 ⅛ × 2 ¾ inches
(41 × 41 × 7 cm)

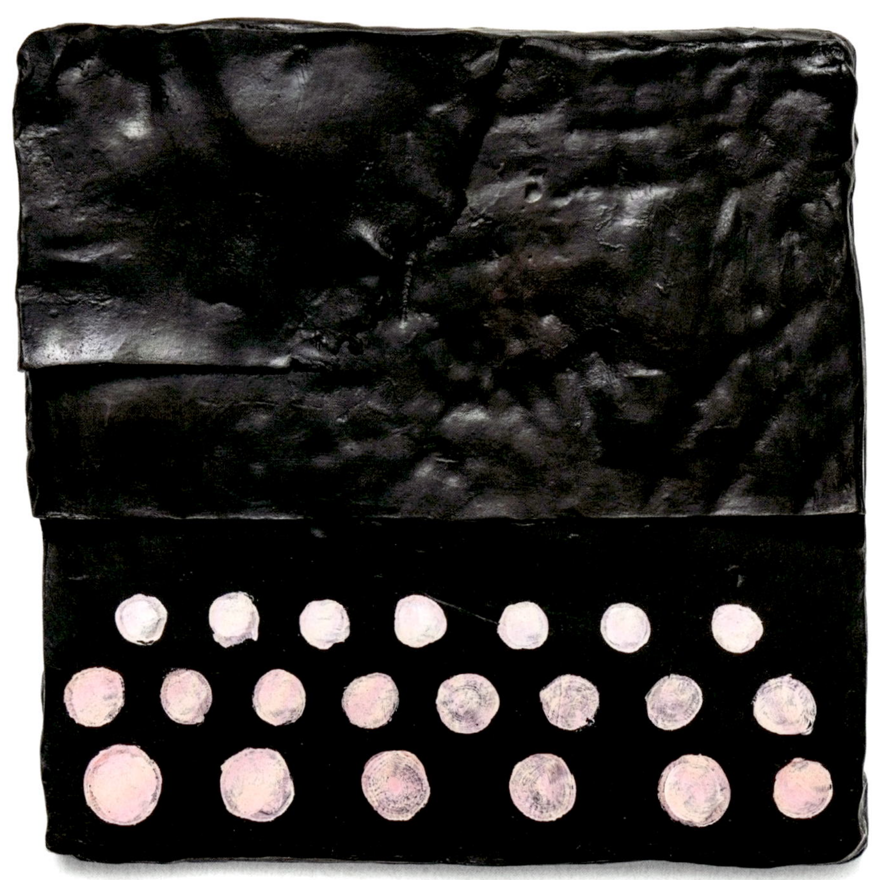

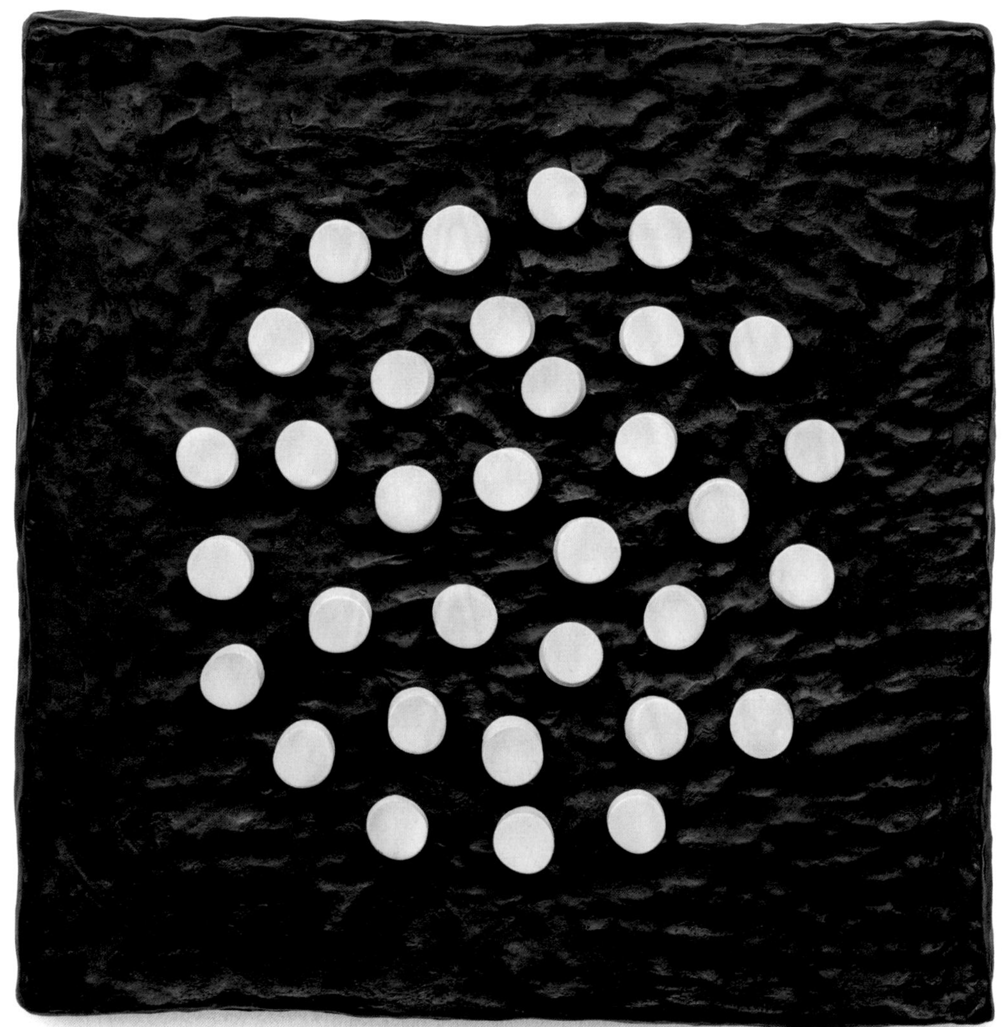

Marshmallow Amazonino, 2019
Bronze, electrostatic painting, and oil
22 $\frac{7}{16}$ × 22 $\frac{7}{16}$ × 3 $\frac{1}{8}$ inches (57 × 57 × 8 cm)

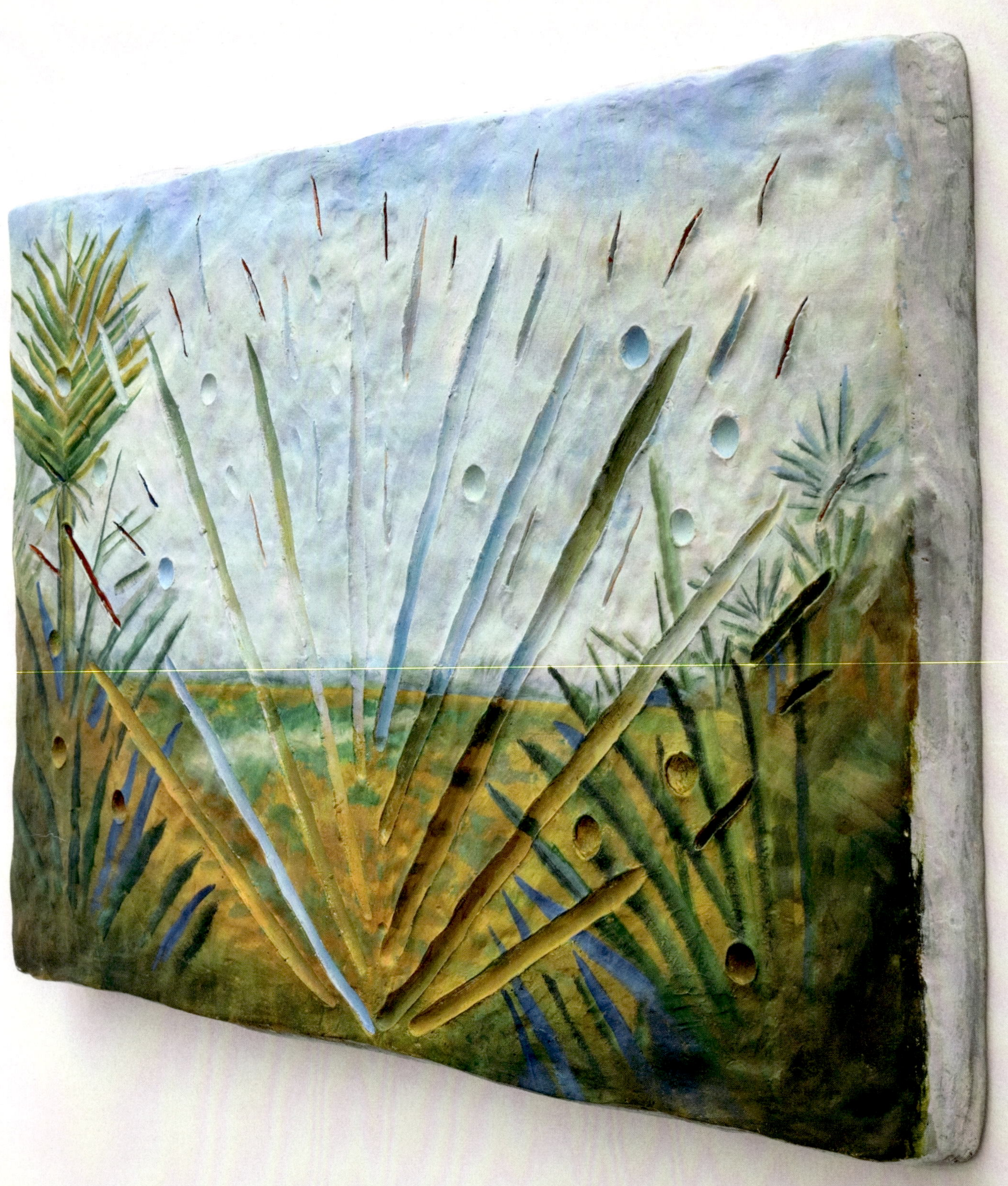

A Guerra do Brasil, 2020
Acrylic and oil on aluminum
24 ¹³⁄₁₆ × 40 ⁹⁄₁₆ × 2 ³⁄₈ inches (63 × 103 × 6 cm)

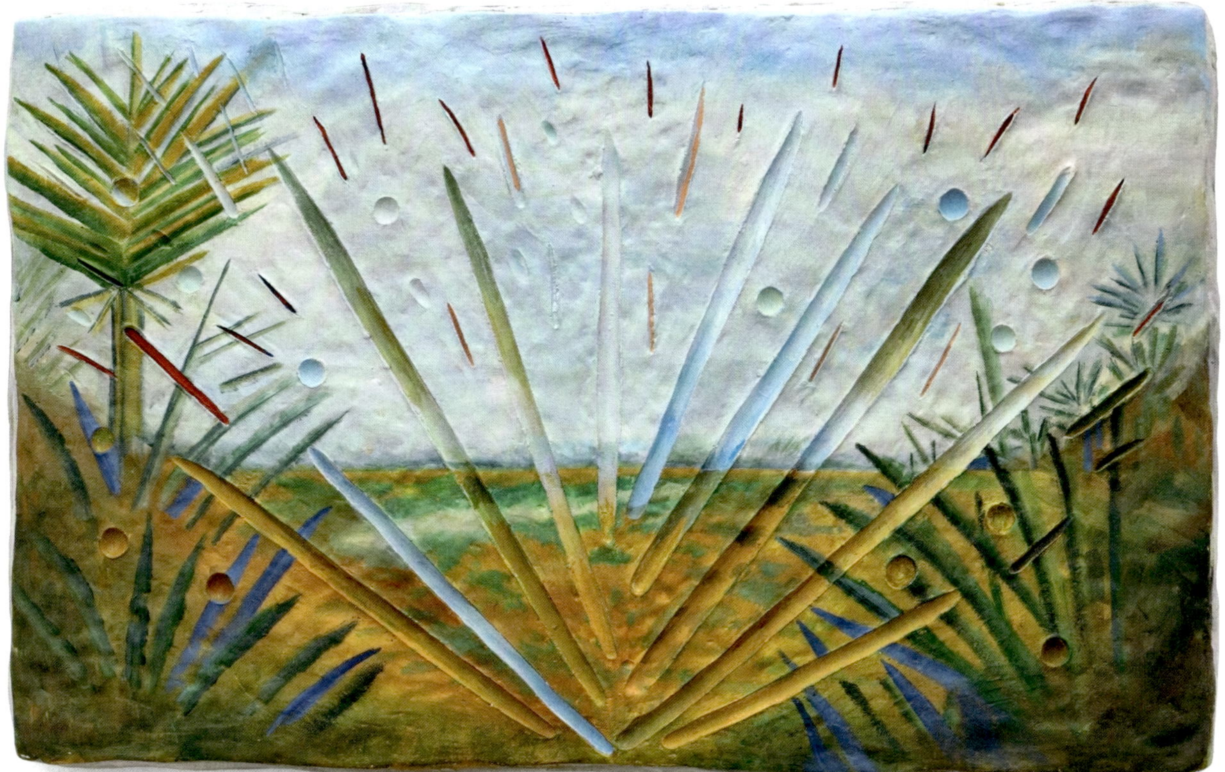

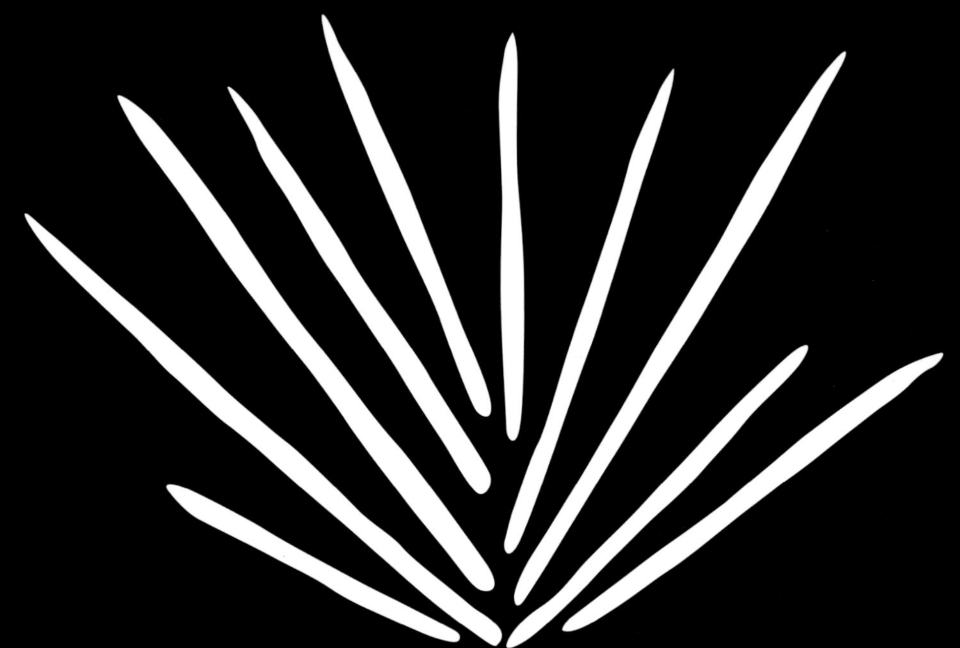

THE WAR OF BRAZIL

We—my brother Elton, other assistants, and I—make rectangular clay plates that look like chocolate cakes. Clay is heavy when wet, and beating down the mass to create a surface is quite physical, as one can tell from the ripples and finger marks in the finished works.

A Guerra do Brasil (2020) is the second life of a clay plate made for a work called *Abraham* (2017) that was related to my disbelief in positive

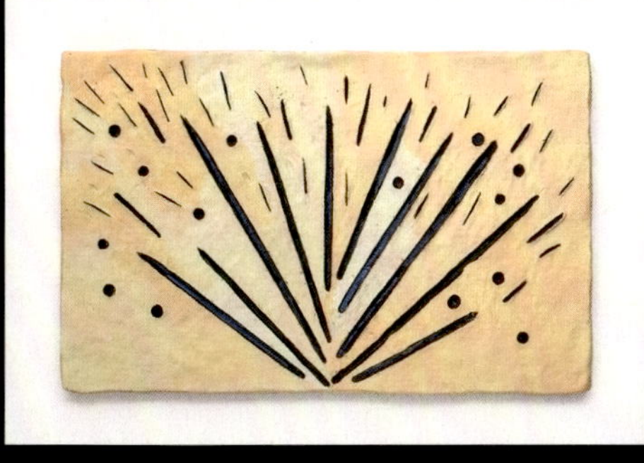

Abraham, 2017. Acrylic on bronze, 15 ³⁄₁₆ × 40 ⅛ × 2 ³⁄₁₆ inches (64 × 102 × 5.5 cm)

thinking. To convey rays or the dissipation of energy, I carved vectors into the clay plate in a fanlike arrangement. *Abraham* was cast in bronze; *A Guerra do Brasil* in aluminum.

I've been experimenting with aluminum lately because it is significantly less detrimental to the environment. Aluminum recycling is big in Brazil—entire families support themselves by collecting soda cans. But as a base surface, aluminum doesn't embrace color as warmly as bronze does. The color of bronze without any patina is golden or reddish gold, depending on the copper-to-tin ratio. Painted and unpainted areas can coexist gently on bronze, while the naked aluminum surface repels the eye. So I tend to cover more and more of the silver "canvas," and in the end the aluminum works are totally coated with color.

I made *A Guerra do Brasil* in June 2020. I was working without leaving my apartment, as Indigenous people were severely impacted by the COVID-19 pandemic. I was trying to learn something by reading Lilia M. Schwarcz and Heloisa M. Starling's *Brazil, a Biography* (2015), which relates the history of Brazil's brutal colonization that reduced the Indigenous populations from millions of people to just thousands. The situation of Brazil's remaining Indigenous peoples, who thrive in many ways through self-determination, is also affected by the legacies of colonialism and extraction.

A chapter of the book narrates the development of the sugar trade and its direct connection to the enslavement of African and Indigenous people. It's illustrated by a seventeenth-century painting by Frans Post, depicting a sugar plantation as an idyllic landscape. I saw the horizon in the painting as if it were the sea, only to later realize it is land—the Atlantic Ocean is behind the painter as he admires the "new world." I chose Post's caramelized sugar plantation to structure my background, but in my version we are looking from Brazil out.

The paint navigated the flat, the carved, and the crunchy surfaces of the aluminum relief. Among the many complicated questions this brought up was: Should the landscape sometimes move into the foreground, with paint covering the ditches and making some cuts invisible? Of course, it should. The game of paint versus topography becomes more complex as things progress. I spent months at home with this work, negotiating its colors, looking at that horizon, eyeing the array of spikes as a sign of imminent violence.

—E.V.

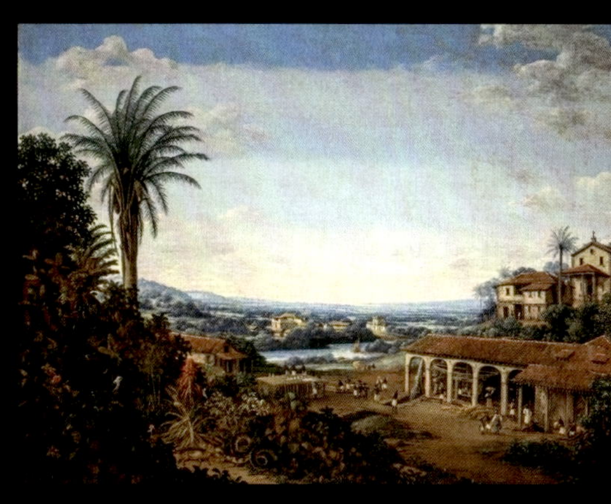

Frans Post, *Landscape with Plantation*, 1660.
Oil on wood, 28 ⅛ × 36 inches (71.5 × 91.5 cm).
Museum Boijmans Van Beuningen, Rotterdam

Espelho, 2020
Bronze and oil
11 ¹³⁄₁₆ × 11 ⁷⁄₁₆ × 1 ³⁄₁₆ inches (30 × 29 × 3 cm)

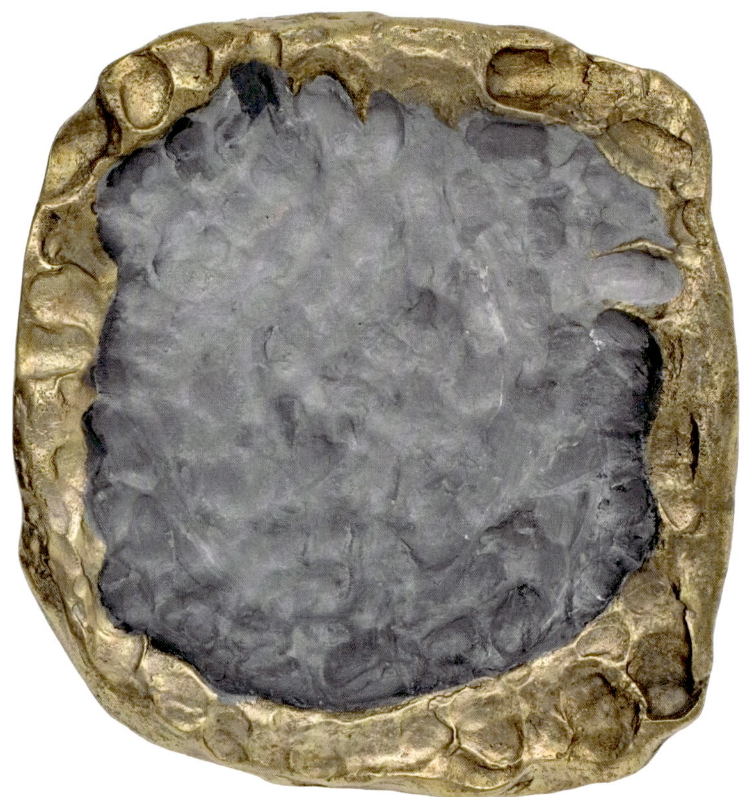

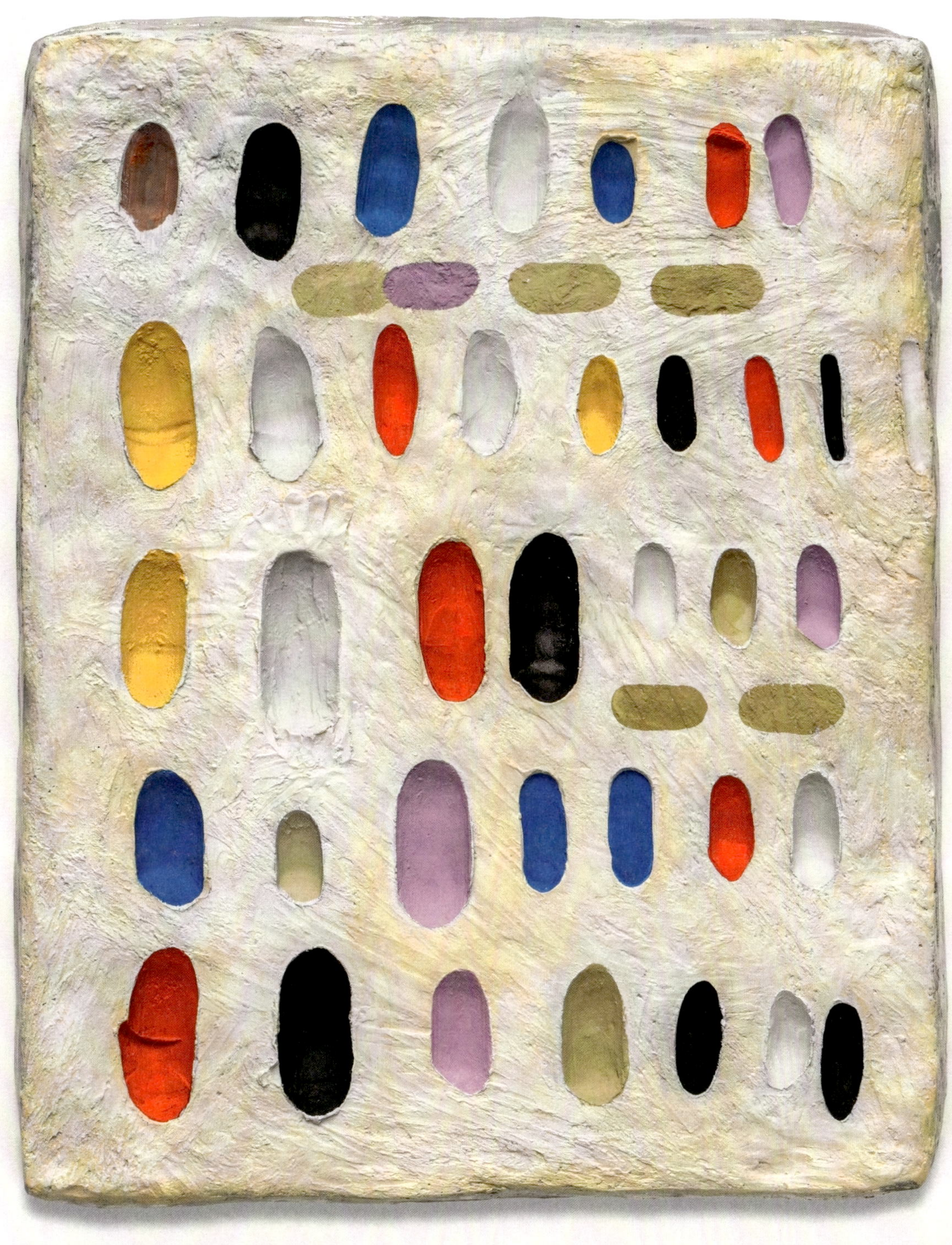

Homeopatia Mondrian, 2020
Acrylic on aluminum
38 9/16 × 31 7/8 × 3 1/8 inches (98 × 81 × 8 cm)

HOMEOPATIA MONDRIAN

For the 2018 exhibition *Ex-Gurus* at Andrew Kreps Gallery in New York, I explored abstract representations of philosophical concepts, presenting works themed on belief systems that I had moved away from, such as astrology, Bach flower remedies, the Baptist Church, and homeopathy. The last relief I made for the show was *Homeopatia* (2018), composed simply of rows of carved marks, as if different-colored homeopathic substances had been scooped out of nature. I used a metal arch-cutting tool like an ice-cream scoop. It felt as if I were creating a coloring book for myself, with

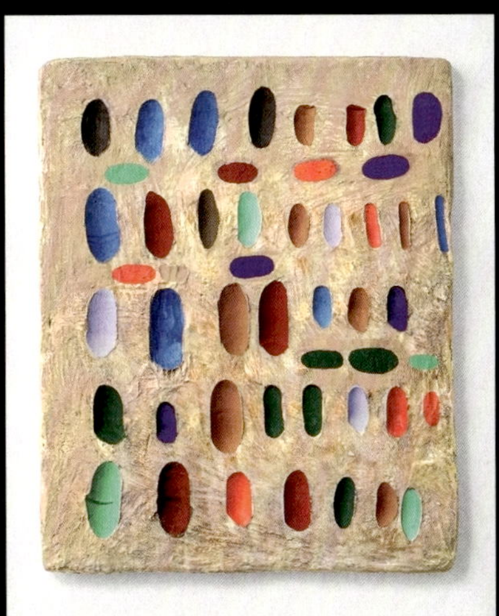

Homeopatia, 2018. Acrylic on bronze, 40 ³⁄₁₆ × 32 ⁵⁄₁₆ × 2 ¾ inches (102 × 82 × 7 cm)

Homeopatia Mondrian was created two years after *Homeopatia*, on an aluminum casting made from the bronze template of *Homeopatia*. In *Homeopatia*, the background color is the golden shade of naked bronze, which unifies high-contrast colors that would otherwise be difficult to combine. *Homeopatia Mondrian* stems from an opposite process: I covered the entire aluminum surface in different shades of white to neutralize its visual coldness and create a quirky "blank canvas." The white field seemed to bring out the grid structure of the work, instantly reminding me of Piet Mondrian, father of all grids.

Mondrian's canvases are often referred to as "clean" and "flat," but when I had the chance to see them in person I was absorbed by the flesh of the paint and the small cracks that give body to the surface. I wanted to have some creamy substance for my background, too, so I chose cold and warm whites, four in all. When the time came to fill the oval slots with color, it felt reassuring to start from predetermined hues that we know by heart from Mondrian—red, yellow, blue, and black—which I soon tempered with beiges and lavender.

This was during the pandemic lockdown, and I was painting at home and spending time choosing which color would go in which nest. This made me feel purposeful and somehow protected. Colors have their own intricate dynamics. While the grid structure appeared simplistic, the colors refused to be confined to their designated spaces. At one point, they rebelled and ventured horizontally, swimming on top of the white surface.

Venus of Cream, 2020
Bronze
82 ¹¹⁄₁₆ × 31 ⅛ × 31 ⅛ inches (210 × 79 × 79 cm)

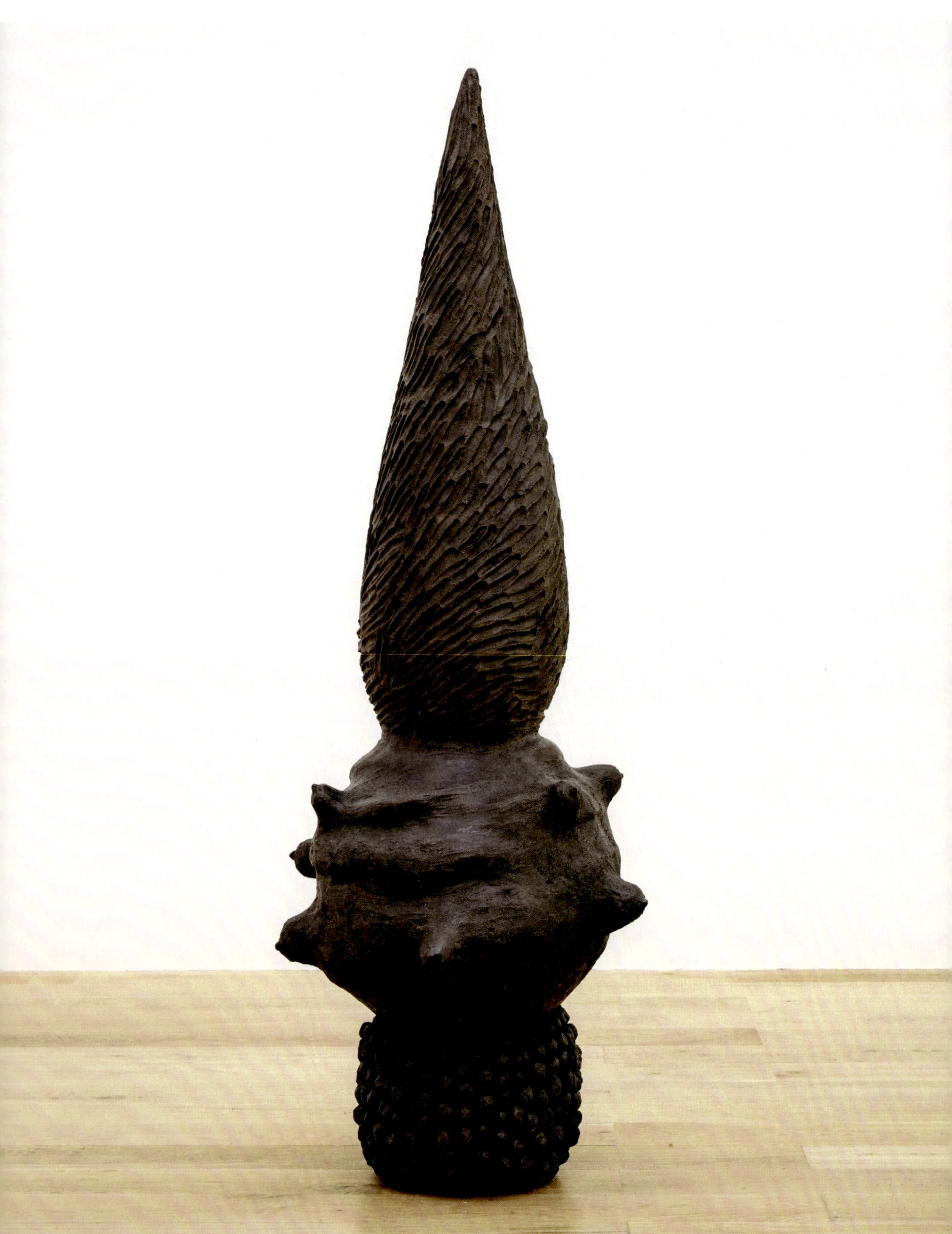

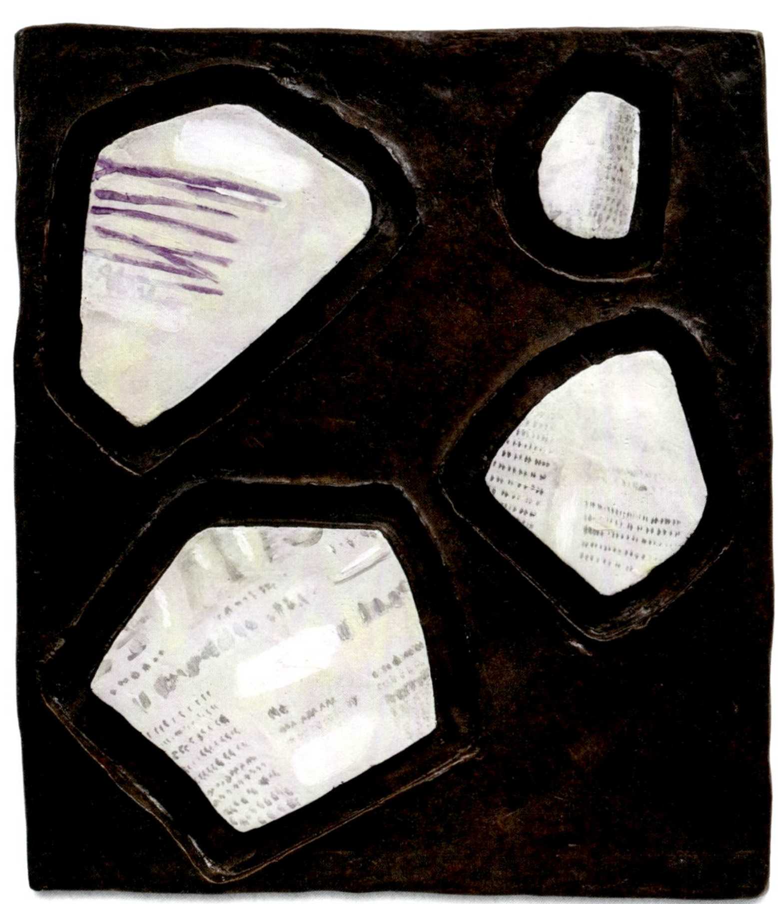

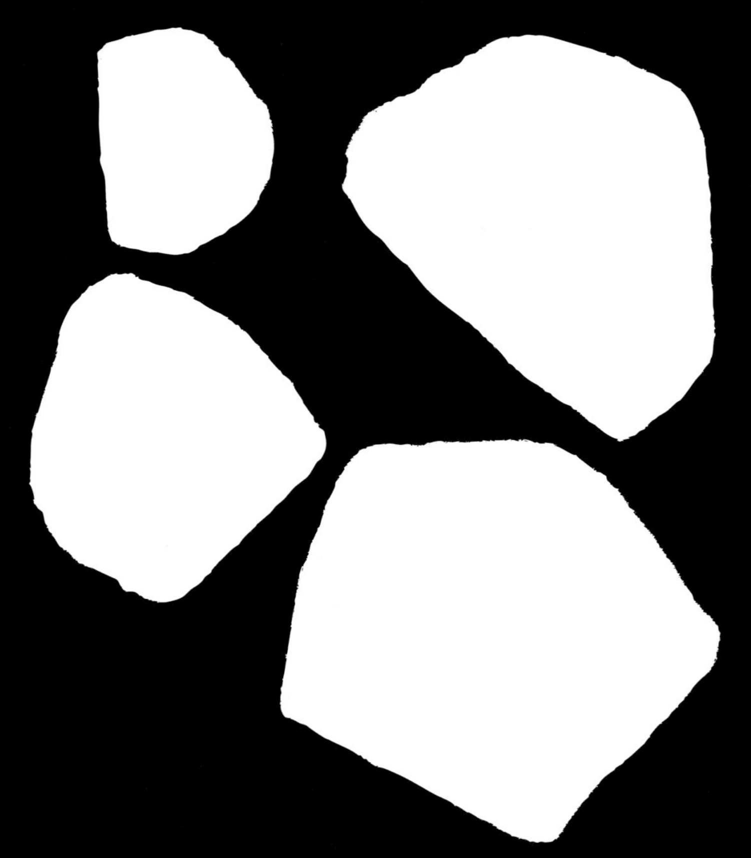

WHITE OUT AND NEWS

Four outlines carved on clay gave me four flat shapes. They were trapezoids with smooth corners, as if they had rolled in time like pebbles. My ambition was for them to be torn pieces of newspaper flying in the wind. I left the plates inside the shapes, flat and smooth, to paint later—I like to give myself tasks that are physically satisfying. I painted the predetermined slices in a very light gray that appears white (because real white has too much contrast for the eye). I waited for them to dry so I could paint newspaper lettering on top, to resemble a page of the news.

The insertion of lettering came from the desire to make my artworks permeable to what is happening in real life, and this was especially true during the abhorrent political period when Jair Bolsonaro was Brazil's president, from 2019 to 2022. Initially the works were quite literal: the first, *A Era da Inocência Acabou* (*The Age of Innocence Is Over*, 2020; page 73), was based on the front page of *Folha de São Paulo*, Brazil's largest daily paper. I copied its lettering and invented a headline that read "Impeachment and Vaccine – Sunday, 26 of July 2020." On top of that I painted a Cubist drawing fragment—I needed to resort to the Cubists, to their paintings of collaged pages, to help in my quest to connect art and bad news.

Later that year, I was in London painting the tiny stock-market ciphers of the *Financial Times* with the thinnest brush, a number zero. The title suggests a character in crisis: *Lady with Newspaper and Coins (Crying?)* (2020). Fingermarks serve as the hair, clothing, hands, and perhaps even tears of a woman in profile. It was September 2020 and there was not yet a vaccine for COVID-19. I painted an article announcing "Christmas to be anticipated" as an example of the dismantling of social structures.

The *Financial Times* title dissipated into a Cubist-style drawing. In the pieces that followed, references to the news become more abstract, as lines blurred and disconnected brushstrokes took over. Yet the perception of printed matter is still there, floating behind, conveying both beauty and anxiety.

White Out stands for Liquid Paper, the old-school correction fluid for typewritten text. Here it feels as if the news had been covered over, erased in the manner of George Orwell's *1984*, as in today's fake news galore, wiped away to the point of abstraction. The application of the corrective white might also be associated with Velature glaze in painting, which involves changing the value of colors, so that a range of blacks and grays now includes dark browns and lavenders.

—E.V.

Lady with Newspaper and Coins (Crying?), 2020. Acrylic, oil, and pigmented wax on bronze, 22 ⅞ × 18 ⅞ × 2 ³⁄₁₆ inches (57 × 48 × 5.5 cm)

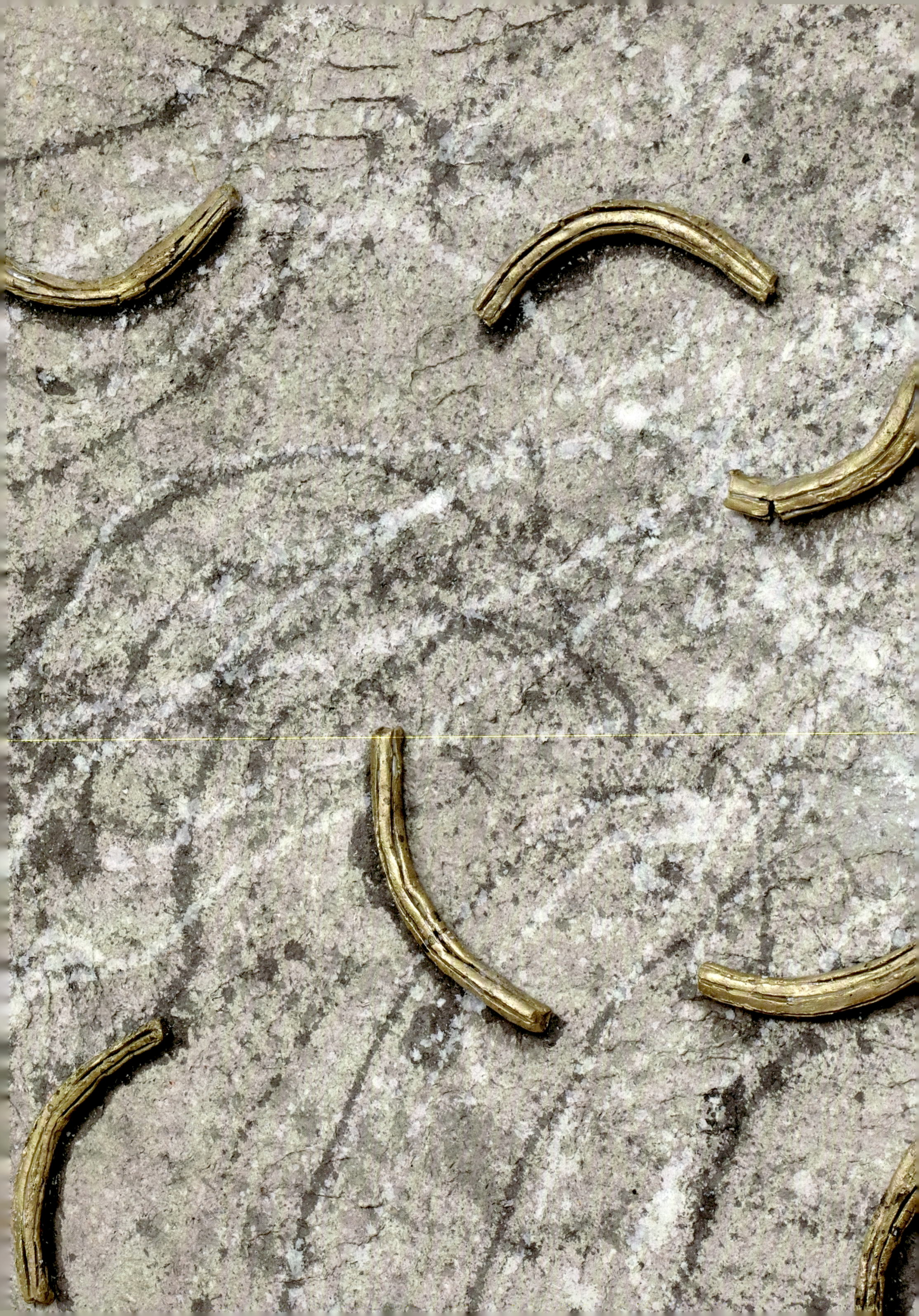

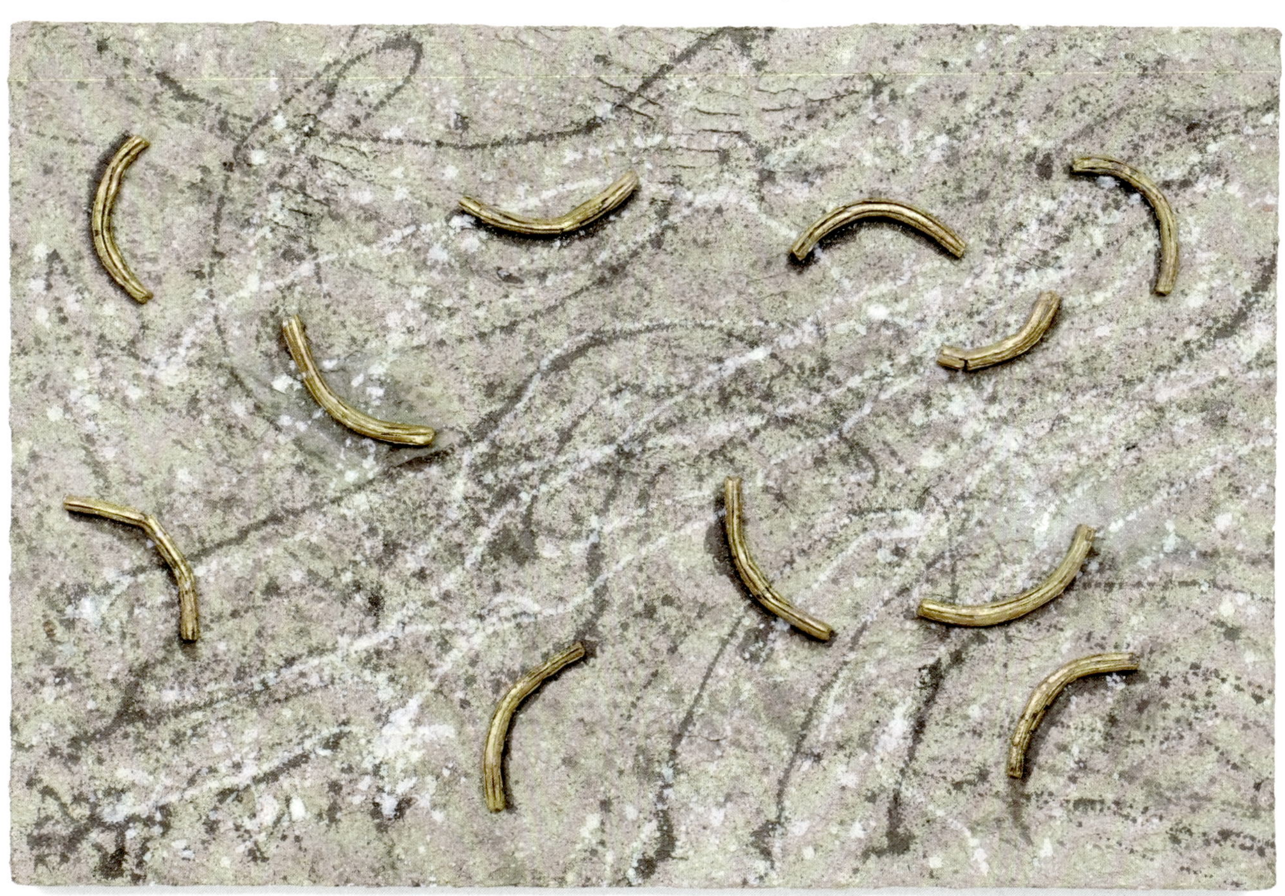

Churros com Vento (*Churros with Wind*), 2022
Papier-mâché, polystyrene, bronze, and oil
39 ⅜ × 59 ¹⁄₁₆ × 3 ⅛ inches (100 × 150 × 8 cm)

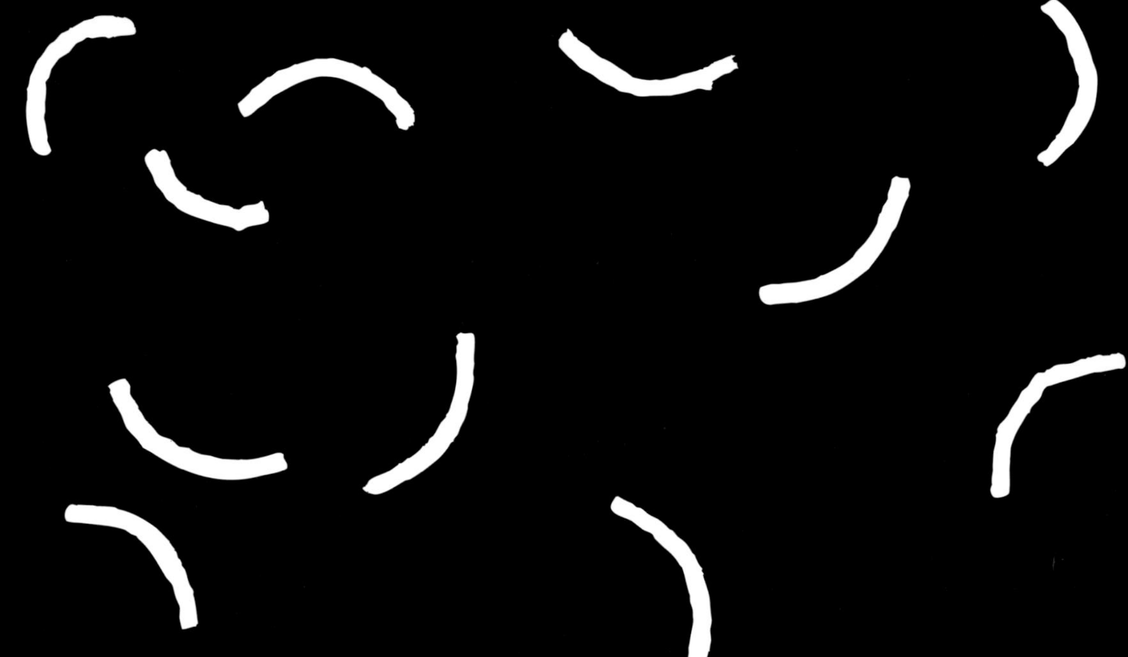

CHURROS AND THE WEATHER

It's curious to retrace how the connection between churros and the weather came about. I had made strips of whipped cream out of clay for works that play with extrusion and cake decoration, as in *Picasso with Strawberries* (2019). I realized churros also involve extrusion, but I faked the pastry-bag mechanics by simply rolling clay snakes and drawing lines on them with a wooden knife. These loose churros don't have as predetermined a path as the cake decorations. Their charm lies in the choice of the curve, ranging from a C shape to an I shape, and avoiding L as much as possible.

There were some elegant bronze churros in the studio—golden, without any patina. I didn't really know what to do with them until I looked and saw sun rays. Their curve was a very open C, which, placed around a circle, could set the composition in motion. *Sol de Churros* (*Sun of Churros*, 2019) was the first weather picture formed by these curved sections. Since then, I've adopted churros as if they were a classic geometric shape. Once spread around a field, they generate all kinds of dynamic compositions. The curves don't settle—they circle, they fly. The connection to weather conditions comes from that energy.

When it came to *Churros com Vento* (*Churros with Wind*, 2022), I felt like I wasn't doing anything but following the curves flying in a disorganized flow, like how leaves and plastic bags blow through big cities. The gray papier-mâché background feels urban, and the loose drips of oil paint seem scattered by the wind or like an apparition of Jackson Pollock's drips, testifying to the ample gesture of the artist's arm.

Splashes of paint are even more Pollockian and vigorous in *Umbrellas and Chaos* (2022; page 117), in which churros seem to have animated themselves into umbrella-handle shapes. The rain here seems stormier, its splashes more assertive. These umbrella handles are made of stoneware, not bronze, and the background is not the usual gray but rather greige. They recall rainy Brussels, where the work was made.

In *Churros Turbulence* (2022; page 116), the drippings seem to have gained speed. Here, swirls of white paint mimic *Starry Night* (1889), Vincent van Gogh's possible envisioning of turbulence, or the confounding phenomena physicists characterize as fluid motion, which appears as what we call spiraling or twirling.

—E.V.

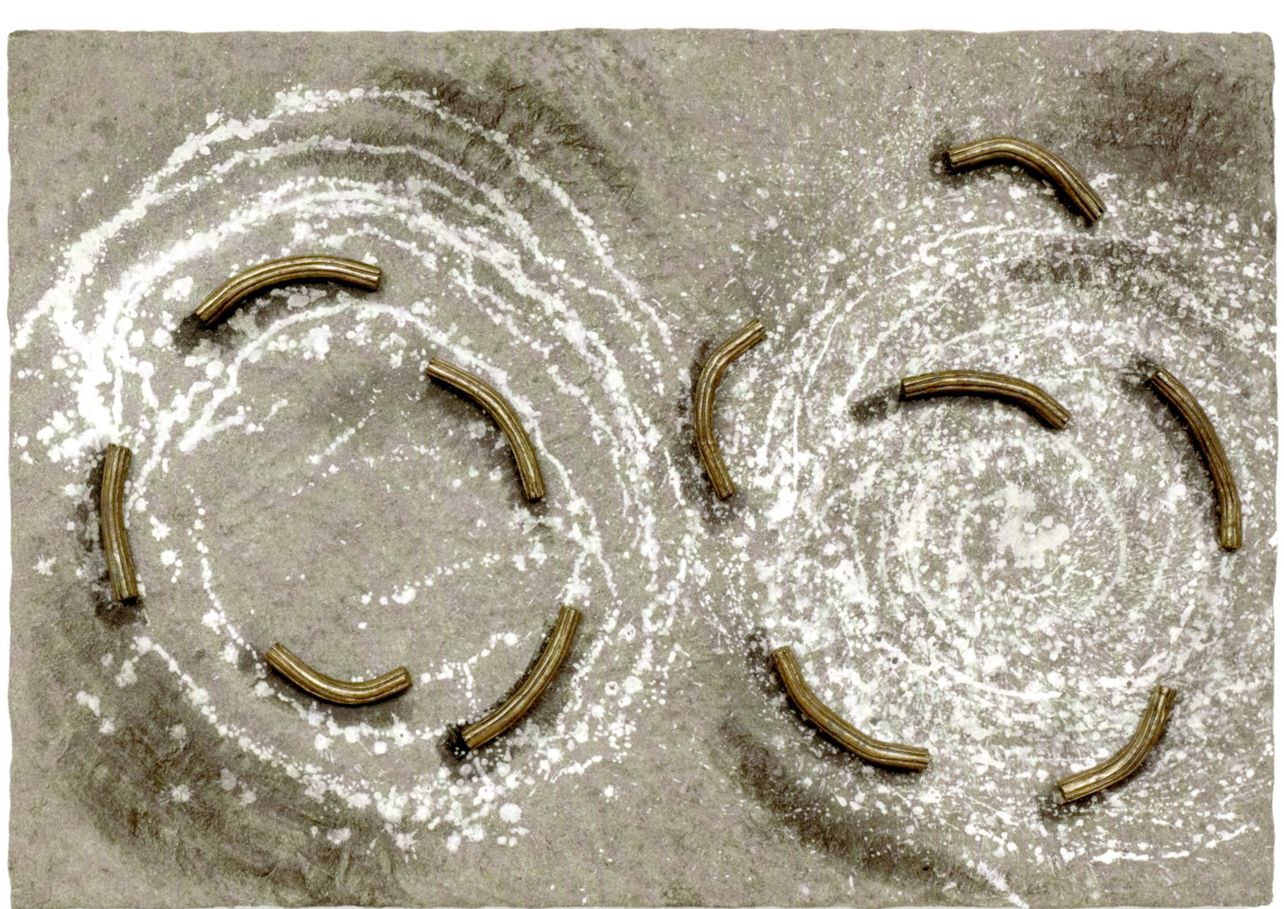

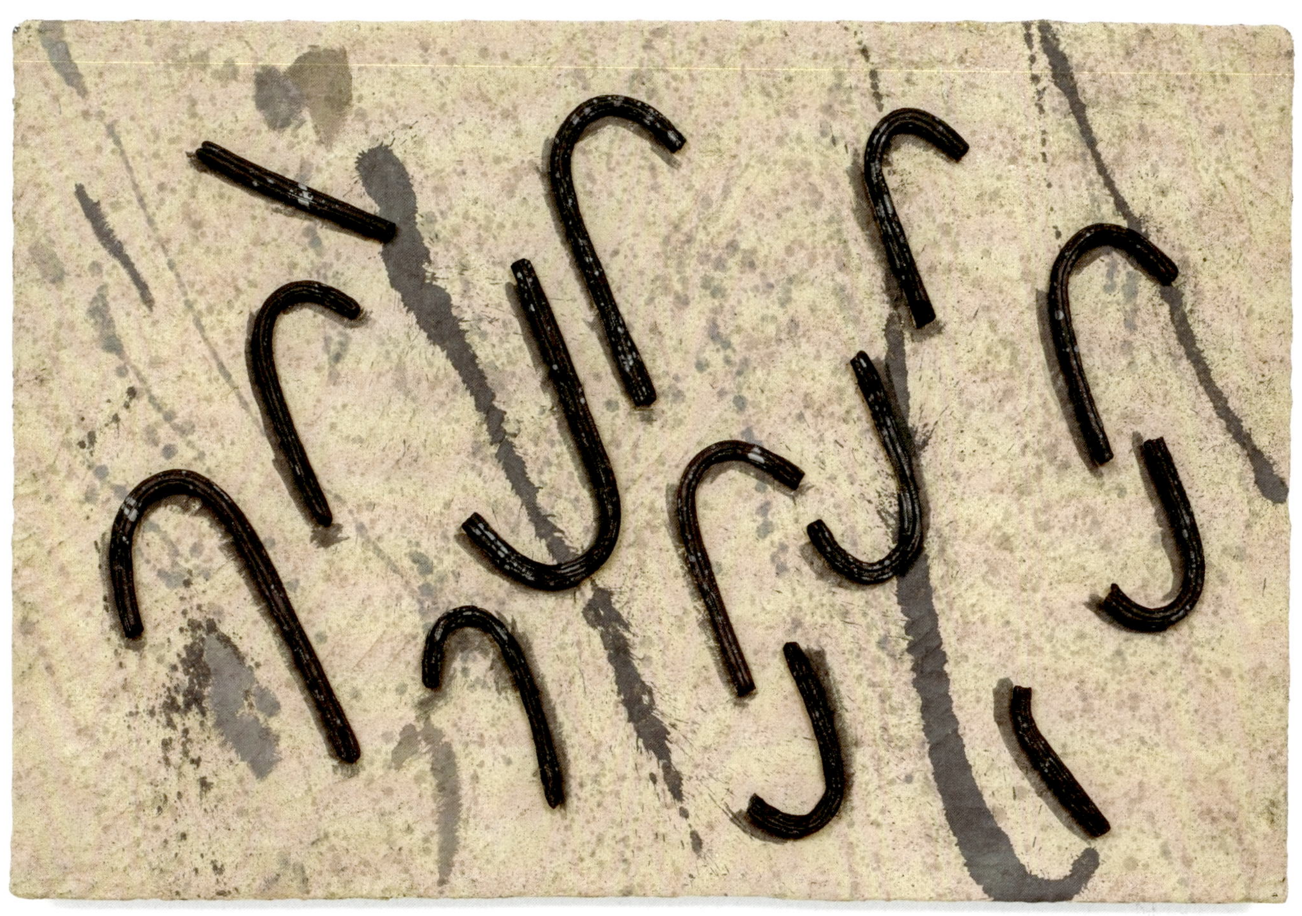

Umbrellas and Chaos, 2022
Papier-mâché, polystyrene, ceramics, and oil
39 ⅜ × 59 1/16 × 3 ⅛ inches (100 × 150 × 8 cm)

Torre de Cacau, 2021
Bronze and oil
134 ¼ × 14 ¹⁵⁄₁₆ × 14 ¹⁵⁄₁₆ inches (341 × 38 × 38 cm)

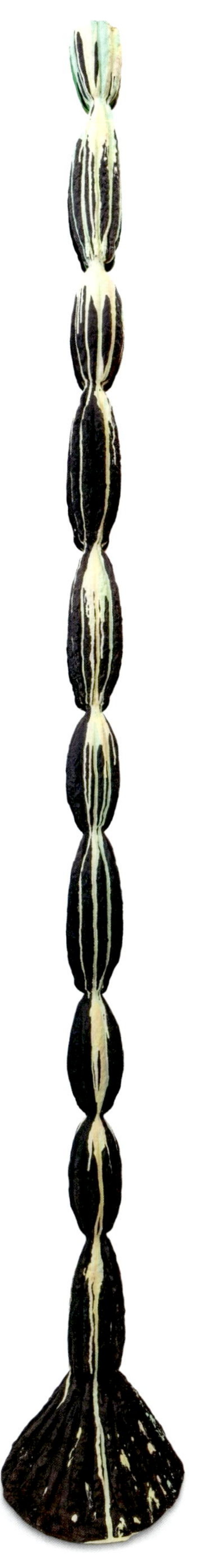

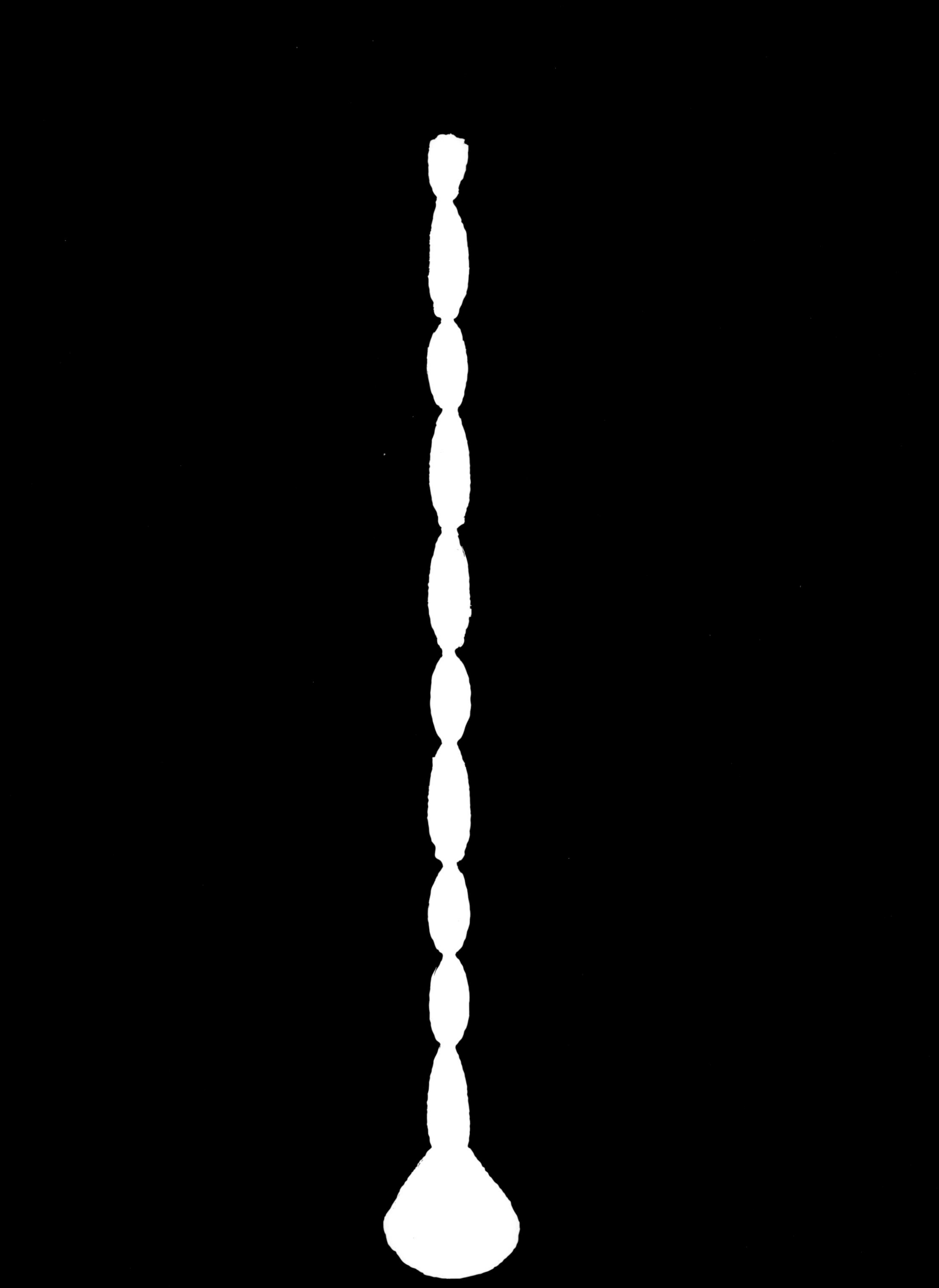

CACAO TOWER

Torre de Cacau (2021) feels as if the work existed before I made it. The shape of the cacao fruit lends itself as a "Brancusian" element that can pile up to infinity. I hear the work say, "I am column, I am fruit, I am sculpture."

My first tower of fruit was *Porn Star* (2011; page 87), made of star fruits cast in bronze. The top fruit was almost twelve feet above the floor, and I cut it in half to make a little cup, into which I poured white paint until it flooded out and down the fruits. This "ejaculation" of white paint animated the tower's verticality. The association of a star fruit with *Endless Column* helped me understand that the Brancusi tower is not just a reference, but more like a legacy, an achievement of language now available for art and artists.

The cacao fruit being much bigger than the star fruit, *Torre de Cacau* offers more surface for the eye to rest on. This column, too, received a performative paint application. If in *Porn Star* I was thinking about sex, here the drive was politics. The viscous paint looks as if it were coming up from the inside, as if the sculpture were bleeding. The blood in this case is yellow and green, and it drips down the cacao fruits' bumpy skins. I wanted to rescue Brazil's national colors. They have been kidnapped by the extreme right in recent years, to the point that the egg-yolk yellow of the Brazilian football shirt seems a repulsive reference to Bolsonarism. For *Torre de Cacau*, I chose very pale shades of green and yellow. The colors could be fading out in decay or fading in as they slowly come back.

—E.V.

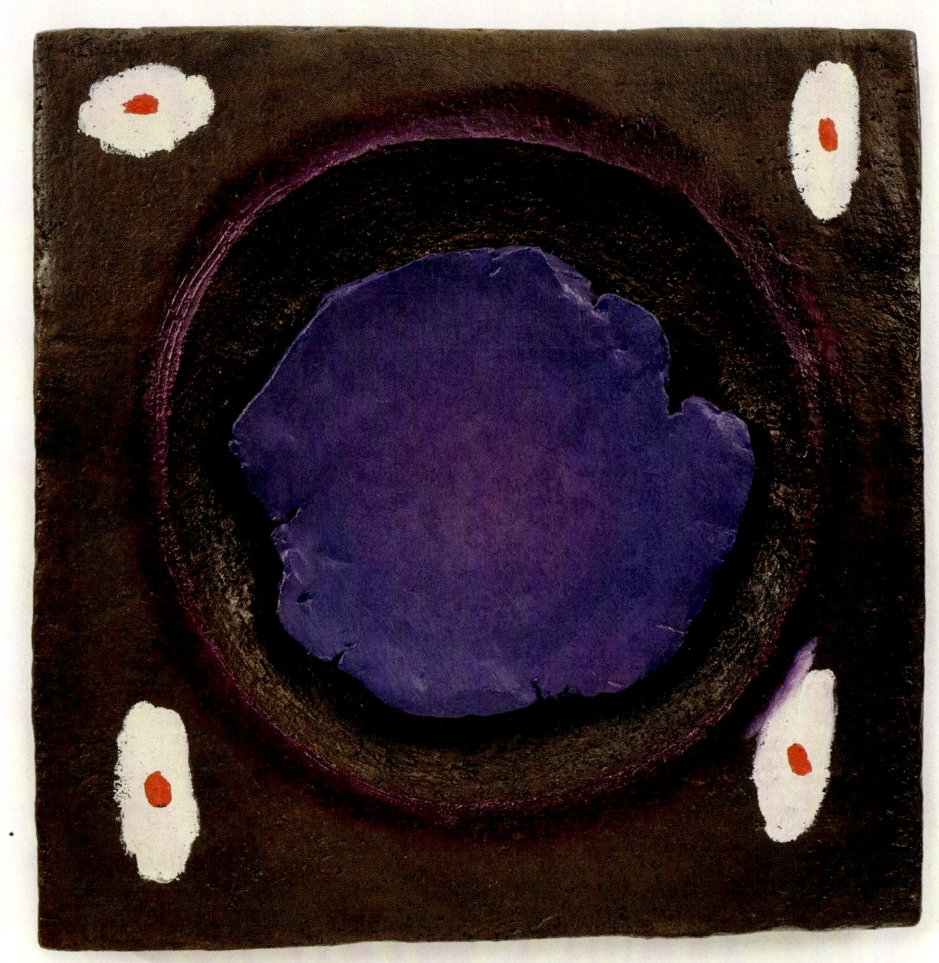

Tantra Roxo (*Purple Tantra*), 2022
Bronze and oil
16 ¹⁵⁄₁₆ × 16 ¹⁵⁄₁₆ × 2 ⅜ inches (43 × 43 × 6 cm)

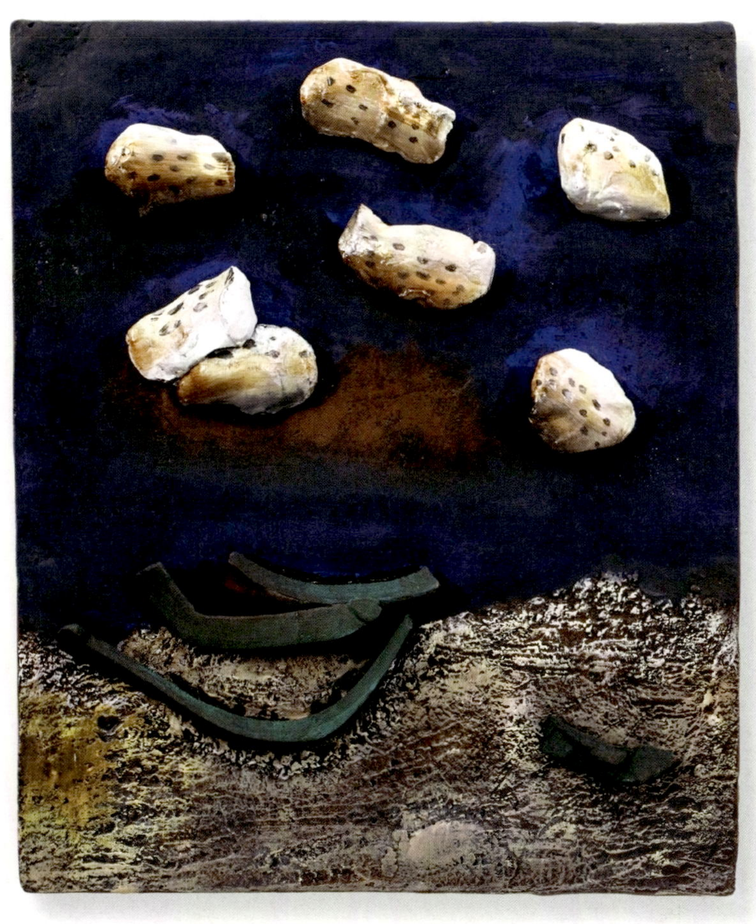

*Vênus Abelha (**Bee Venus**)*, 2022
Bronze, acrylic, and macrame
43 5/16 × 23 5/8 × 23 5/8 inches (110 × 60 × 60 cm)

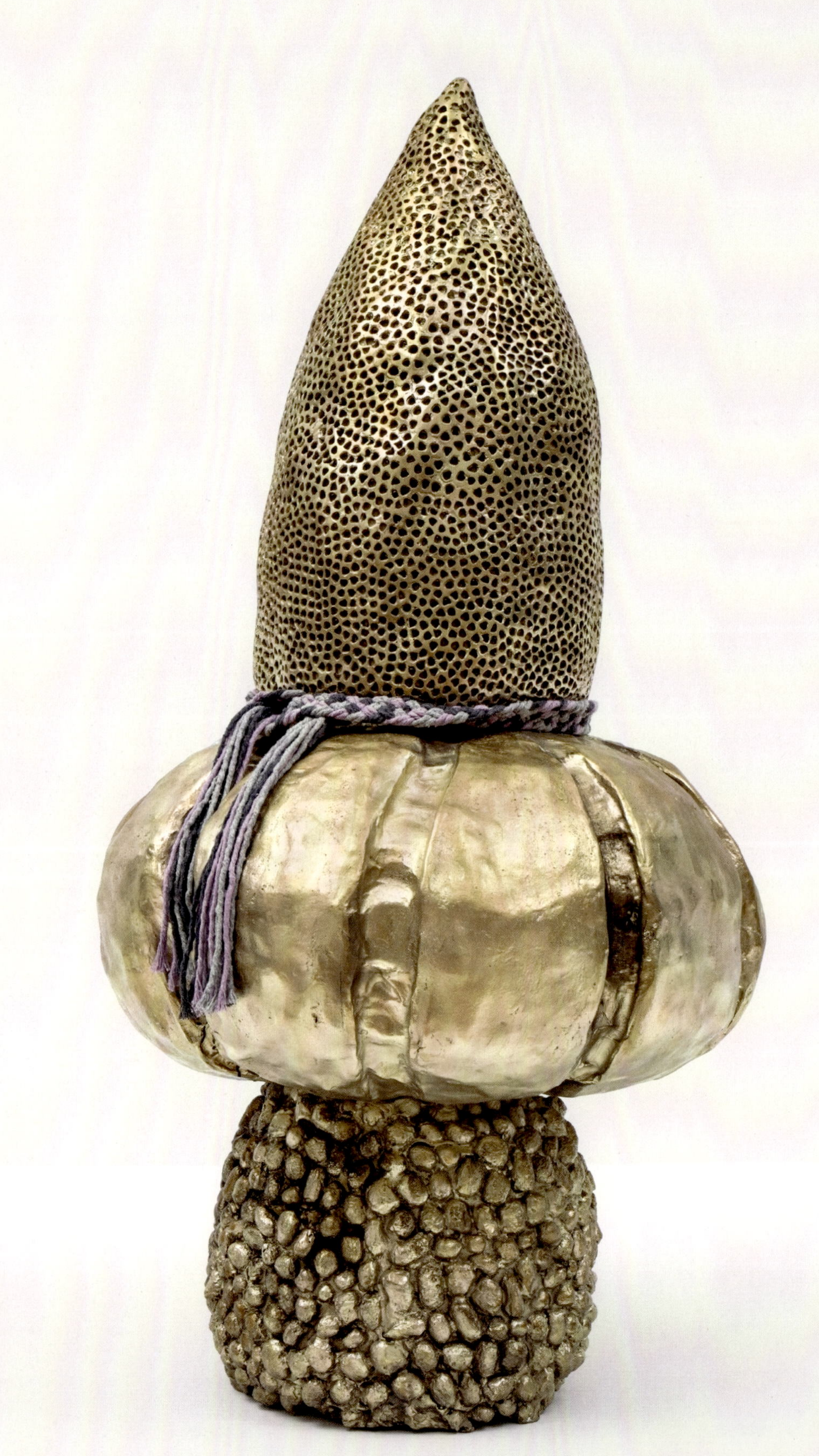

Venus Doll, 2022
Bronze
15 ¾ × 7 ⅞ × 7 ⅞ inches (40 × 20 × 20 cm)

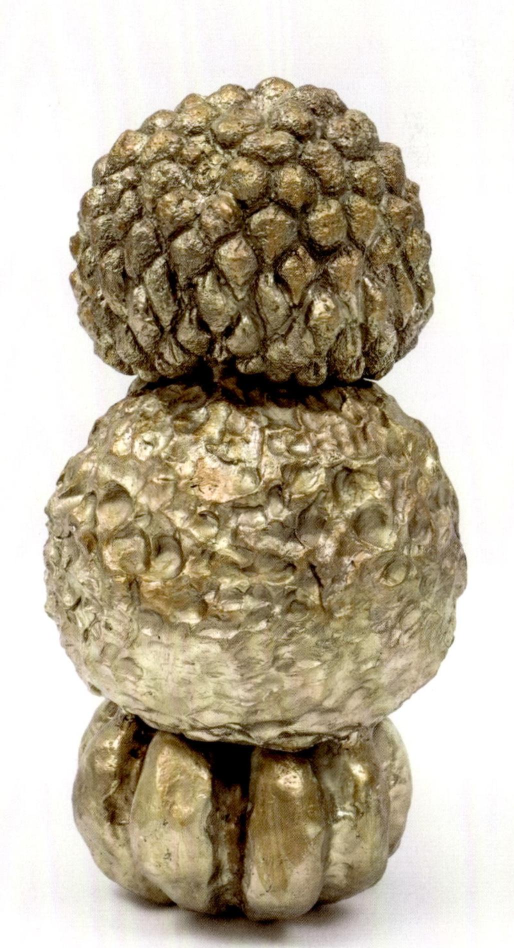

Venus Gokula, 2022
Bronze, acrylic, and macrame
29 ¹⁵⁄₁₆ × 15 ⅜ × 15 ⅜ inches (76 × 39 × 39 cm)

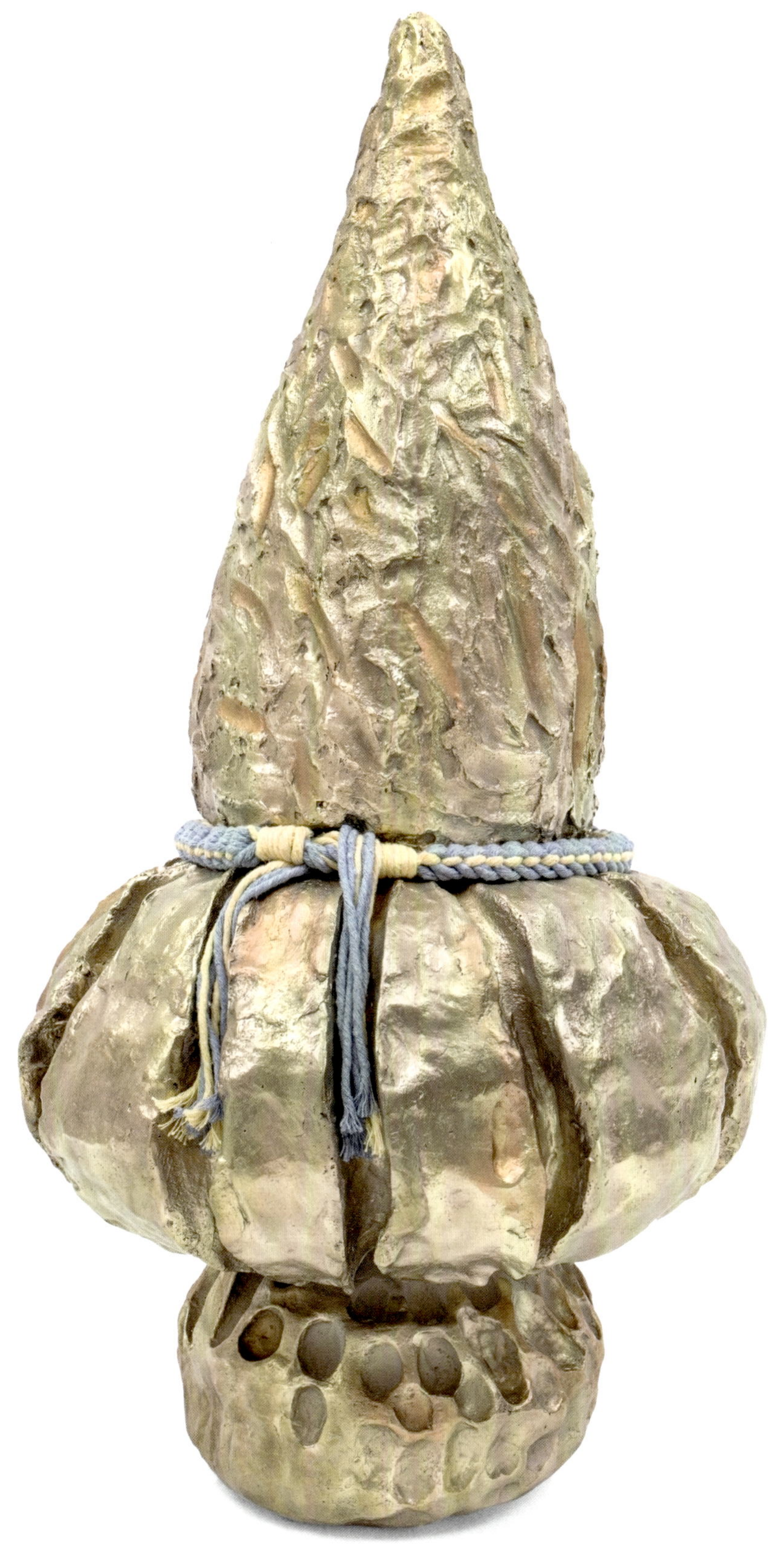

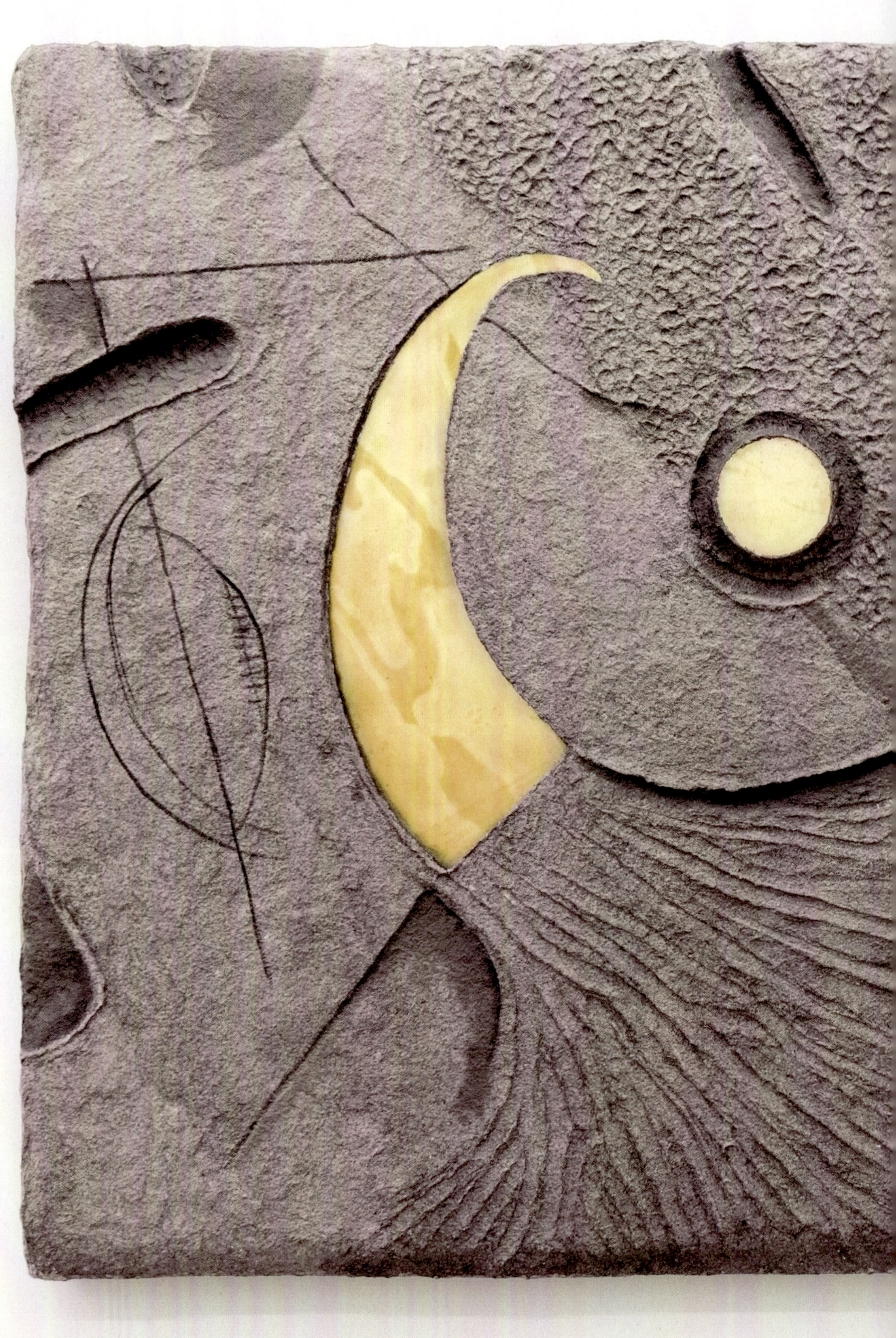

Crisis of Sculpture, 2023
Polystyrene, papier-mâché, brass, and oil
56 ¹¹⁄₁₆ × 84 ¼ × 7 ¹⁄₁₆ inches (144 × 214 × 18 cm)

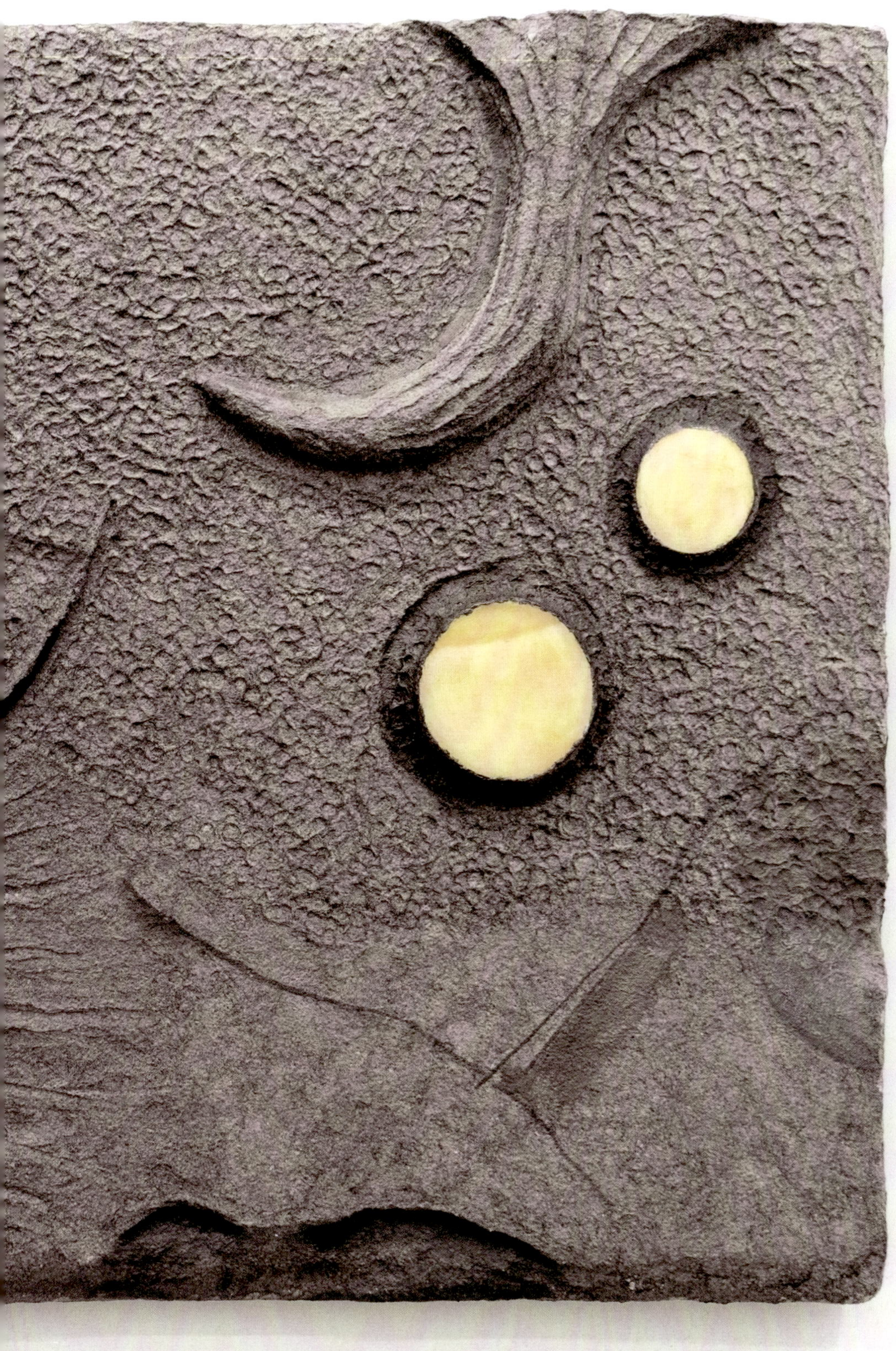

ERIKA VERZUTTI:
RHYTHM AND DELIRIUM

Bernardo Mosqueira

For Erika Verzutti, irreverence and insubordination serve as the foundation of a constructive practice at odds with the world as structured by modernity, where such tendencies are more likely associated with negation, destruction, and deconstruction. Using a particular vocabulary of formal and conceptual strategies, Verzutti investigates the ways in which material encounters can affect people's lives by orienting or disorienting our symbolic and spatial relationships with the world. Her work brings together references from widely various contexts—vernacular culture, art histories, domestic daily life, the digital sphere, contemporary political conflicts—without affirming categories and hierarchies. At the center of her artistic practice is an experimental and speculative study of the survival of images, of how forms are endowed with their own intelligence, desire, and resilience. Disobedience and autonomy also characterize the unusual ways in which the artist takes up materials as diverse as clay, bronze, stone, wood, paint, wax, fabric, papier-mâché, polystyrene, fiberglass, and found objects. Ultimately, her indecipherable techniques generate contradictions and uncertainties for our visual perception, often making us aware of our too-hasty search for meaning and forcing us to develop new ways of feeling, thinking, and being with the world.

Verzutti's artistic trajectory started with studying industrial design at the Universidade Presbiteriana Mackenzie, São Paulo. Following her graduation in 1991, she developed a series of works involving gestural marks, geometric shapes, and graphemes on paper, influenced by the neo-Expressionist practice of the members of Casa 7,[1] a São Paulo–based artists group, as well as certain artists with whom she studied, such as Leda Catunda and Sérgio Romagnolo. Despite the impact of these artists, Verzutti came to feel that the formalism of the older generation was uncomfortably disconnected from the world, an impression that pushed her experimental inquiries forward in the nineties. It was only after receiving her master's in fine arts from Goldsmiths College, London, in 2000 that she found the field of sculpture to be fertile ground for advancing her practice. Following a short experimental period of making vases out of paper, the material encounter between her body and clay opened a mysterious and prolific passage to shapes from the past, present, and future, as she finally realized what she had been searching for: intertwinement with the world.

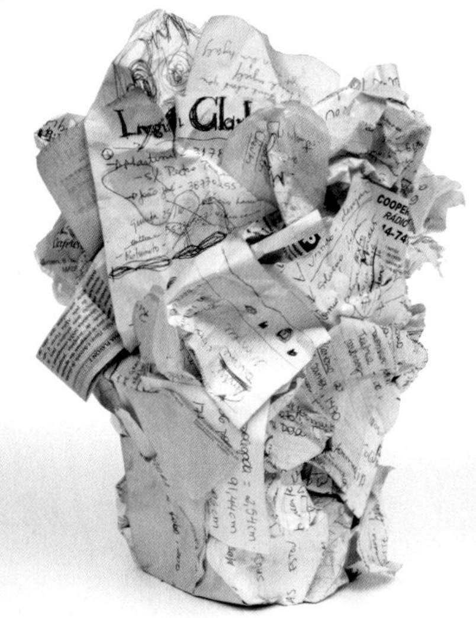

Erika Verzutti, *Vaso Chinês* (*Chinese Vase*), 2001. Found paper, 15 × 14 9/16 × 14 3/16 inches (39 × 37 × 36 cm)

1 Between 1982 and 1985, the artistic group Casa 7 (Rodrigo Andrade, Carlito Carvalhosa, Fabio Miguez, Paulo Monteiro, and Nuno Ramos) experimented with cheap industrial paint on large pieces of kraft paper. The group was directly influenced by artists such as Philip Guston and Markus Lüpertz, whose works they had encountered in the 1981 and 1983 editions of the Bienal de São Paulo.

Since then, this passage, like a gigantic and ravenous mouth, has been devouring ancient artifacts, modern art, fresh fruits and vegetables, esteemed poetry, countless hours of electronic music, urgent political struggles, the most disparate of movies, sensual-slime ASMR videos, assorted makeup palettes, and so forth, to then regurgitate enthralling monsters constituted of memories of these ingested sources of luscious wonder—parts of their shapes, names, movements, opposites, reverses, echoes, rumors, shadows, distortions, and secrets. Decomposing, recomposing, and finding new positions, Verzutti's constructive irreverence plays with ideas of value and meaning while giving unpredictable afterlives to her cultural references, disregarding arbitrary divisions between high and low culture. Over the years, the artist has become more and more attracted to investigating how images circulate in contemporary life and manipulate our bodies, especially in relation to a world dominated by constant, captivating, and exhaustive digital interactions and marked by instability, dispute, and uncertainty.

Verzutti has structured her practice through the establishment of aesthetic-conceptual games, unspoken personal rules, and a singular heuristic system that arises from her laborious journeys in the studio. For most of her career, she has kept her working space in her own residence, and a strong sense of intimacy endows her poetics, even in her large-scale pieces. A subversive gaze always pays special attention to the incorrect or inadequate, and with Verzutti it is no different. Her process errors, failures, mishaps, and frustrations often inaugurate new paths, creating opportunities for her to go further, closer to the state of delirium.

The word *delirium* derives from the Latin *de*, meaning "outside," and *lira*, referring to the lines a plow furrows in soil; it is thus connected to the idea of sowing in deviation, of growing from the unexpected to flourish in contradiction. There are few words as generative as this one to reflect Verzutti's practice. Two major examples of how Verzutti has been using delirium to give life to her works are the series *Cemitérios* (*Cemeteries*, 2008–present) and *Bicho de Sete Cabeças* (*Seven-Headed Monster*, 2007–10).

The *Cemitérios* series debuted in 2008 in the solo exhibition *Pet Cemetery* at Galeria Fortes Vilaça, São Paulo. The exhibition was named to echo the iconic punk-rock song "Pet Sematary," written by the Ramones for the 1989 film adaptation of the eponymous Stephen King novel, about a group of children who discover a mysterious burial site in the woods, where the soil has the magical power to resurrect the deceased. The kids start bringing their pets back to life there, naming the site "Pet Sematary," its misspelling apparent on the sign they install in the woods. Verzutti's *Cemitérios* also continue from mistakes: they are made from broken pieces and process debris she collects in a corner of her studio. She resurrects these pieces by arranging them together and eventually adding other objects as small interventions. At the original *Pet Cemetery* exhibition, she also had her own group of cool kids play resurrection with her: she invited artists Efrain Almeida, Tonico Lemos Auad, Alexandre da Cunha, Tiago Carneiro da Cunha, and Leda Catunda to collaborate on specific pieces, with each bringing something representative of their own poetics and studio practices.

Another rare and remarkable collaborative occasion happened three years later for a work from Verzutti's *Bicho de Sete Cabeças* series, which takes as its title a popular phrase used in Brazil to refer to complex and scary situations that seem to require difficult solutions. (It's believed that the expression refers to the many-headed Hydra of Lerna, whom Hercules defeated as the second of his twelve labors.) In 2007, Verzutti exhibited her first versions of *Bicho de Sete Cabeças* at the London gallery Blow de la Barra. These sculptures have seven long necks, each ending in a vegetable- or fruit-shaped head. In 2010, aiming to condense the experience of a group exhibition into a single sculpture, Verzutti invited the artists Efrain Almeida, Carlos Bevilacqua, Alexandre da Cunha, Jac Leirner, Ernesto Neto, Damián Ortega, Nuno Ramos, and Adriana Varejão to each make a head according to their own artistic practice. The resulting, large-scale *Bicho* was a dynamic and fragmented monster resembling a postapocalyptic coral reef of accumulated heads, like a Frankenstein technology.

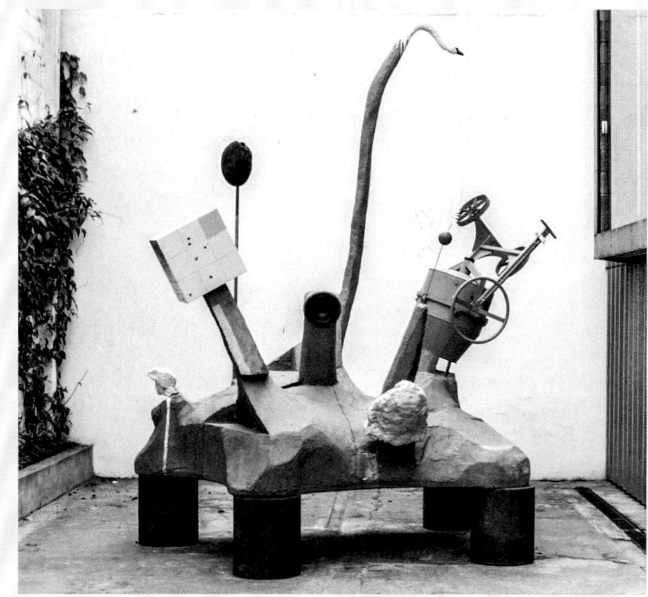

Erika Verzutti, collaboration with Efrain Almeida, Carlos Bevilacqua, Alexandre da Cunha, Jac Leirner, Ernesto Neto, Damián Ortega, Nuno Ramos, and Adriana Varejão, *Bicho de Sete Cabeças* (*Seven-Headed Monster*), 2010. Mixed media, 159 ⅞ × 86 ⅝ × 122 1⁄16 inches (406 × 220 × 310 cm). Exhibition view, Galeria Fortes Vilaça, São Paulo, 2010–11

Astutely, Verzutti's practice amalgamates iconoclasm and iconography. Her *Cemitérios* and *Bicho de Sete Cabeças* evidence how she plays with delirium to give life, new life, and afterlife to what intrigues her, whether it is debris from her own studio practice, works by other artists, or images taken from the internet. Precisely because of the playful, intimate, and untethered ways through which she engages with images as living beings, an exhibition of her work at an institution dedicated to curatorial studies—the Center for Curatorial Studies, Bard College—is especially powerful.

In the fields of curatorial theory and teaching, there are three particularly problematic but recurrent tendencies. The first is a common urge to define what curatorial practice *is* or *must be*, rather than encouraging the invention or imagination of what curating *can be* or *may yet become*. The second is the treating of artworks as objects, without considering their own agency, intelligence, subjectivity, mutation, life, and—why not?—spiritual dimensions. The third is believing that to organize an exhibition is to create a static display, a simple and rigid relationship between measurable objects and measurable space, for this neglects the most important part of our work, which is the preparation of fertile territory for the presence, movement, and transformation of the public, with the aim of inspiring many dance improvisations instead of enforcing a unique choreography.

Occupying the CCS Bard Galleries, *New Moons*, Verzutti's first major museum exhibition in the United States, can contribute enormously to a meditation on these points. Especially for the community that returns to the building daily, the exhibition offers the chance to observe audience behaviors and to learn how each encounter between a person and a work is a unique intersubjective experience, impossible to predict or standardize. The exhibition prompts an awareness of an ungraspable, opaque, complex experience, an uncontained glance toward the infinite. The cosmos manifested in the face of art inspires, in singular ways, recognition, projection, doubt, and reflection. Verzutti's works are questioning, and they make us question ourselves—our subjectivities, abilities, limitations, and ways of being together. They welcome and reject us, comfort and disturb us. Sometimes, they pretend to ignore our presence; at others, they perform unapologetically.

As does any living being, each of these sculptures communicates with us in ways that are more or less comprehensible, while actively manipulating our bodies—inviting us to move closer and farther away; to twist our necks and torsos; to step up and down, point our cameras, find the best angle; to relax for a hot second before launching ourselves into myriad movements of crouching, stretching, reclining . . . If one is paying attention, it's clear that Verzutti's sculptures are not silent. These pieces are talking

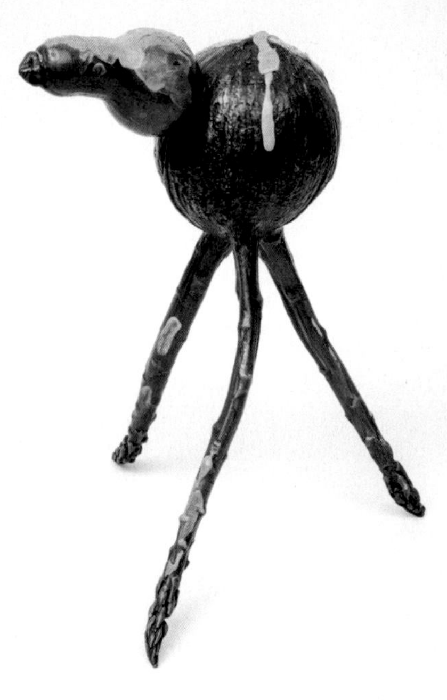

Erika Verzutti, *Maria*, 2007. Bronze and acrylic, 12 ¹⁄₁₆ × 8 ¼ × 7 ⅞ inches (31 × 21 × 20 cm)

and inviting us to talk. Neither are they still. Verzutti created them while constantly dancing in the studio, and from that they learned well. If we're improvising our movements around them, that's because they're dancing and inviting us to dance. They've opened the floor to us. They're party monsters, enfants terribles, fleurs du mal, busy conspirators, carnival ghosts, lousy visionaries, badass bitches, rebels with and without a cause. They're untamable. These statues are not dead. They're clearly more than objects. They're not here to be interpreted, defined, categorized, or explained. Instead, they are generously but impatiently teaching us a pedagogy of perception subversive to how art institutions have been built. Indeed, Verzutti is aware that multidirectional possibilities of presence are much richer than linear models—she plays with fractal paths of affection.

Her works engage with our fantasies, guts, and muscles and ask us to imagine how to be in the world beyond the old Western divisions of subjects/objects, agents/materials, and animate/inanimate beings. Opting for porosity and irregularity, Verzutti creates works that express characteristics of living beings. The discipline of art history has been thinking a lot about the contextual conditions in which works of art are produced. However, what could we learn by reflecting on what works of art actively produce? Which changes will arise in our field when we truly understand that we have always been products of them?

Engaging with Verzutti's works, we face the heterogeneity and elasticity of the temporal dimension. She is always digging in time to fabricate beings that exhibit a combination of the desire for fixation and the certainty of impermanence. When the shape of a fruit, an egg, or a fingerprint takes on the temporality of different materials, whether metal or clay, how does it change our perception of the duration of a lifetime? Of an encounter? Of a desire? Of a fantasy? In this way, Verzutti's creatures skew certain fundamental ideas of the world as ordered and structured by spatial and temporal dimensions.

Perhaps accordingly, the idea of the "monster" is often used to discuss her poetics. In the nineteenth century, when the world was changing at a seemingly unprecedented pace, monsters became important metaphors of modern subjectivity in Gothic literature.[2] As expressions of a society obsessed with evolving forms of production and consumption, they echoed a desire for the establishment of a new social order. The representation of monsters contributed to the formation of modern collective imaginaries; they operated as new myths, or new mirrors, and guided society in both the search for more new things and in the conservation of old values. They fundamentally embodied deviant behavior, an existence that de-monstrates a corruption of the order of things as maintained through binary categories of female/male, proletariat/aristocrat, creator/creature, native/foreign, body/soul, culture/nature, and subject/object. Monsters inspire fear and desire, profoundly affecting people and disrupting our most basic feelings and beliefs.

Verzutti's practice opens passages to ambiguous monsters, composed of simultaneously recognizable and unrecognizable, whole and fragmented, derived and newly synthesized elements. The results affect us viscerally: these entities are never completely graspable, apprehensible, comprehensible, or decipherable, but they are nonetheless moving. They are mesmerizing and seductive and often deceive us; they make us laugh at them and ourselves; they create generative contradictions in our ways of perceiving and understanding—thus encouraging us to expand our ways of being with the world.

2 Anne Bannerman's "The Mermaid" (1800), Mary Shelley's *Frankenstein* (1818), Joseph Sheridan Le Fanu's *Carmilla* (1872), Bram Stoker's *Dracula* (1897), and Robert Louis Stevenson's *The Strange Case of Dr. Jekyll and Mr. Hyde* (1886) are extremely influential examples of the portrayal of monsters in Gothic literature.

As a result of her elaborate, mysterious techniques, Verzutti's works are almost opaque; they often produce illusions about their materiality, density, weight, point of balance, and, above all, personalities, thoughts, and inner dimensions. With works arising from the intimacy and alchemy of studio practice, her creative processes seem to halt only when her meaningful titles meet her material creatures. The words sometimes arrive as impregnations, setting the tone for the vitality of that matter. Or they rub against the bodies of the works, creating sparks that trigger our imagining machines, opening portals to nonconforming worldliness. They can short-circuit to different points on the grid of the ordered world, functioning as destabilizing nominations that alternately increase opacity or shed light on its potentially inconspicuous aspects. Playing with the limits of the survival of images and experimenting with the expansion of our ways of feeling, Verzutti's work proposes a type of a mythical reorganization, playing with how shapes orient us and help us to lend temporary meanings to the experience of being alive in chaos.

On view in *New Moons*, *Cemitério com Franja* (*Cemetery with Fringe*, 2014; pages 60–61) is another gathering of sculptural fragments from the studio, supplemented with bulky stones, drawings, and a rhythmic adornment of paintbrushes and hand chisels along one edge. Looking at this work and reflecting on the sculptor's labor, I am reminded of a legend about Michelangelo: it is said that, just after completing one of his masterpieces, the Italian artist hit the sculpture on the knee with a chisel saying, "Now, speak, Moses!" While this story may be apochryphal, five centuries later his giant *Moses* is speaking in the most different of languages—beautifully, yet maybe too loud. In *New Moons*, we are invited to enter the realm of delirium, to perceive life manifested through Verzutti's forms. The sheer vitality of these pieces offers the opportunity to go beyond thinking about how we might move them around in space and what we know about them, to instead consider how they move us in space and what they know about us. But never forget how untamable these sculptures are. It is possible that any day now, frustrated by our lack of sensitivity and agency as we hurry through the galleries, one of them is going to throw a chisel at us and shout, "Now, listen, Moses!"

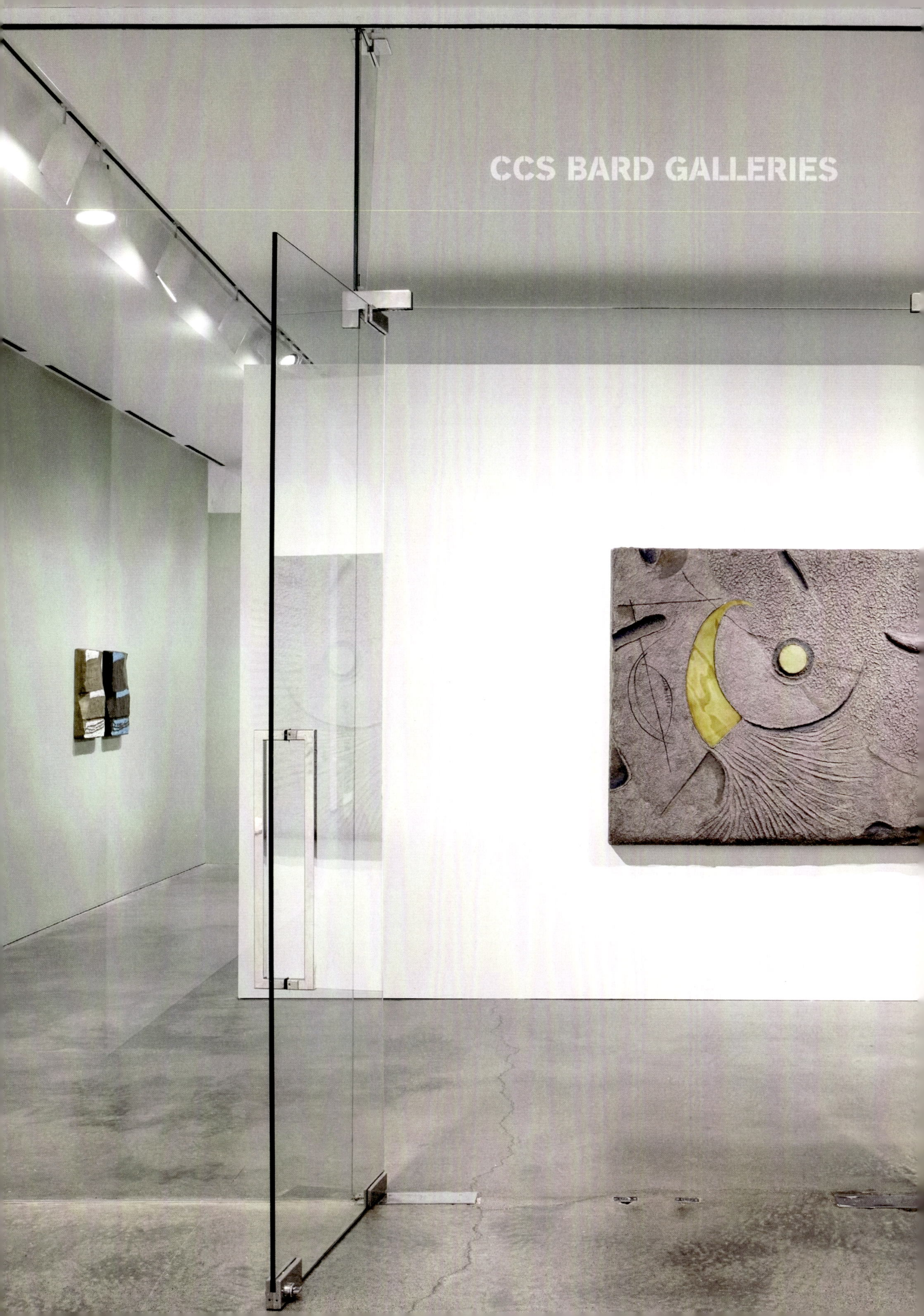

CCS BARD GALLERIES

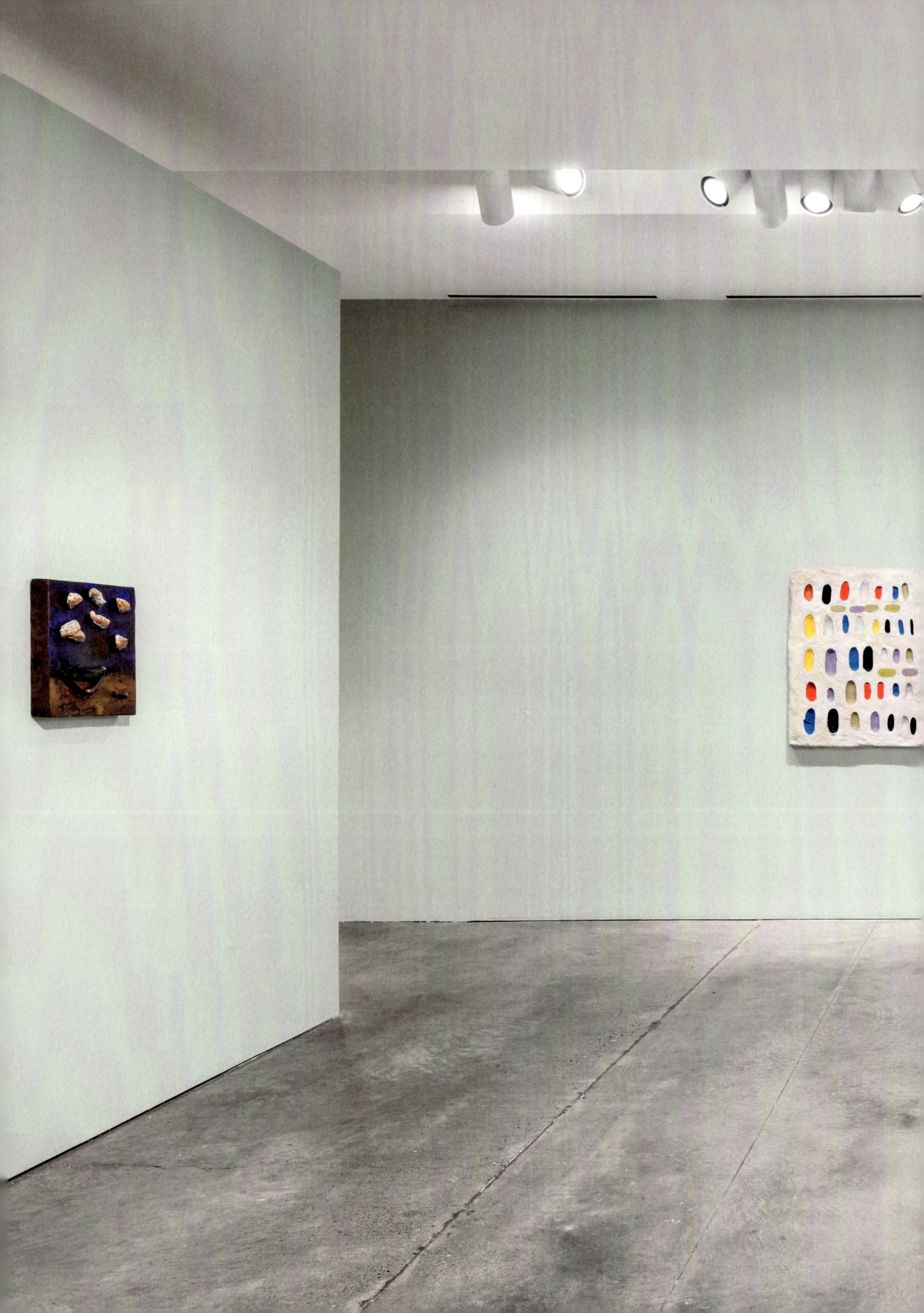

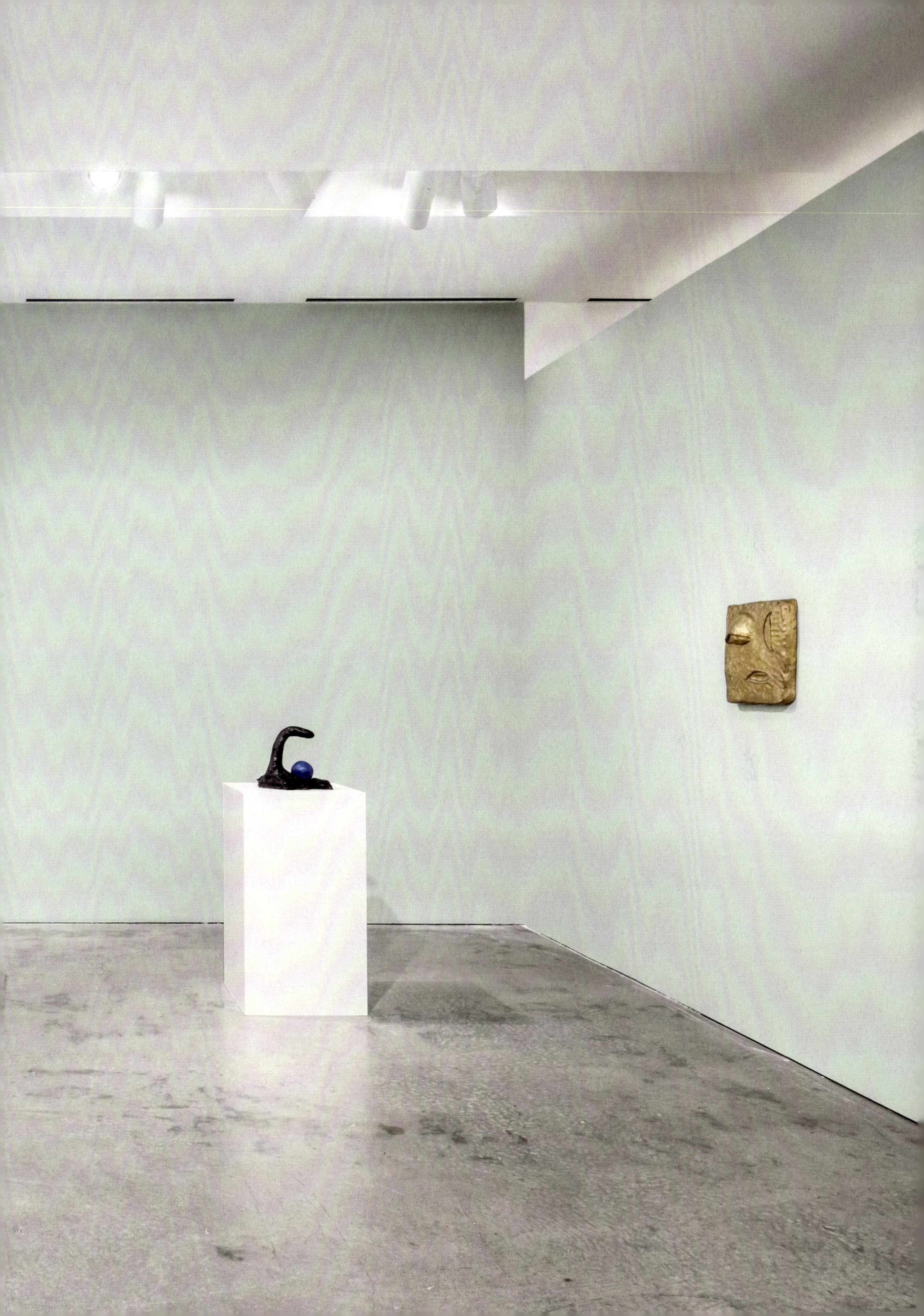

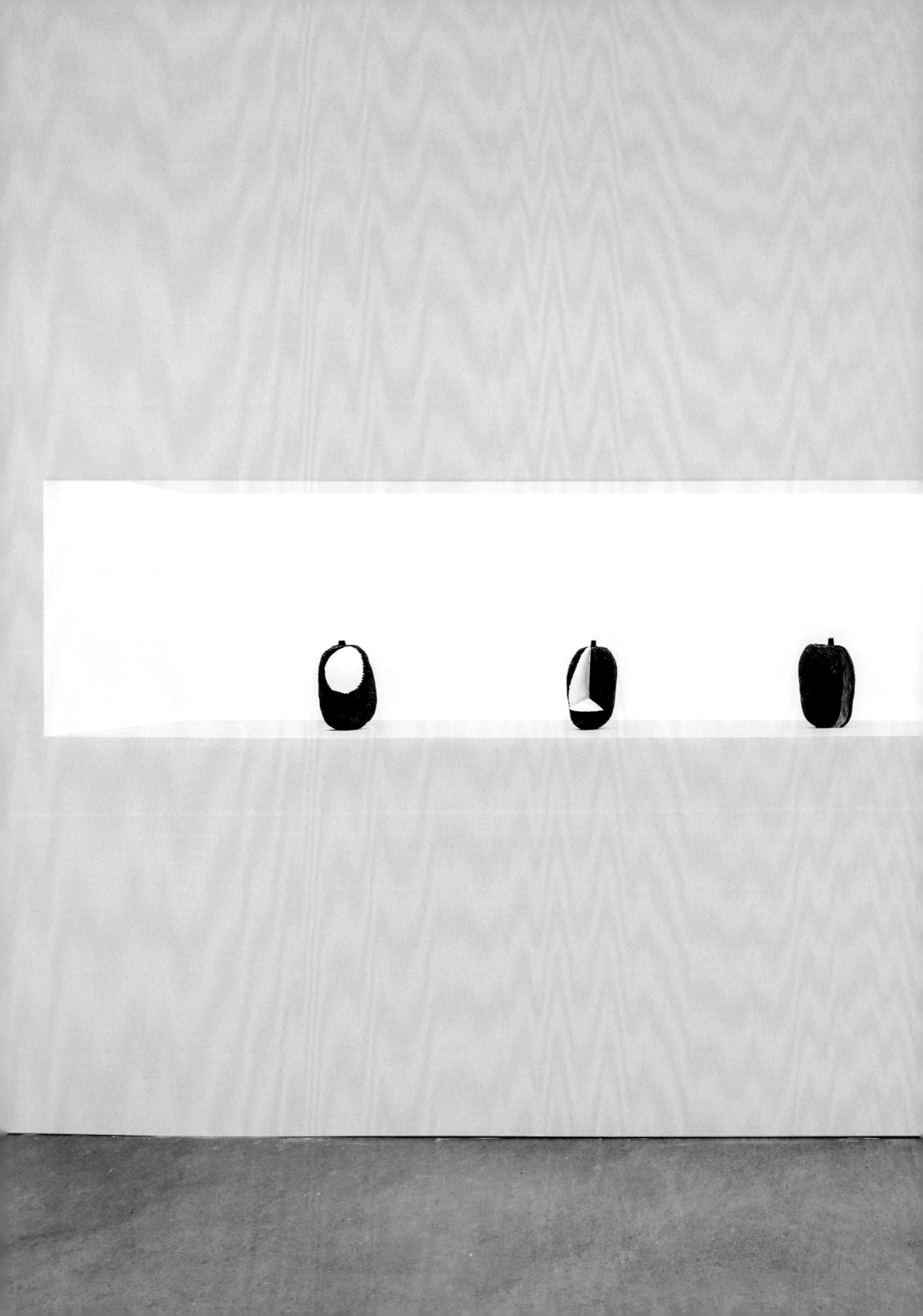

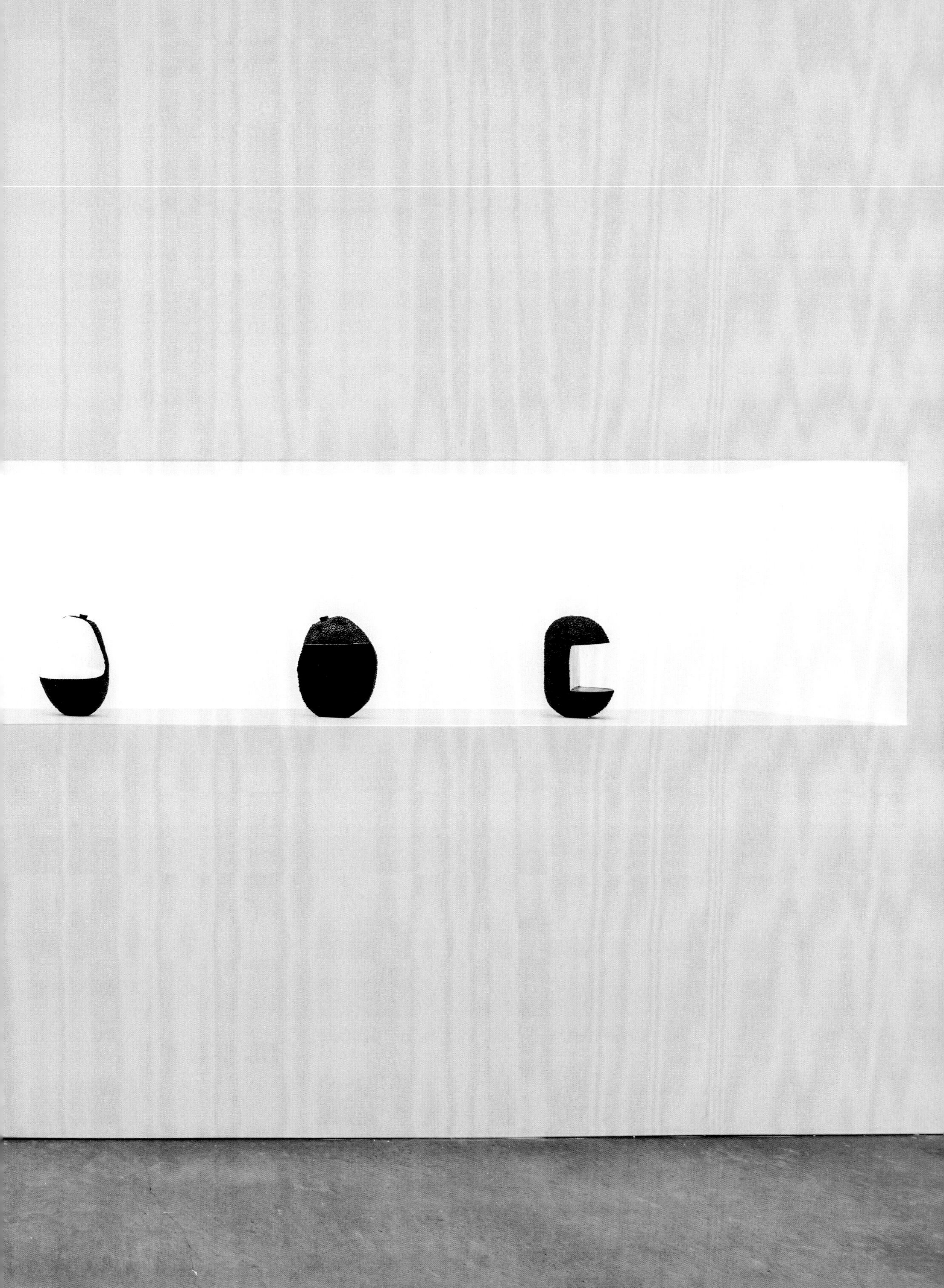

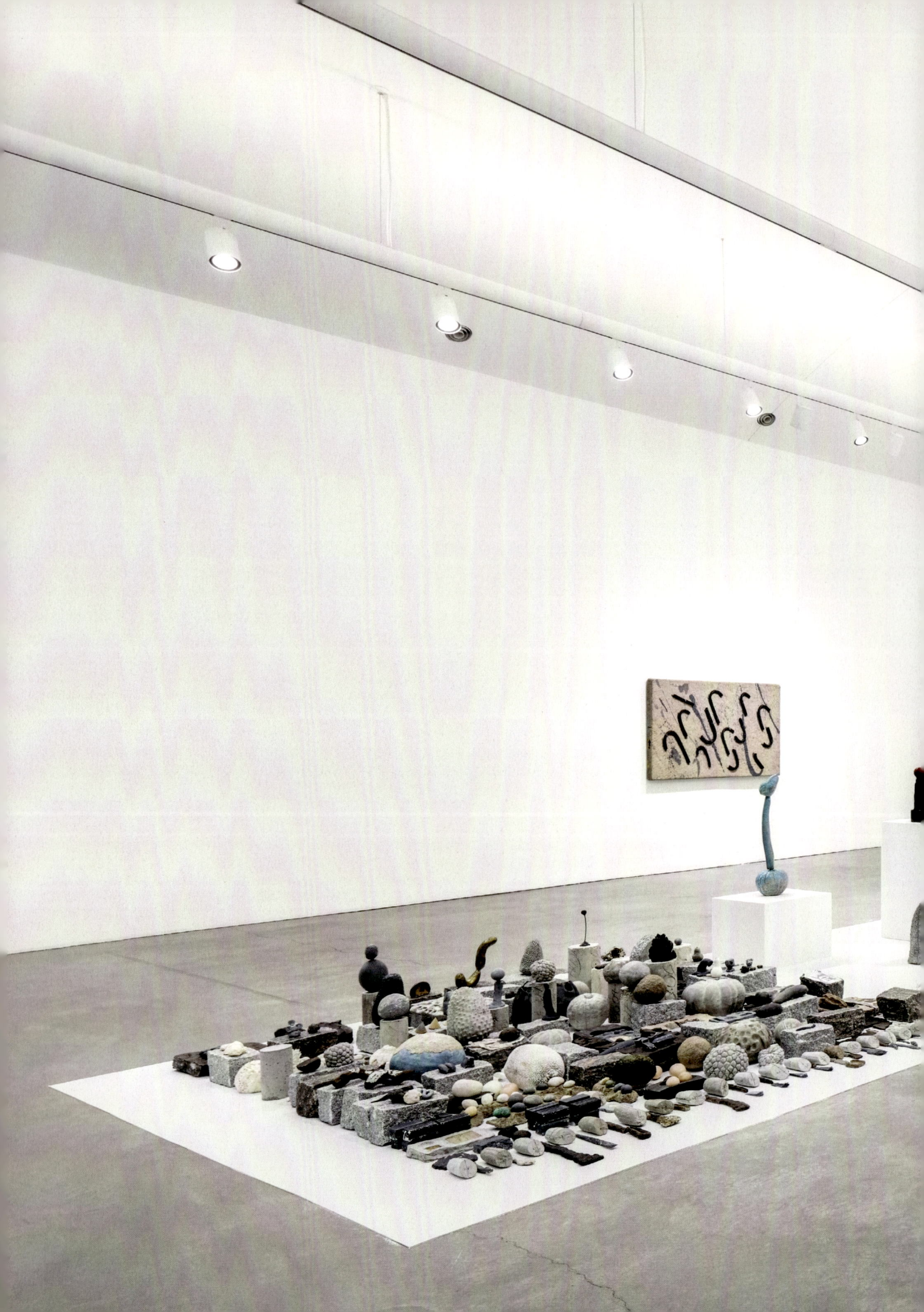

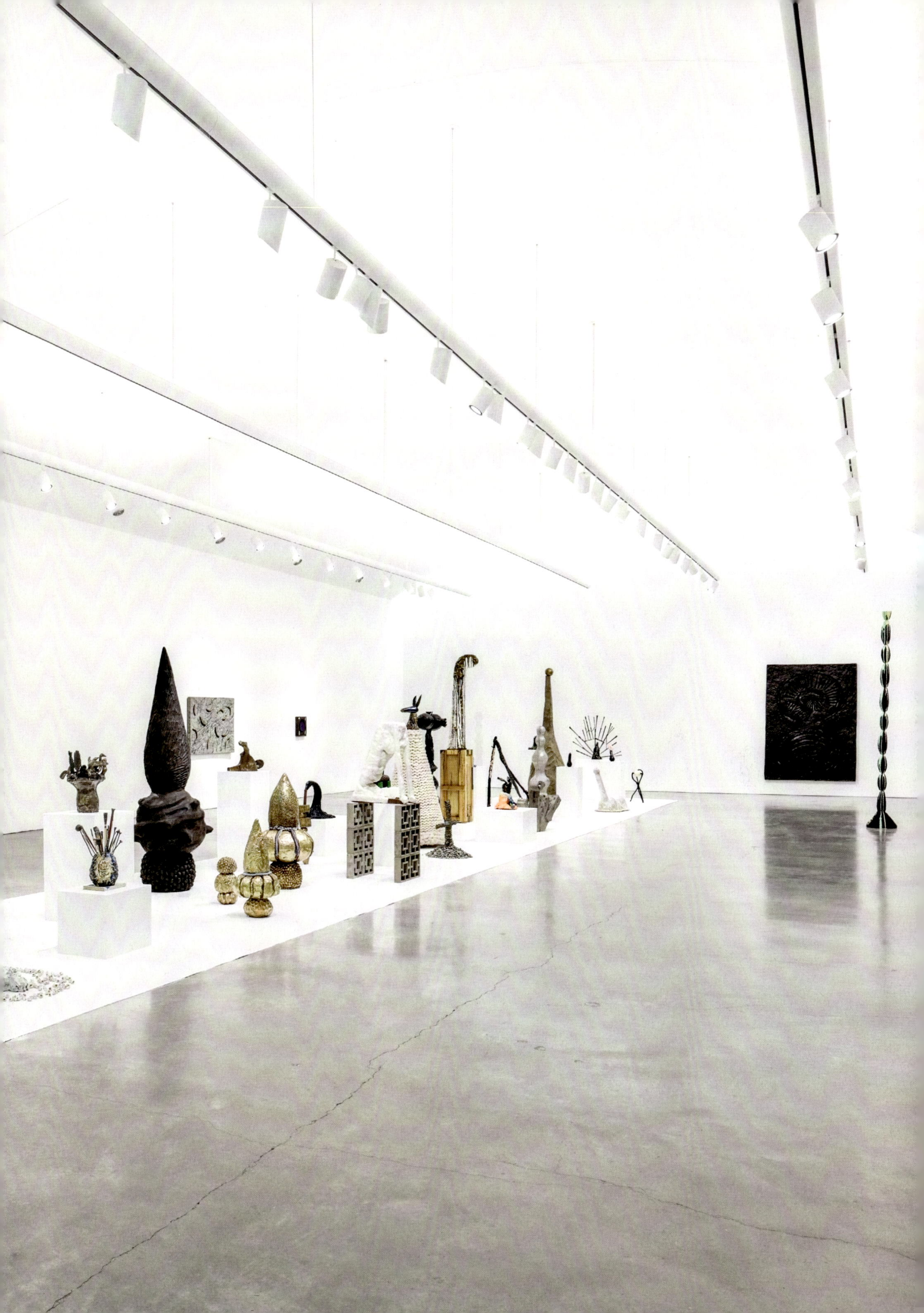

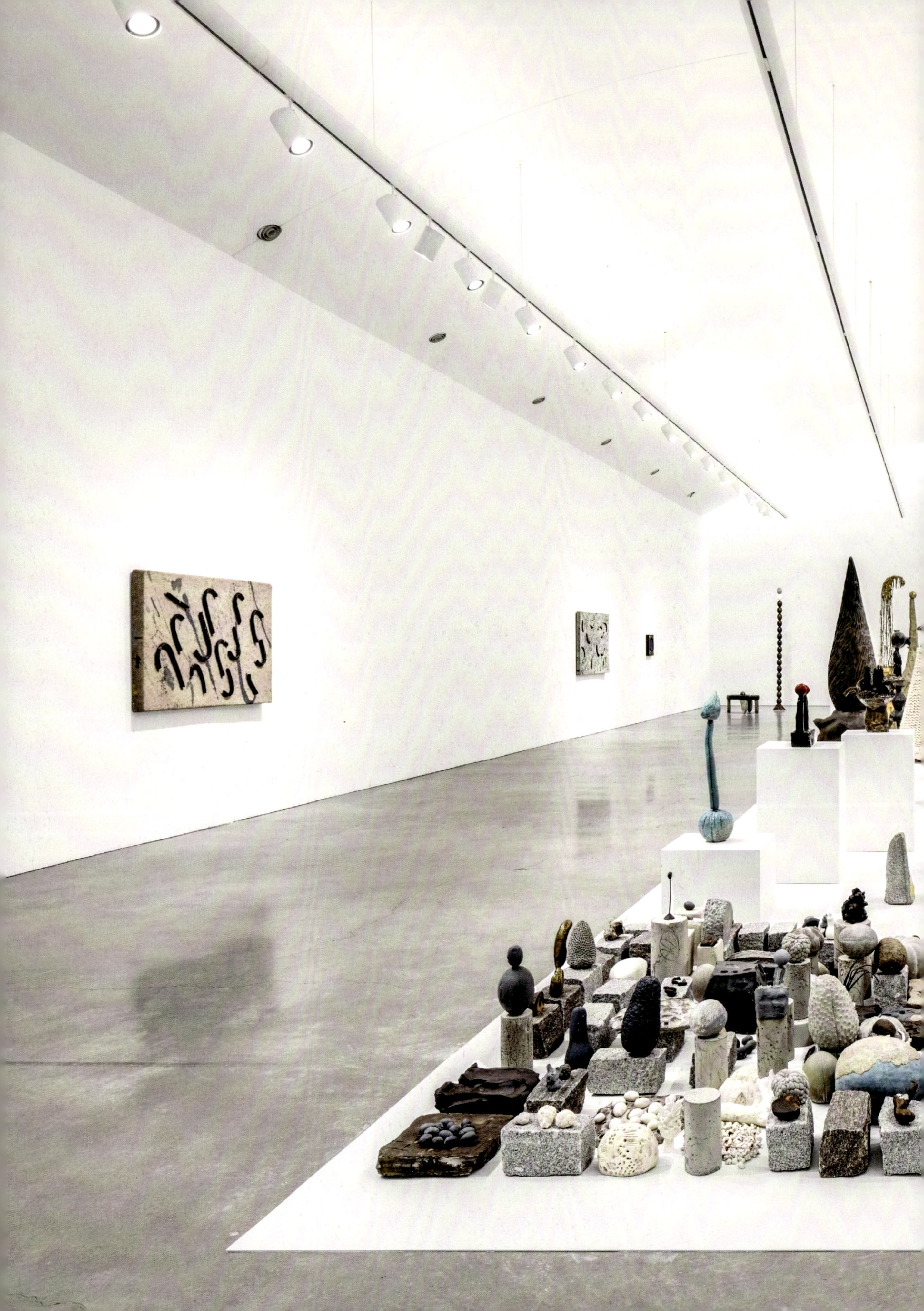

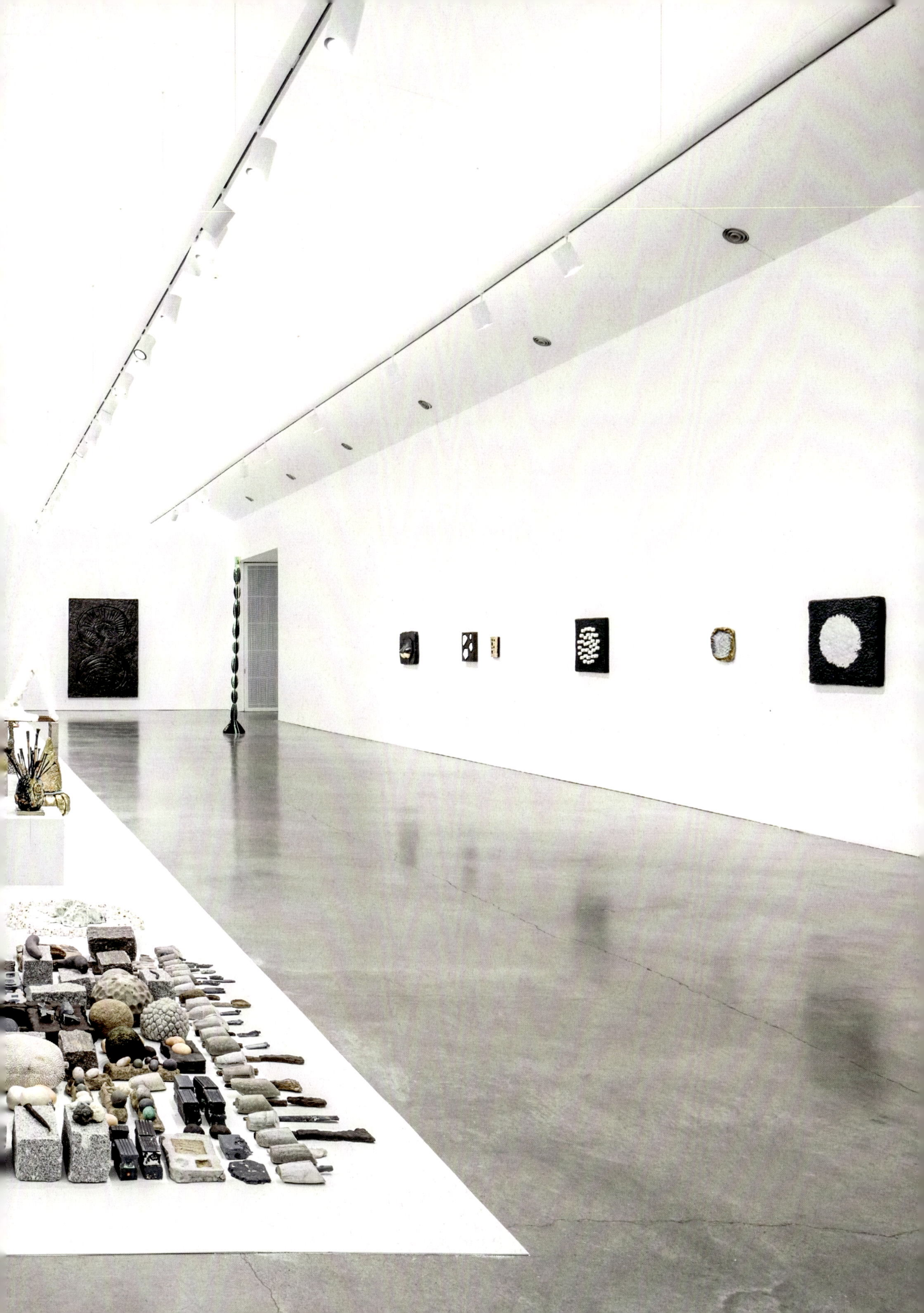

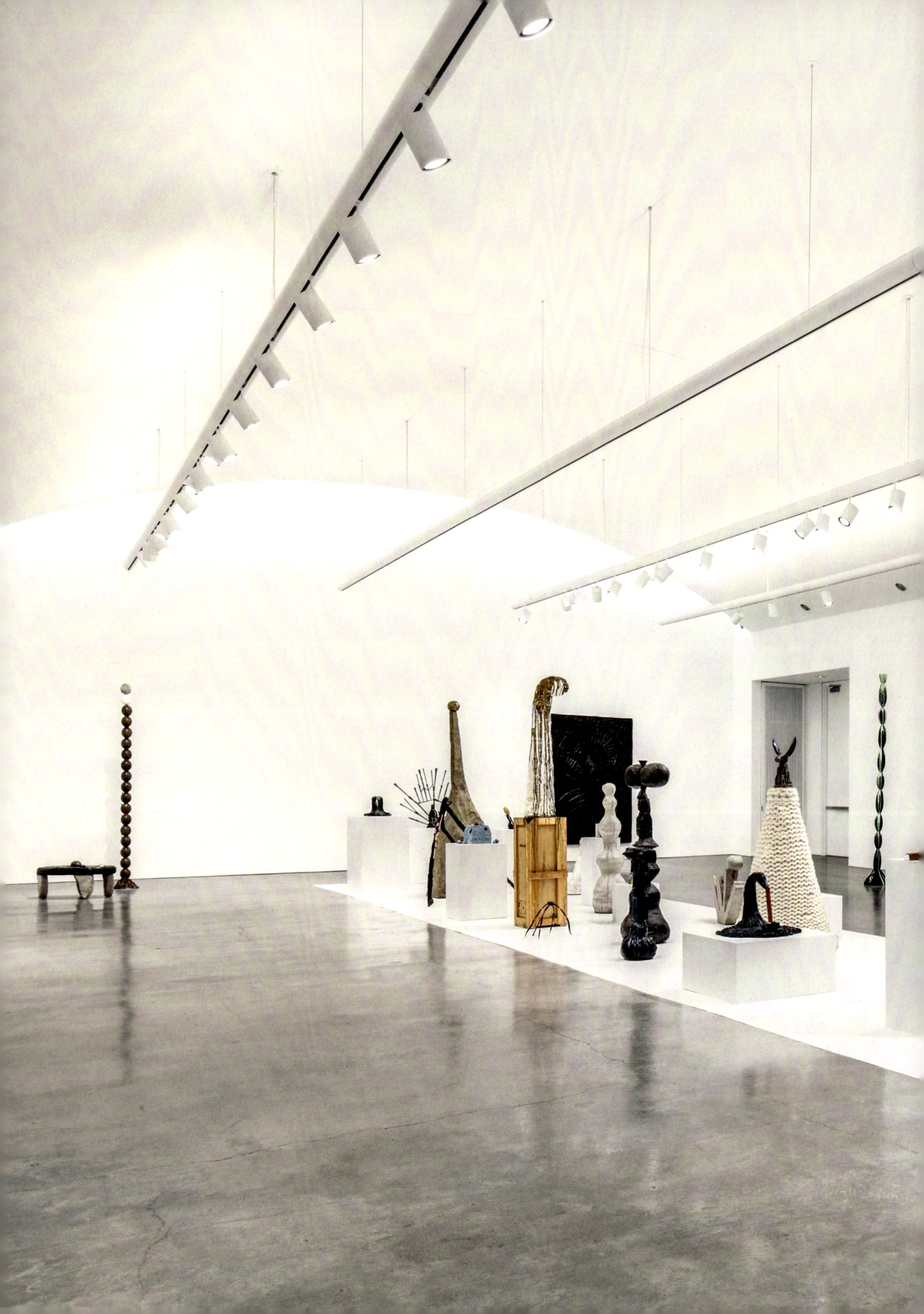

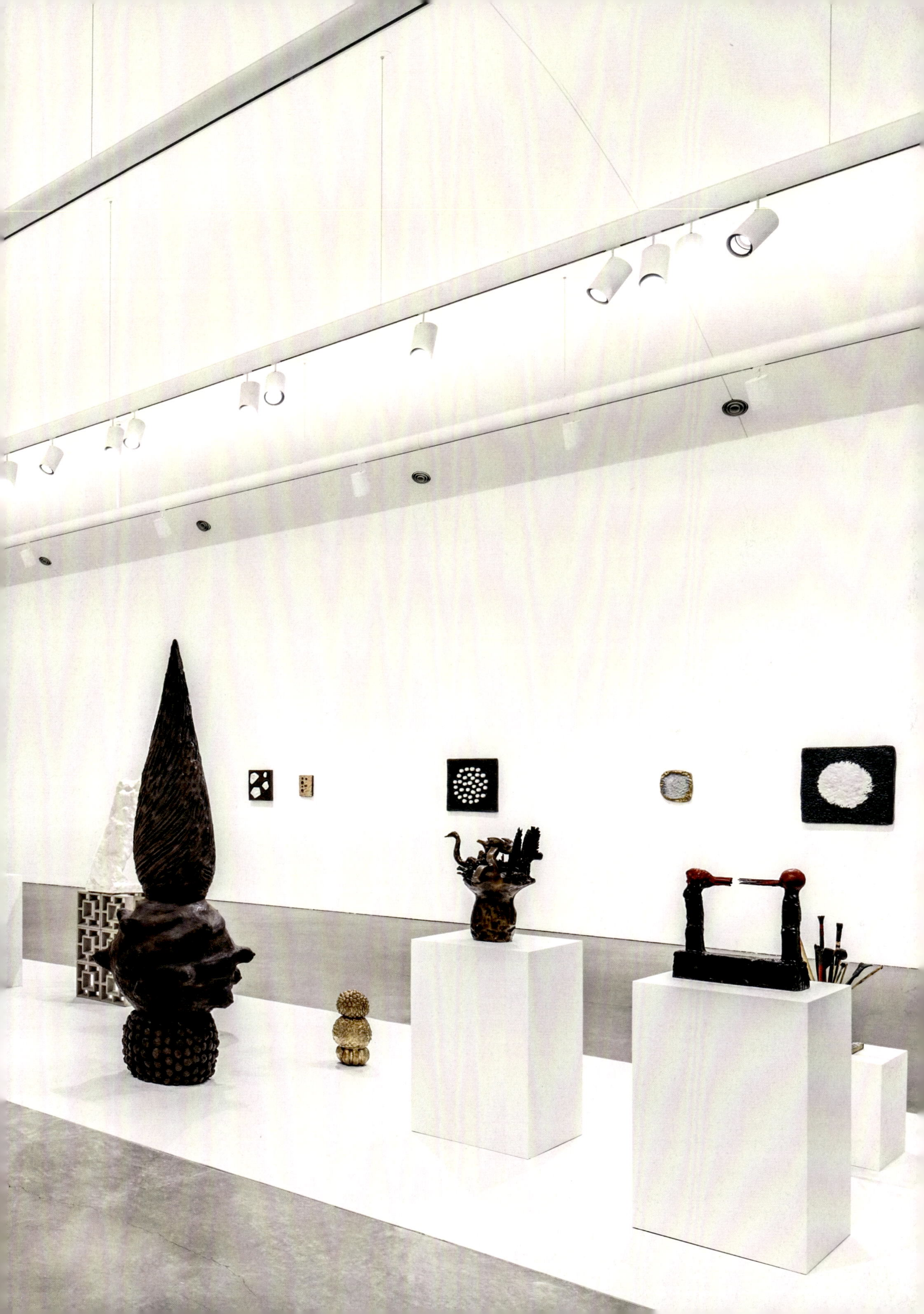

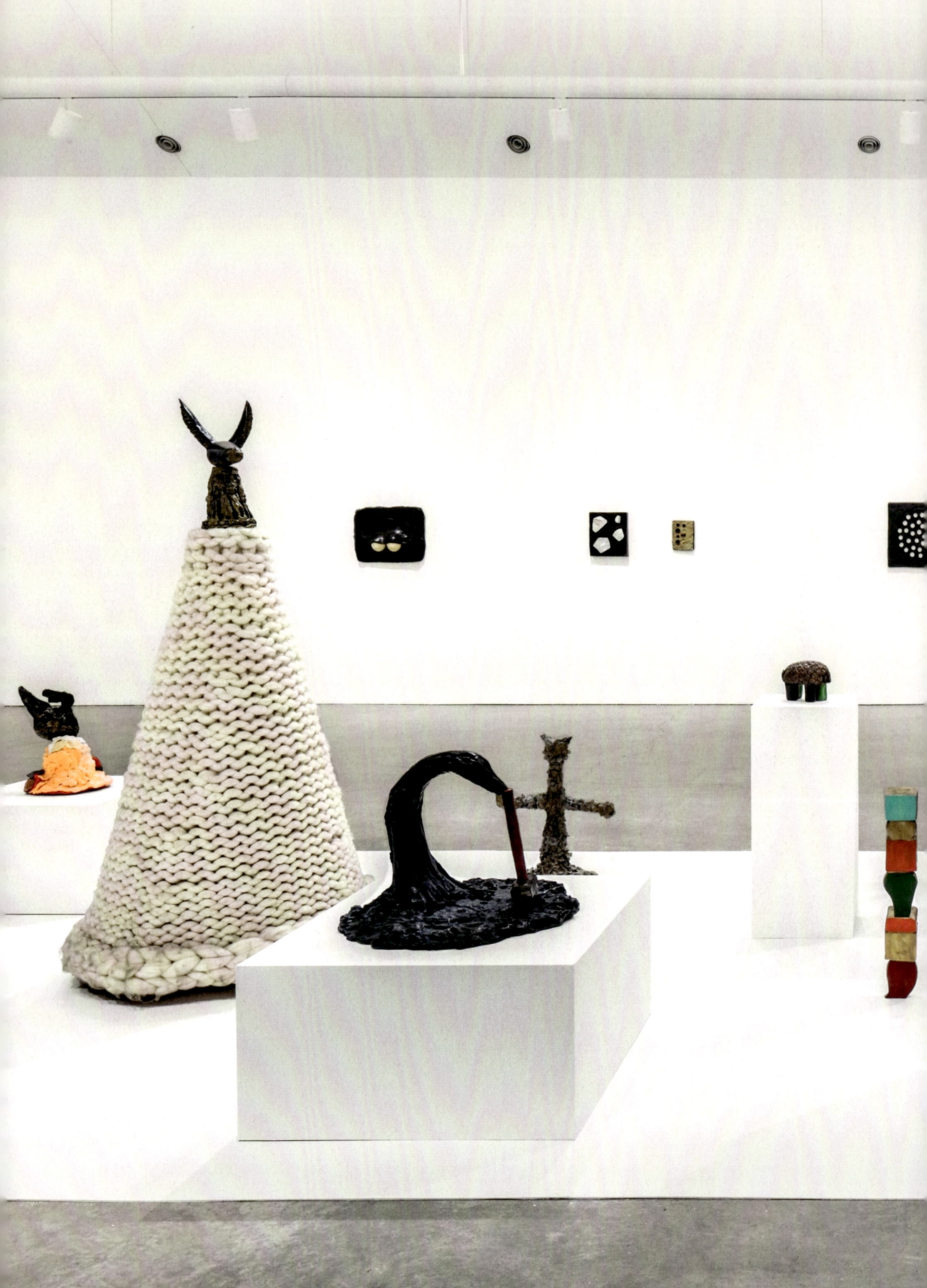

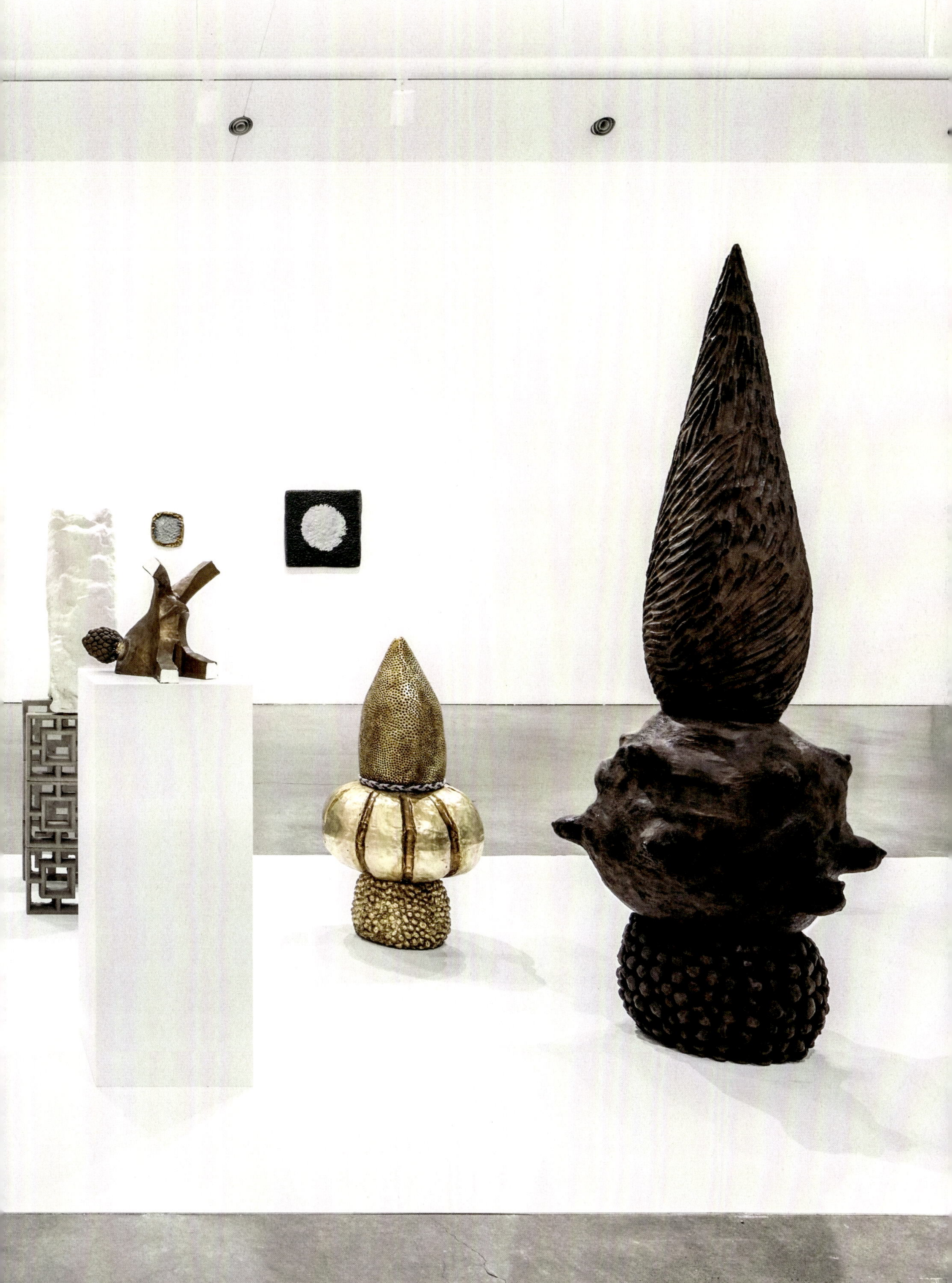

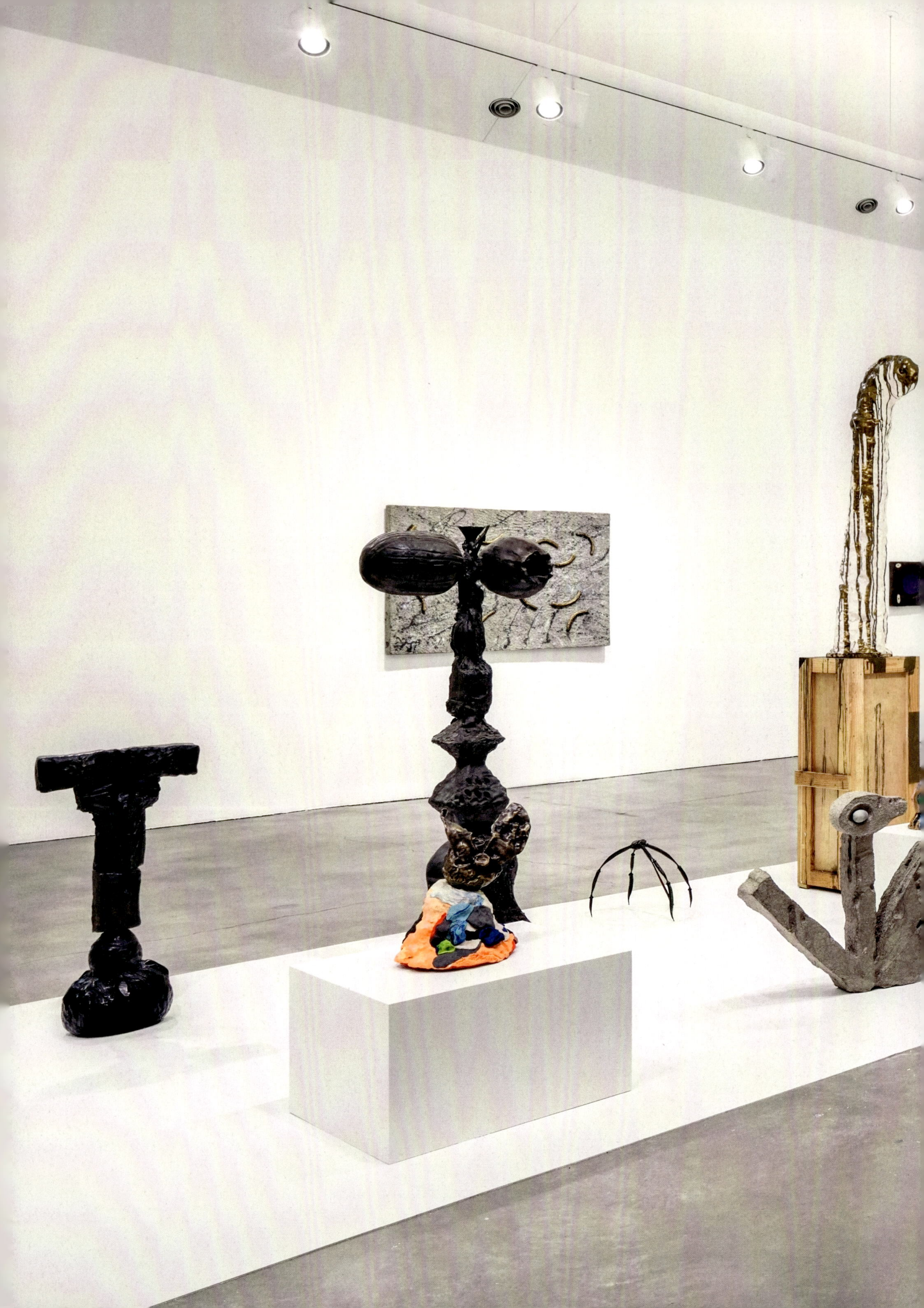

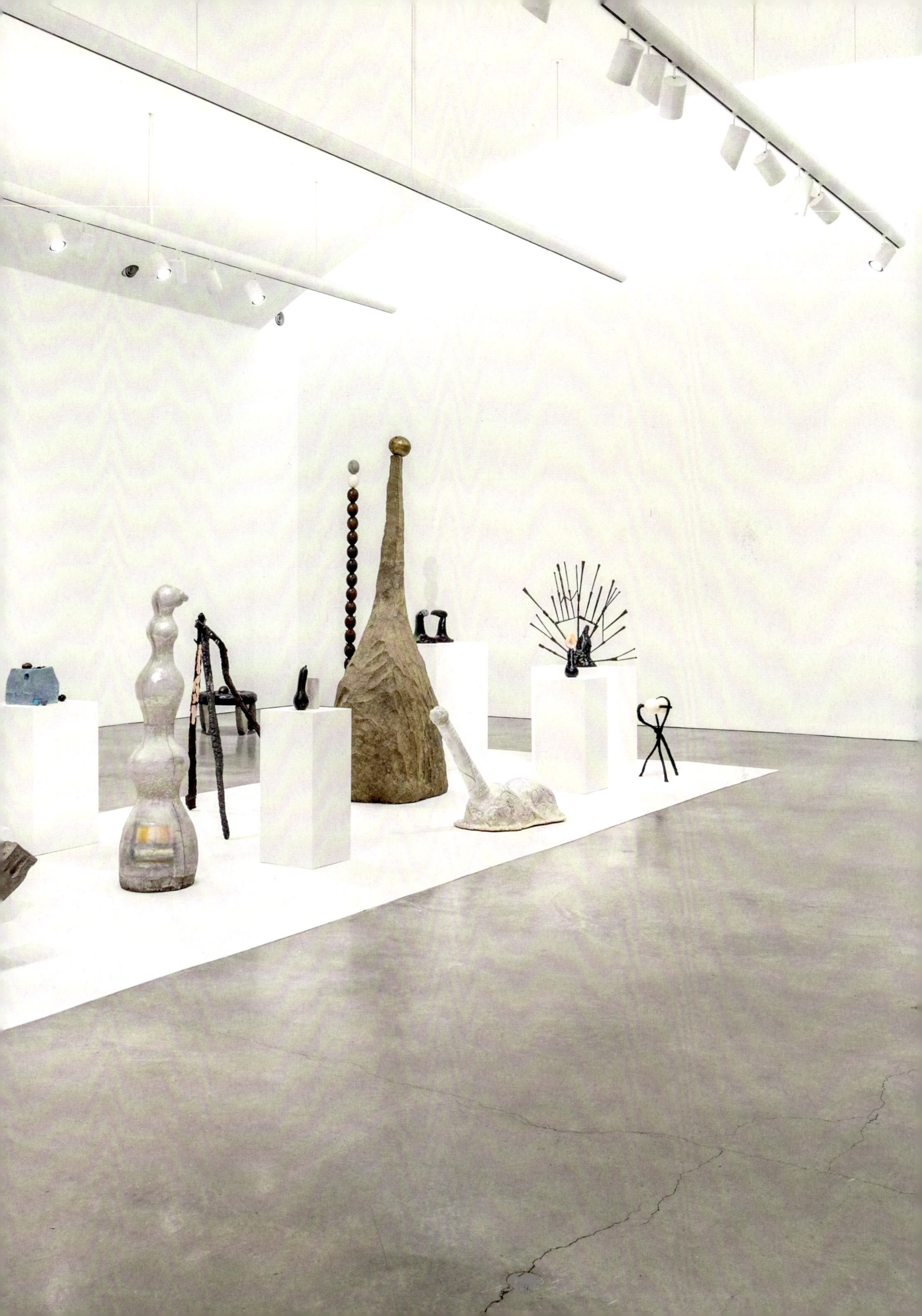

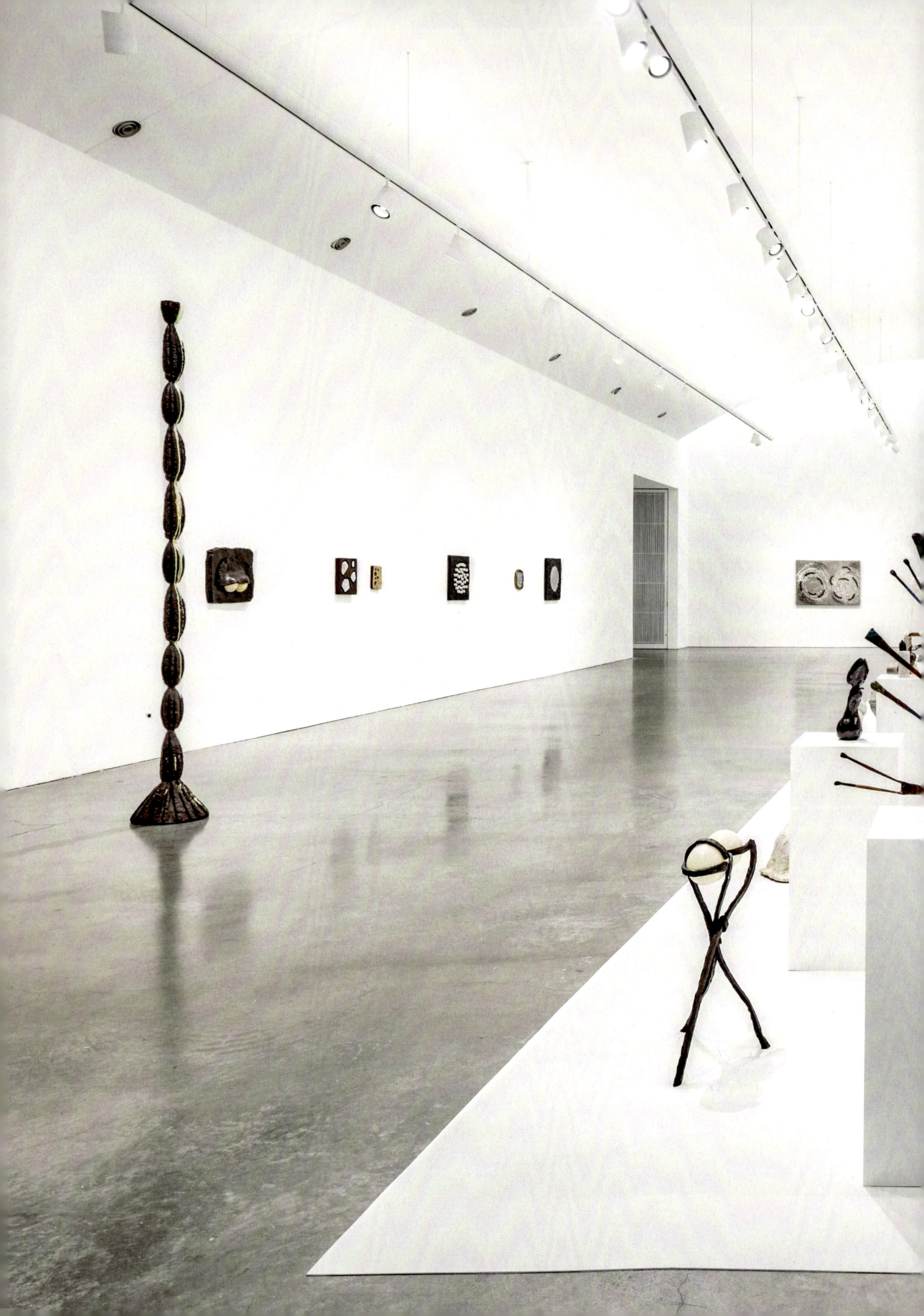

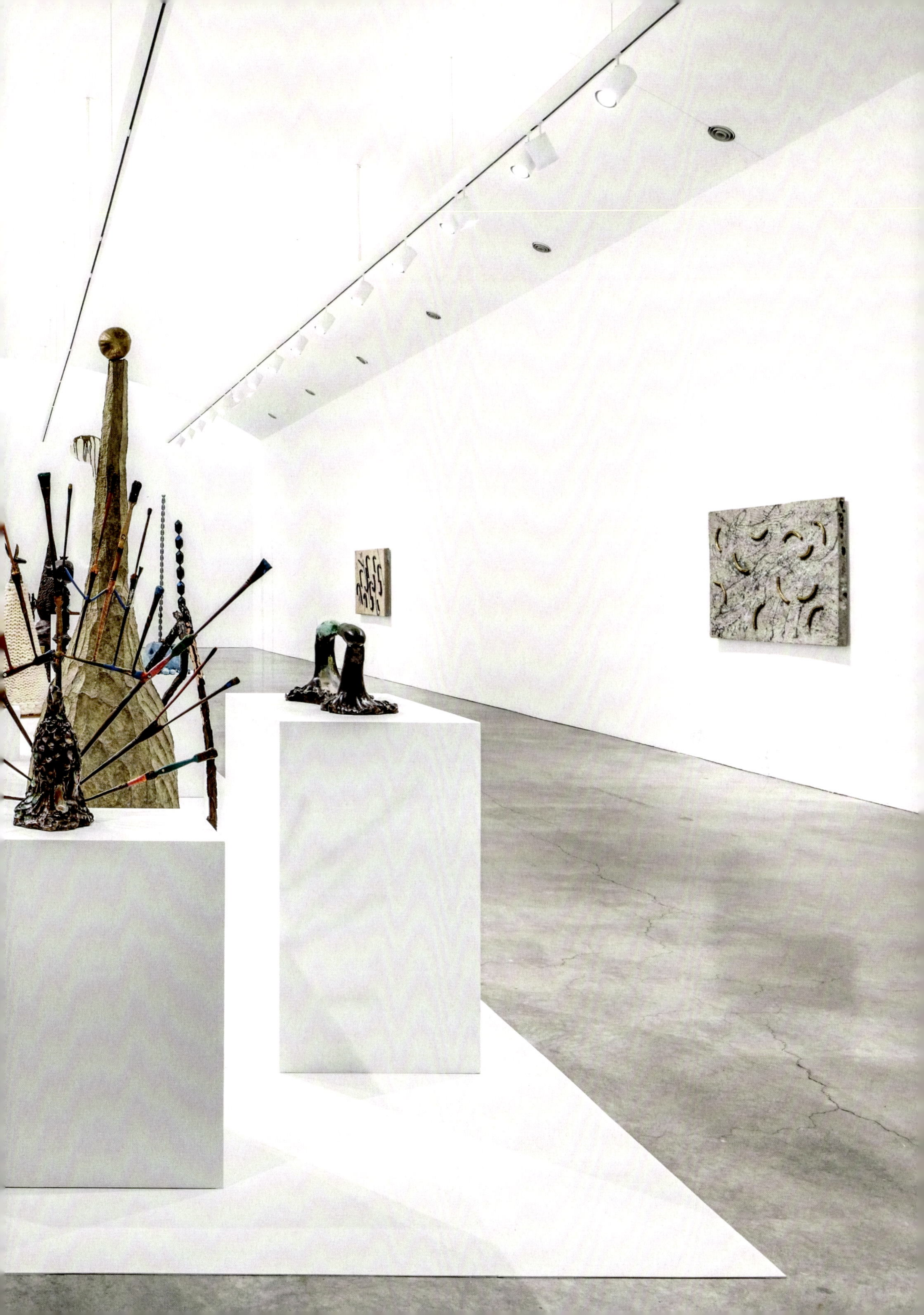

EXHIBITION CHECKLIST

p. 20
Miami, 2005
Clay, acrylic, and copper enamel
8 ¼ × 5 ⅞ × 5 ⅞ inches (21 × 15 × 15 cm)
Private Collection

p. 17
Saramandaia, 2006
Polychromatic bronze
18 ⅞ × 14 ³⁄₁₆ × 17 ¹¹⁄₁₆ inches (48 × 36 ×
45 cm)
Edition 3/3 + 1 AP
Andrea and José Olympio Pereira Collection

p. 16
Jaspera na Escola (*Jaspera at School*),
2006–8
Bronze, acrylic, and paper
21 ⅝ × 9 ¹³⁄₁₆ × 9 ¹³⁄₁₆ inches (55 × 25 × 25 cm)
1 of 1 AP, edition of 3
Adriana Varejão Collection

p. 21
Rabisco, 2007
Bronze and cold porcelain clay
18 ⅛ × 14 ³⁄₁₆ × 10 ¼ inches (46 × 36 × 26 cm)
Ricard Akagawa Collection

p. 27
Turtle Modern, 2007
Bronze and plasticine
6 ⅛ × 5 ⅛ × 7 ⅞ inches (15.5 × 13 × 20 cm)
Edition 4/5
Private Collection

p. 33
Avestruz (*Ostrich*), 2008
Bronze and acrylic
51 ³⁄₁₆ × 39 ⅜ × 46 ⁷⁄₁₆ inches (130 × 100 ×
118 cm)
Second of a series of 3 + 1 AP
Paola Ricci and Henrique Miziara Collection

pp. 28 (detail), 29
Egito, 2008
Bronze, wood, and wool
72 ¹⁄₁₆ × 39 ⅜ × 39 ⅜ inches (183 × 100 ×
100 cm)
First of a series of 3
Andrea and José Olympio Pereira Collection

p. 32
Gato, 2008
Bronze and gravel
25 ³⁄₁₆ × 21 ⅝ × 21 ⅝ inches (64 × 55 × 55 cm)
Third of a series of 3 + 1 AP
Cecilia Tanure Collection, Los Angeles

p. 30
Neo Rex, 2008
Concrete, cold porcelain clay, wood, and
acrylic
59 ¹⁄₁₆ × 25 ³⁄₁₆ × 18 ⅞ inches (150 × 64 ×
48 cm)
Private Collection

p. 23
Nessie, 2008
Cold porcelain clay, wood, and acrylic
101 ³⁄₁₆ × 15 ¾ × 19 ¹¹⁄₁₆ inches (257 × 40 ×
50 cm)
Courtesy of the artist

pp. 26–27
Pavão (*Peacock*), 2008
Bronze and acrylic
35 ⁷⁄₁₆ × 39 ⅜ × 9 ⁷⁄₁₆ inches (90 × 100 × 24 cm)
Third of a series of 3 + 1 AP
Rodman Primack and Rudy Weissenberg
Collection

p. 31
Chicken, 2008/2017
Bronze, cold porcelain clay, and acrylic
Dimensions variable
Courtesy of the artist

p. 38
Brasília Quitanda, 2010
Bronze and acrylic
11 ¹³⁄₁₆ × 7 ¹⁄₁₆ × 7 ¹⁄₁₆ inches (30 × 18 × 18 cm)
Edition 2/3 + 1 AP
Hollander-Yehudi Collection

p. 37
Henry Branco, 2010
Bronze and acrylic
12 ⅝ × 14 ⁹⁄₁₆ × 15 ¾ inches (32 × 37 × 40 cm)
Second of a series of 3 + 1 AP
Private Collection, São Paulo

p. 41
Beijo (*Kiss*), 2011
Bronze and acrylic
14 ¹⁵⁄₁₆ × 14 ³⁄₁₆ × 4 ¾ inches (38 × 36 × 12 cm)
Edition 3/3 + 1 AP
Private Collection

p. 39
Brasília Acústica (*Acoustic Brasília*), 2011
Bronze and acrylic
11 ¹³⁄₁₆ × 9 ⁷⁄₁₆ × 6 ⁵⁄₁₆ inches (30 × 24 × 16 cm)
Edition 1/3 + 1 AP
Private Collection

p. 38
Brasília Jóia (*Jewel Brasília*), 2011
Bronze and acrylic
11 ¹³⁄₁₆ × 7 ¹⁄₁₆ × 6 ⁵⁄₁₆ inches (30 × 18 × 16 cm)
1/1 AP, edition of 3
Private Collection

p. 40
Brasília Parede (*Brasília Wall*), 2011
Bronze and acrylic
12 ⅝ × 8 ¼ × 6 ¹¹⁄₁₆ inches (32 × 21 × 17 cm)
Edition 1/3 +1 AP
Private Collection

p. 39
Brasília Skate, 2011
Bronze and acrylic
12 ⅝ × 8 ¼ × 6 ¹¹⁄₁₆ inches (32 × 21 × 17 cm)
Edition 1/3 + 1 AP
Private Collection

p. 40
Brasília TV, 2011
Bronze and acrylic
12 ⅝ × 8 ¼ × 6 ¹¹⁄₁₆ inches (32 × 21 × 17 cm)
1/1 AP, edition of 3
Sergio Renault and Junio Oliveira Collection

p. 45
Desenho (*Drawing*), 2011
Bronze and acrylic
12 ⅝ × 17 ⁵⁄₁₆ × 12 ³⁄₁₆ inches (32 × 44 ×
31 cm)
Edition 3/3 + 1 AP
Private Collection

pp. 48 (detail), 49
Missionary, 2011
Bronze and acrylic
12 ³⁄₁₆ × 3 ¹⁵⁄₁₆ × 6 ⁵⁄₁₆ inches (31 × 10 × 16 cm)
Edition 3/3 + 1 AP
Private Collection, San Francisco

p. 87
Porn Star, 2011
Bronze and acrylic
129 ¹⁵⁄₁₆ × 3 ⁹⁄₁₆ × 3 ⁹⁄₁₆ inches (330 × 9 × 9 cm)
Edition 3/3 + 1 AP
Private Collection

p. 46
Romana (Blue), 2011
Concrete
30 ⁵⁄₁₆ × 7 ¹⁄₁₆ × 7 ¹⁄₁₆ inches (77 × 18 × 18 cm)
Beth Rudin DeWoody Collection

p. 50
Scale Drawing (*Escala Desenho*), 2011
Bronze, concrete, and oil pastel
9 ¹⁄₁₆ × 7 ⅞ × 3 ¹⁵⁄₁₆ inches (23 × 20 × 10 cm)
Edition 2/3 + 1 AP
Private Collection

p. 47
Tarsila com Novo (*Tarsila with New*), 2011
Bronze, acrylic, and graphite
11 × 21 ¼ × 11 ⁷⁄₁₆ inches (28 × 54 × 29 cm)
Edition 1/3 + 1 AP
Private Collection

p. 51
Dino Pot, 2012
Concrete and wax
59 ¹⁄₁₆ × 17 ¹¹⁄₁₆ × 17 ¹¹⁄₁₆ inches (150 × 45 × 45 cm)
Third of a series of 3 + 1 AP
Private Collection

p. 53
Cisne com Martelo (*Swan with Hammer*), 2013
Bronze and sledgehammer
25 ⁹⁄₁₆ × 27 ⁹⁄₁₆ × 27 ⁹⁄₁₆ inches (65 × 70 × 70 cm)
Edition 3/3 + 1 AP
Private Collection

pp. 54, 55 (detail)
Egg Tower, 2013
Bronze, ostrich eggshell, concrete, and wax
110 ¼ × 15 ¾ × 15 ¾ inches (280 × 40 × 40 cm)
Edition 3/3 + 1 AP
Jay and Claudia Khalifeh Collection

p. 56
Boyfriend, 2014
Bronze and ostrich eggshell
19 ¹¹⁄₁₆ × 24 × 5 ½ inches (50 × 61 × 14 cm)
Edition 1/3 + 1 AP
Laura Skoler Collection

pp. 60–61
Cemitério com Franja (*Cemetery with Fringe*), 2014
Studio remains: bronze, concrete, clay, cold porcelain clay, and stone
632 pieces: 11 ¹³⁄₁₆ × 86 ⅝ × 94 ½ inches (30 × 220 × 240 cm) overall
Courtesy of the artist

p. 58
Lápis, 2014
Bronze and wax
112 ³⁄₁₆ × 7 ⅞ × 7 ¹⁄₁₆ inches (285 × 20 × 18 cm)
Edition 1/3 + 1 AP
Courtesy of Compound LB, Long Beach, California

pp. 58, 59 (detail)
Torre Lápis (*Pencil Tower*), 2014
Bronze and wax
74 ¹³⁄₁₆ × 7 ⅞ × 6 ¹¹⁄₁₆ inches (190 × 20 × 17 cm)
1/1 AP, edition of 3
Private Collection

p. 52
Turner, 2014
Concrete and acrylic
14 ³⁄₁₆ × 9 ¹³⁄₁₆ × 5 ⅛ inches (36 × 25 × 13 cm)
Martin and Rebecca Eisenberg Collection

p. 63
Black Sun, 2015
Bronze and wax
25 ⁹⁄₁₆ × 26 × 1 ¹⁵⁄₁₆ inches (65 × 66 × 5 cm)
Edition 3/3 + 1 AP
Luiz Antonio Campos Collection

pp. 74–75
The Dress, 2015
Bronze and acrylic
Two parts: 23 ⅝ × 35 ⁷⁄₁₆ × 3 ⅜ inches (60 × 90 × 8.5 cm) overall
Edition 3/3 + 1 AP
Patrícia and Ricardo Lacaz Martins Collection, São Paulo

p. 77
Mexicana, 2015
Bronze, acrylic, and wax
35 ⁷⁄₁₆ × 19 ¹¹⁄₁₆ × 11 ¹³⁄₁₆ inches (90 × 50 × 30 cm)
Edition 2/3 + 1 AP
Paulus Magnus Collection, São Paulo

p. 98
The Painter's Wife, 2015
Bronze and wax
16 ⅛ × 16 ⅛ × 2 ¾ inches (41 × 41 × 7 cm)
Ernesto Poma Family Collection

p. 78
Star Without Makeup, 2015
Bronze and wax
15 ¾ × 15 ¾ × 3 ⁹⁄₁₆ inches (40 × 40 × 9 cm)
Edition 1/3 + 1 AP
Maria Rita and Rodolfo Barreto Collection

p. 62
Stone Washed, 2015
Concrete, bronze, and stone
9 ¾ × 9 ¼ × 9 inches (25 × 23.5 × 23 cm)
Beth Rudin DeWoody Collection

p. 76
Surrealista, 2015
Bronze, acrylic, and wax
66 ⅛ × 25 ³⁄₁₆ × 17 ¹¹⁄₁₆ inches (168 × 64 × 45 cm)
Edition 2/3 + 1 AP
Luiz Antonio Campos Collection

p. 67
Tarsila com Koons, 2015
Bronze and acrylic
10 ⅝ × 10 ⅝ × 12 ³⁄₁₆ inches (27 × 27 × 31 cm)
Edition 1/3 + 1 AP
Courtesy of the artist

p. 66
Turtle, 2015
Bronze, concrete, raku ceramics, wax, and acrylic
18 ⅞ × 39 ⅜ × 26 ⅜ inches (48 × 100 × 67 cm)
Edition 3/3 + 1 AP
Tracy O'Brien and Thaddeus Staber Collection

p. 82
Van Gogh with Eggs, 2015
Bronze and acrylic
22 ¹⁄₁₆ × 18 ⅛ × 3 ⁹⁄₁₆ inches (56 × 46 × 9 cm)
Beth Rudin DeWoody Collection

p. 88
Camelo, 2016
Papier-mâché, polystyrene, bronze, and acrylic
101 ³⁄₁₆ × 29 ½ × 33 ⁷⁄₁₆ inches (257 × 75 × 85 cm)
Marcelino Rafart de Seras Collection

p. 83
Gober, 2016
Bronze, wax, beeswax, cold porcelain clay, and acrylic
23 ⅝ × 14 ¹⁵⁄₁₆ × 2 ¾ inches (60 × 38 × 7 cm)
Hollander-Yehudi Collection

p. 79
God Flower Brain Flower, 2016
Bronze
98 ⁷⁄₁₆ × 70 ⅞ × 2 ¾ inches (250 × 180 × 7 cm)
Edition 3/3 + 1 AP
Private Collection, São Paulo

p. 89
Camel, 2017
Ceramic
36 ¼ × 47 ¼ × 20 ⅞ inches (92 × 120 × 53 cm)
Edition 2/3 + 1 AP
Courtesy of the artist

pp. 92 (detail), 93
Dias da Semana (*Days of the Week*), 2017
Bronze and oil
24 ⁷⁄₁₆ × 3 ¹⁵⁄₁₆ × 3 ¹⁵⁄₁₆ inches (62 × 10 × 10 cm)
Edition 2/3 + 1 AP
Ana Luiza and Gregory Reider Collection

pp. 90–91
Flat Grandpa, 2017
Papier-mâché, polystyrene, concrete, and oil
27 ¾ × 38 ³⁄₁₆ × 7 ¹¹⁄₁₆ inches (70.5 × 97 ×
19.5 cm)
Courtesy of the artist

p. 91
Sex, 2017
Bronze and ostrich eggshell
25 ⁹⁄₁₆ × 13 ¾ × 13 ¾ inches (65 × 35 × 35 cm)
Edition 3/3 + 1 AP
Luís Paulo Montenegro Collection

pp. 99
Marshmallow Amazonino, 2019
Bronze, electrostatic painting, and oil
22 ⁷⁄₁₆ × 22 ⁷⁄₁₆ × 3 ⅛ inches (57 × 57 × 8 cm)
Edition 3/3 + 1 AP
Private Collection

p. 97
Skin Moon, 2019
Oil and acrylic on bronze
10 ¼ × 7 ½ × 1 ⁹⁄₁₆ inches (26 × 19 × 4 cm)
Camille Henrot Collection

p. 104
Espelho, 2020
Bronze and oil
11 ¹³⁄₁₆ × 11 ⁷⁄₁₆ × 1 ³⁄₁₆ inches (30 × 29 × 3 cm)
Edition 2/3 + 1 AP
Private Collection, São Paulo

pp. 100, 101
A Guerra do Brasil, 2020
Acrylic and oil on aluminum
24 ¹³⁄₁₆ × 40 ⁹⁄₁₆ × 2 ⅜ inches (63 × 103 × 6 cm)
Inhotim Institute Collection, Minas
Gerais, Brazil

p. 105
Homeopatia Mondrian, 2020
Acrylic on aluminum
38 ⁹⁄₁₆ × 31 ⅞ × 3 ⅛ inches (98 × 81 × 8 cm)
Third of a series of 3 + 2 AP
Andrea and José Olympio Pereira Collection

p. 96
Lady Sneezing with Fur and Coins (Praying?),
2020
Oil and wax on cast aluminum
22 ⁷⁄₁₆ × 18 ⅞ × 2 ³⁄₁₆ inches (57 × 48 × 5.5 cm)
Kaitlyn and Mike Krieger Collection,
San Francisco

p. 108
Venus of Cream, 2020
Bronze
82 ¹¹⁄₁₆ × 31 ⅛ × 31 ⅛ inches (210 × 79 ×
79 cm)
Edition 3/3 + 2 AP
Courtesy of the artist

p. 119
Torre de Cacau, 2021
Bronze and oil
134 ¼ × 14 ¹⁵⁄₁₆ × 14 ¹⁵⁄₁₆ inches (341 × 38 ×
38 cm)
1/2 AP, edition of 3
Courtesy of the artist

pp. 112 (detail), 113
Churros com Vento (*Churros with Wind*),
2022
Papier-mâché, polystyrene, bronze, and oil
39 ⅜ × 59 ¹⁄₁₆ × 3 ⅛ inches (100 × 150 × 8 cm)
Courtesy of the artist

p. 116
Churros Turbulence, 2022
Papier-mâché, polystyrene, bronze, and oil
39 ⅜ × 59 ¼ × 4 ½ inches (100 × 150.5 × 11.4
cm)
Courtesy of the artist

p. 123
Praia Noturna com Jangadas (*Nocturne
Beach with Rafts*), 2022
Oil on bronze
16 ⁹⁄₁₆ × 13 ¾ × 1 ⁹⁄₁₆ inches (42 × 35 × 4 cm)
Edition 2/3 + 2 AP
Marieluise Hessel Collection, Hessel Museum
of Art, Center for Curatorial Studies, Bard
College, Annandale-on-Hudson, New York

p. 122
Tantra Roxo (*Purple Tantra*), 2022
Bronze and oil
16 ¹⁵⁄₁₆ × 16 ¹⁵⁄₁₆ × 2 ⅜ inches (43 × 43 × 6 cm)
Edition 1/3 + 2 AP
Courtesy of the artist

p. 117
Umbrellas and Chaos, 2022
Papier-mâché, polystyrene, ceramics, and oil
39 ⅜ × 59 ¹⁄₁₆ × 3 ⅛ inches (100 × 150 × 8 cm)
Courtesy of the artist

p. 124
Vênus Abelha (*Bee Venus*), 2022
Bronze, acrylic, and macrame
43 ⁵⁄₁₆ × 23 ⅝ × 23 ⅝ inches (110 × 60 ×
60 cm)
Edition 3/3 + 2 AP
Courtesy of the artist

p. 125
Venus Doll, 2022
Bronze
15 ¾ × 7 ⅞ × 7 ⅞ inches (40 × 20 × 20 cm)
Edition 1/3 + 2 AP
Courtesy of the artist

p. 127
Venus Gokula, 2022
Bronze, acrylic, and macrame
29 ¹⁵⁄₁₆ × 15 ⅜ × 15 ⅜ inches (76 × 39 × 39 cm)
Edition 1/3 + 2 AP
Courtesy of the artist

p. 109
White Out 1, 2022
Bronze and oil
15 ¾ × 13 ¾ × 2 ⅜ inches (40 × 35 × 6 cm)
Courtesy of the artist

pp. 128–29
Crisis of Sculpture, 2023
Polystyrene, papier-mâché, brass, and oil
56 ¹¹⁄₁₆ × 84 ¼ × 7 ¹⁄₁₆ inches (144 × 214 ×
18 cm)
Courtesy of the artist

CONTRIBUTORS

Lauren Cornell is the director of the graduate program and chief curator at the Center for Curatorial Studies, Bard College (CCS Bard), Annandale-on-Hudson, New York. At CCS Bard, she has organized monographic surveys including *Dara Birnbaum: Reaction* (2022); *Martine Syms: Grio College* (2022); *Sky Hopinka: Centers of Somewhere* (2020–21); *Leidy Churchman: Crocodile* (2019); *Nil Yalter: Exile Is a Hard Job* (coorganized with the Museum Ludwig, 2019); and *Daniel Steegmann Mangrané: A Transparent Leaf Instead of a Mouth* (2018); as well as the group exhibitions *Phantom Plane: Cyberpunk in the Year of the Future,* with Tobias Berger, Dawn Chan, Xue Tan, and Jeppe Ugelvig, at Tai Kwun Contemporary in Hong Kong (2020–21); and *Invisible Adversaries*, with Tom Eccles (2016). Previously, Cornell was curator and associate director of technology initiatives at the New Museum, New York. As a curator at the New Museum, she cocurated the 2015 and 2009 triennials; organized multiple exhibitions, performances, and screenings; and cofounded the Seven on Seven conference. From 2005 to 2012, Cornell served as executive director of Rhizome, an organization affiliated with the New Museum supporting born-digital art. She is coeditor, with Ed Halter, of *Mass Effect: Art and the Internet in the Twenty-First Century* (MIT Press, 2015). Cornell is the recipient of ArtTable's 2017 New Leadership Award.

Ruba Katrib is curator and director of curatorial affairs at MoMA PS1, New York. At PS1, she has curated exhibitions such as *Jumana Manna: Break, Take, Erase, Tally* (2022), *Greater New York* (2021), *Niki de Saint Phalle: Structures for Life* (2021), Simone Fattal's retrospective in 2019, and solo shows by Edgar Heap of Birds (2019), Karrabing Collective (2019), Fernando Palma Rodríguez, and Julia Phillips (2018). From 2012 to 2018, she was the curator at SculptureCenter in New York, where she organized over twenty exhibitions, including *74 million million million tons* (2018, co-organized with artist Lawrence Abu Hamdan) and solo shows of the work of Kelly Akashi, Sam Anderson, Teresa Burga, David Douard, Anthea Hamilton, Nicola L., Rochelle Goldberg, Charlotte Prodger, Araya Rasdjarmrearnsook, Magali Reus, Carissa Rodriguez, Aki Sasamoto, Gabriel Sierra, Erika Verzutti, and Cosima von Bonin. In 2018, Katrib cocurated SITE Santa Fe's biennial, *Casa Tomada*, with José Luis Blondet and Candice Hopkins. She regularly writes for periodicals and museum catalogues.

Bernardo Mosqueira is a curator, writer, and researcher based in New York. He is chief curator at the Institute for Studies on Latin American Art (ISLAA), founder and artistic director at Solar dos Abacaxis, Rio de Janeiro (since 2015), and director at Prêmio FOCO ArtRio, Rio de Janeiro (since 2012). Between 2021 and 2023, Mosqueira was the ISLAA Curatorial Fellow at the New Museum, New York. In 2017, he received the Premio Lorenzo Bonaldi per l'Arte, an international award for young curators, organized by GAMeC, in Bergamo, Italy. His recent exhibitions include *Wynnie Mynerva: The Original Riot* (2023), *Pepón Osorio: My Beating Heart/Mi corazón latiente* (cocurated with Margot Norton, 2023), *Vivian Caccuri and Miles Greenberg: The Shadow of Spring* (2022), and *Daniel Lie: Unnamed Entities* (2022), at the New Museum, New York; *Eros Rising: Visions of the Erotic in Latin American Art* (co-curated with Mariano López Seoane, 2022) at ISLAA, New York; *Nascente* (2022) at Solar dos Abacaxis, Rio de Janeiro; *Castiel Vitorino Brasileiro: Eclipse* (2021) at the Hessel Museum of Art, Bard College, Annandale-on-Hudson, New York; and *Miriam Inez da Silva* (2021) at Museu da República, Rio de Janeiro. In 2021, he was part of the curatorial team of the fifth New Museum Triennial, *Soft Water Hard Stone*. Mosqueira holds a masters' in curatorial studies (CCS Bard, 2021).

Erika Verzutti was born in 1971 in São Paulo, where she lives and works. She has a bachelor's degree in industrial design from the Universidade Presbiteriana Mackenzie, São Paulo (1991) and a master's degree in fine art from Goldsmiths College, University of London (2000). She has had solo exhibitions at MASP—Museu de Arte de São Paulo (2021); Nottingham Contemporary, Nottingham, England (2021); Centre Pompidou, Paris (2019); Aspen Art Museum, Colorado (2019); Pivô, São Paulo (2016); SculptureCenter, New York (2015); Tang Museum, Saratoga Springs, New York (2014); and Centro Cultural São Paulo (2012). Group exhibitions include the 57th Venice Biennale (2017); 32nd Bienal de São Paulo (2016); 34th Panorama of Brazilian Art, Museu de Arte Moderna de São Paulo (2015); 2013 Carnegie International, Pittsburgh (2013); 9th Bienal do Mercosul, Porto Alegre, Brazil (2013); and the 11th Biennale de Lyon (2011). Her work is in the collections of Carnegie Museum of Art, Pittsburgh; Museu de Arte Moderna de São Paulo; Pinacoteca do Estado, São Paulo; Solomon R. Guggenheim Museum, New York; and Tate Modern, London; among other institutions.

Institute for Studies on Latin American Art (ISLAA)

The Institute for Studies on Latin American Art (ISLAA) expands scholarship and public engagement with art from Latin America through our program of exhibitions, publishing, research, and partnerships.

ISLAA Staff

Ariel Aisiks
Founder

Jordi Ballart
Project Director

Olivia Casa
Curator and Exhibition Program Manager

Mercedes Cohen
Director of Operations

Natacha del Valle
Collection Manager

Guadalupe González
Project Director

Lucy Hunter
Executive Director

Nicole Kaack
Editorial Program Manager

Rebecca Miralrio
Exhibition Assistant

Bernardo Mosqueira
Chief Curator

Blanca Serrano Ortiz de Solórzano
Research and Partnerships Manager

Magali Trench
Collection Assistant

Lenders to the Exhibition

Adriana Varejão Collection
Ana Luiza and Gregory Reider Collection
Andrea and José Olympio Pereira Collection
Beth Rudin DeWoody Collection
Camille Henrot Collection
Cecilia Tanure Collection, Los Angeles
Compound LB, Long Beach, California
Ernesto Poma Family Collection
Hollander-Yehudi Collection
Inhotim Institute Collection, Minas Gerais, Brazil
Jay and Claudia Khalifeh Collection
Kaitlyn and Mike Krieger Collection, San Francisco
Laura Skoler Collection
Luís Paulo Montenegro Collection
Luiz Antonio Campos Collection
Marcelino Rafart de Seras Collection
Maria Rita and Rodolfo Barreto Collection
Marieluise Hessel Collection, Hessel Museum of Art, Center for
    Curatorial Studies, Bard College, Annandale-on-Hudson, New York
Martin and Rebecca Eisenberg Collection
Paola Ricci and Henrique Miziara Collection
Patrícia and Ricardo Lacaz Martins Collection, São Paulo
Paulus Magnus Collection, São Paulo
Private Collection
Private Collection, San Francisco
Private Collection, São Paulo
Ricard Akagawa Collection
Rodman Primack and Rudy Weissenberg Collection
Sergio Renault and Junio Oliveira Collection
Tracy O'Brien and Thaddeus Staber Collection

**Hessel Museum of Art
Center for Curatorial Studies
Bard College**

The Center for Curatorial Studies at Bard College (CCS Bard) was founded in 1990 as an exhibition and research center for the study of late-twentieth-century and contemporary art and culture, and to explore experimental approaches to the presentation of these topics and their impact on our world. Since 1994, the graduate program has actively sought perspectives underrepresented in contemporary art and cultivated a student body representing a diverse spectrum of backgrounds in a broad effort to transform the curatorial field. The graduate program is uniquely situated alongside the internationally renowned CCS Bard Library and Archives and the Hessel Museum of Art and its rich permanent collection, which together create one of the world's most forward-thinking teaching and learning environments for contemporary curatorial practice and scholarship. Dynamic and multifaceted in its programming, CCS Bard's annual program consistently explores the critical potential of the institutions and practices of exhibition making, including public events, symposia, exhibitions, and publications.

CCS Bard Board of Governors

Martin Eisenberg, Chair
Leon Botstein, *ex officio*
Amy Cappellazzo
Lori Chemla
John Garcia
Marieluise Hessel, Founding Chair
Maja Hoffmann
Audrey Irmas, *emeritus*
Scott Lorinsky
Patrizia Sandretto Re Rebaudengo
Annabelle Selldorf
Melissa Schiff Soros
Lowery Stokes Sims
Michael Ward Stout
Avery Willis Hoffman

CCS Bard Faculty and Staff

Amanda Bard
Graduate Program Administrator

Ann E. Butler
Director of Library and Archives

Shane Brennan
Director of Administration

Dawn Chan
Senior Lecturer

Victoria Chou
Administrative Coordinator and Development Assistant

Lauren Cornell
Director of the Graduate Program and Chief Curator

Tom Eccles
Executive Director

Andy Gabrysiak
Head Preparator

Martha Hart
Museum Registrar

Candice Hopkins (Tlingit, Citizen of Carcross/Tagish First Nation)
Fellow in Indigenous Art History and Curatorial Studies

Harry Jaycox
Security Manager

Andrés Laracuente
Graduate Program and Exhibitions Assistant

Amy Linker
Head of Collections and Registration

Lara Fresko Madra
Assistant Professor and Luma Fellow

Hannah Mandel
Archivist

William McHenry
Librarian

Kobena Mercer
Charles P. Stevenson Professor of Art History and Humanities

Casey Robertson
Public Engagement Manager

Ramona Rosenberg
Director of External Affairs

Ian Sullivan
Director of Exhibitions and Operations

Evan Calder Williams
Associate Professor

This book was published on the occasion of the exhibition *Erika Verzutti: New Moons*, on view at CCS Bard, June 24–October 15, 2023, curated by Lauren Cornell.

Exhibitions at CCS Bard and the Hessel Museum of Art are made possible with generous support from Lonti Ebers, the Marieluise Hessel Foundation, the Robert Mapplethorpe Foundation, the Board of Governors of the Center for Curatorial Studies, and the Center's Patrons, Supporters, and Friends.

Additional support for *Erika Verzutti: New Moons* has been generously provided by the Institute for Studies on Latin American Art (ISLAA), New York.

Edited by Lauren Cornell, Karen Kelly, and Barbara Schroeder
Copyediting: Deirdre O'Dwyer and Karen Kelly
Proofreading: Polly Watson
Design: Giulio Ferrarella with Mattia Tomasi, for Leftloft, Milan
Exhibition photography: Olympia Shannon Studio

This book is typeset in Neue Haas Unica Pro and printed on Magno Volume 135 gsm.

Photo Credits
All works © the artists unless otherwise noted.

All images of works by Erika Verzutti courtesy of Fortes D'Aloia & Gabriel, Andrew Kreps Gallery, Alison Jacques Gallery, and Misako&Rosen.

pp. 9, 63, 74, 75, 79, 82, 83, 96, 98, 111: photo by Michael Brzezinski; p. 10: © Tarsila do Amaral Licenciamentos; p. 12: photo by Henri Stahl; pp. 13, 69: © Succession Brancusi / Artists Rights Society (ARS), New York; pp. 14, 16, 23, 25 (left), 28, 29, 30, 31, 32, 33, 37, 38, 39, 40, 41, 46, 47, 48, 49, 50, 51, 53, 54, 55, 62, 65 (both images), 66, 67, 76, 77, 78, 87, 88, 89, 99, 100, 101, 104, 105, 119, 131, 133, 134: photo by Eduardo Ortega; pp. 17, 21, 27: photo by Denise Andrade; p. 19 (right): created by Dias Gomes, produced and aired by TV Globo; pp. 20, 45, 95: image courtesy of the artist; pp. 25 (right), 90, 91, 92, 93, 103 (left), 107: photo by Everton Ballardin; pp. 26, 97: photo by Bryan Zimmerman, courtesy CCS Bard; p. 43: © Estate of Maria Martins; p. 52: photo by Dawn Blackman; p. 56: photo by Thomas Strub; p. 58 (left): photo by Jean Vong; pp. 58 (right), 59, 60–61: photo by Sebastiano di Persano; p. 70: © Jasper Johns / VAGA at Artists Rights Society (ARS), New York; p. 71: photo by Dario Lasagni; p. 72: photo by Jason Mandella; p. 73: photo by Ding Musa; pp. 123, 128–29: photo by Connor Creagan; p. 108: photo by Stuart Whipps, courtesy Nottingham Contemporary; pp. 109, 112, 113, 116, 117, 122, 123: photo by Kristien Daem; pp. 124, 125, 127: photo by Lance Brewer; pp. 137–53: photo by Olympia Shannon, courtesy CCS Bard

Published in 2023 by Dancing Foxes Press, Brooklyn, New York; Center for Curatorial Studies, Bard College, Annandale-on-Hudson, New York; Institute for Studies on Latin American Art (ISLAA), New York.

Library of Congress Control Number: 2023941292
ISBN: 978-1-954947-08-5

III CCS BARD

Center for Curatorial Studies
Hessel Museum of Art
Bard College
Annandale-on-Hudson, New York 12504
ccs.bard.edu

INSTITUTE FOR STUDIES ON LATIN AMERICAN ART

Institute for Studies on Latin American Art (ISLAA)
142 Franklin Street
New York, New York 10013
islaa.org

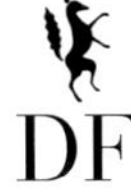

Dancing Foxes Press
16 Lefferts Place
Brooklyn, NY 11238
dfpress.org

Distributed by
ARTBOOK |D.A.P.
75 Broad Street, Suite 630
New York, NY 10004
artbook.com

Printed and bound in Spain by Brizzolis, Madrid